FUTURES

Cultural Memory
in
the
Present

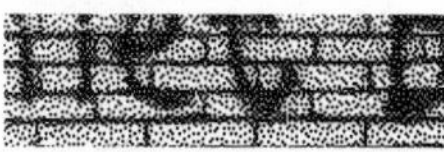

Mieke Bal and Hent de Vries, Editors

FUTURES

Of Jacques Derrida

Edited by Richard Rand

STANFORD UNIVERSITY PRESS

STANFORD, CALIFORNIA 2001

Stanford University Press
Stanford, California

This book is printed on acid-free, archival quality paper.

Library of Congress Cataloging-in-Publication Data

Futures : of Jacques Derrida / edited by Richard Rand.
p. cm.—(Cultrual memory in the present)
ISBN 0-8047-3955-2 (alk. paper)—ISBN 0-8047-3956-0 (paper : alk. paper)
1. Derrida, Jacques—Contributions in criticism—Congresses.
2. Deconstruction—Congresses. I. Rand, Richard II. Series.

PN98.D43 F88 2001
801'.95'092—dc21 00-050483

Original Printing 2001
Last figure below indicates year of this printing:
10 09 08 07 06 05 04 03 02 01

Typeset by Robert C. Ehle in 11/13.5 Adobe Garamond.

Acknowledgments

These papers were read at the twenty-second annual English Department symposium of the University of Alabama, held in Tuscaloosa on September 28–30, 1995. The editor wishes to thank first and foremost his cohost for the occasion, Professor J. P. Hermann, whose unstinting assistance was essential to its taking place. For material support, our heartfelt thanks as well go to James Taaffe, provost; James Yarbrough, dean of the College of Arts and Sciences; Sara de Saussure Davis, chair of the English Department; and our graduate student assistants, especially Allyson Fulmer and Elizabeth Howells. For the publication of this book, particular thanks are due to Willis Regier, Werner Hamacher, Hent de Vries, Helen Tartar, and Elizabeth Berg. For the preparation of the manuscript, particular thanks as well to Toby Whitman and Nancy Young. To Yve-Alain Bois and Sarah Henry of the Barnett Newman Foundation go our thanks for permission to reproduce the drawing on the cover of this volume.

Contents

Contributors

Geoffrey Bennington teaches French literature at the University of Sussex.

Paul Davies teaches philosophy at the University of Sussex.

Jacques Derrida teaches philosophy at the École des Hautes Études en Sciences Sociales, Paris.

Peter Fenves teaches comparative literature at Northwestern University.

Werner Hamacher teaches German literature at Princeton University.

Jean-Michel Rabaté teaches English at the University of Pennsylvania.

Elisabeth Weber teaches German and comparative literature at the University of California, Santa Barbara.

Advertisement

This book is a gathering of papers read at a symposium entitled "Futures," held in 1995 at the University of Alabama in Tuscaloosa to mark the occasion of Jacques Derrida's sixty-fifth birthday. They discuss death and birth (Geoffrey Bennington), principles and contradictions (Paul Davies), secrets (Peter Fenves), Marx's commodity language (Werner Hamacher), gambling (Jean-Michel Rabaté), and Jacques Lacan's thoughts on modern science (Elisabeth Weber). All in a spirit of speculation. Jacques Derrida himself contributes the groundwork toward a deconstruction that may never occur—"prolegomena," as he puts it, for "a deconstructive genealogy of the history of the lie." And he says the following about Hannah Arendt's concept of the lie: "Hannah Arendt often recalls that the liar is a 'man of action,' and I would even add: par excellence. Between lying and acting, acting in politics, manifesting one's own freedom through action, transforming facts, anticipating the future, there is something like an essential affinity. . . . The lie is the future." Such "lies" do not have to be *immediately productive*: in the words of Werner Hamacher, "My remarks—even if it is not 'written on their face'—have the character of questions in progress; they are not entirely tied to the hope of passing into effective questions or determinations; they do not mean to be immediately productive, nor aim at achieving predetermined theoretical or practical aims."

Though they may cohere, these essays are presented in no particular order—in the alphabetical order, merely, of their authors' last names. Their futures lie not in our advertisement but in the thoughts of the essays themselves. And to these we therefore turn.

FUTURES

RIP

Geoffrey Bennington

> For the clarity we are aiming at is indeed *complete* clarity. But this simply means that the philosophical problems should *completely* disappear. The real discovery is the one that makes me capable of stopping doing philosophy when I want to. —The one that gives philosophy peace.
>
> —Wittgenstein, *Philosophical Investigations*, §133

Philosophy is a discourse that knows all about the future, or at least about *its* future. It knows, and has always known, that it has no future. Philosophy knows that the future is death. Philosophy is always going to die. Always has been going to die. Always will have been going to die. From the beginning, its future will have been its end: and from this end, its future will have been always to begin its ending again. Philosophy happens in this archeo-teleo-necrological solidarity. The end of philosophy is the end of philosophy.

The concern philosophy has always shown with what we might naively call *literal* death (my death, Socrates' death, the death involved in being-toward-death individuating *Dasein* in its *Jemeinigkeit*) is (also) a displaced figure of what we might equally naively call philosophy's *figural* (or at least nonliteral) death, which death is analytically inscribed in the philosophical concept of philosophy. But this primary possibility of figural displacement, between death and "death," the death of the philosopher and the death of philosophy, leaves the rich philosophical lexicon of death curiously indeterminate as to its sense and reference: is death in philosophy the death of philosophy or the death of the philosopher? What if the concern philosophy has always shown for the latter were a figural precipitate of the necessity of the former? "Death is a displaced name for a linguistic predicament," wrote Paul de Man.[1]

Philosophers traditionally philosophize because their future is death, they philosophize to overcome death, so as not to be afraid of death. The *locus classicus* here is Socrates in the *Phaedo*:

> Ordinary people [other people, i.e., people other than philosophers: τουζαλλουζ] seem not to realize that those who really apply themselves in the right way to philosophy are directly and of their own accord preparing themselves for dying and for death. If this is true, and they have actually been looking forward to death all their lives, it would of course be absurd to be troubled when the thing comes for which they have so long been preparing and looking forward.
>
> Simmias laughed and said, Upon my word Socrates, you have made me laugh, though I was not at all in the mood for it. I am sure that if they heard what you said, most people [τουζαλλουζ] would think—and our fellow countrymen would heartily agree—that it was a very good hit at the philosophers to say that they are half dead [θαναττωσι: moribund, as good as dead] already, and that they, the normal people, are quite aware that death would serve the philosophers right.
>
> And they would be quite correct, Simmias—except in thinking that they are "quite aware." They are not at all aware in what sense true philosophers are half dead [θαναττωσι again] or in what sense they deserve death, or what sort of death they deserve.[2]

That "true" philosophers are half dead will perhaps not come as a surprise to most of us: but it's worth stressing that this "half-death"—and this is no doubt in part why it must escape the awareness of "normal people"—also affects all moral qualities as their condition of logical consistency. Socrates proceeds to argue that only the philosopher thus defined by the relation to death can possess the virtues of courage, self-control, and temperance (and by extension all the others) in a form that is not "illogical": in the nonphilosopher, for example, courage is always dictated by fear (of something worse than that in the face of which courage is shown, and that "worse" taken to an absolute is death)—but that courage be thus dictated by fear is illogical.[3] Only philosophers, in the half-death that defines them *as* philosophers, can exhibit a philosophically acceptable (i.e., logical, noncontradictory) virtue, and they can do so only because of the horizon of death that makes philosophy philosophical in the first place. The half-death of the philosopher is the half-life of philosophy. Taking something philosophically, then, *always* involves this more or less hidden relationship with death.[4] Or, by a slightly violent *contraction*, whatever I take philosophically is death. Death is the only subject of philosophy, by which it knows the future and can allow philosophers to be moral. The philosophers' stone is an inscribed headstone.

The "logic" invoked here by Socrates, and the logic of that invocation of "logic," with the concept of "half-death" that supports it, are both absolutely familiar and extremely disconcerting, as *Unheimlich* as the double of what is most homely and reassuring. In an apparently dialectical pattern, life and death can exchange their attributes to the point where Socrates will depart for a fuller life in death than in life (which was, after all, half-death, and so only half-life), where "those who have purified themselves sufficiently by philosophy live thereafter altogether without bodies" (*Phaedo* 114c). This pattern (which could no doubt be described as dialectical only on the basis of death so conceived)[5] can always pitch catastrophically, like the souls of the damned into Tartarus (113d), into a nondialectizable aporetics that leaves philosophy (or at least the philosopher) in a zone that is less "between" life and death[6] than strictly uncognizable in terms of the concepts "life" and "death." (And here we would have to stress the fact that Socrates' *viva voce* doctrine of life, death, and philosophy—in which those concepts receive a determination definitive of the Western tradition—is relayed, according to the fiction of the dialogue, still *viva voce* by Phaedo to Echecrates, but beyond that in writing by Plato [absent of course on the fateful day], according to the relay structure analyzed in Derrida's "Plato's Pharmacy" and the "Envois" section of *The Post Card*.) In this aporetical reading (and I use the term "aporetical" in homage to Derrida's recent *Aporias*), the soul is *both* essentially separate from the body, free of the body's contingent taint, *and* essentially corruptible or contaminable by the body: the philosopher is half dead because he strives to keep the soul free of such contamination, but *only* half dead in that the soul cannot be free of the body until death, after philosophy. Philosophy is thus also always the fading compromise of its own contamination and taintedness.[7] The philosopher may "practice death," as Socrates says a little later (81e), may rehearse death in life, but cannot ever quite *practice* it until death—the death that philosophy never quite achieves but that releases the philosopher for a pure practice of philosophy as a wisdom that would henceforth be endless and pointless.

Death, then, cuts both ways. Death interrupts, cuts the thread or tears the cloth of living existence, puts an end always too soon, brings up short. Nothing more inevitable, nothing more unpredictable. Death is both absolute necessity and absolute contingency. But death, cutting the thread or ripping the yarn of my life, tearing it off, brings peace or at least repose. Philosophy is organized around or toward death, but also, thereby, around or toward peace. When Kant, for example, opens his text on Perpetual Peace with a joke about the Dutch innkeeper whose inn of that name carried a sign depicting a graveyard, he introduces an image that repeatedly returns to haunt not only that text but his whole philosophy.

This situation generates several paradoxical consequences that mark out the history of philosophy and maybe just are the history of philosophy. I philosophize *for* death and from death, but because I philosophize death as peace or repose, I philosophize that death as life. Transcendental life is death conceived in this way. As transcendentally alive, I am, essentially, dead. Jacques Derrida's demonstrations in "Cogito and the History of Madness," "Freud and the Scene of Writing," *Speech and Phenomena*, and "Signature Event Context" show this, I am tempted to say, *conclusively*, with lethal—mortal—accuracy, and one evaluation of this "early" work would say that its importance lies precisely in this simultaneous confirmation and displacement of the philosophical thinking of death or of philosophy as a thinking of death. Deconstruction would, on this view, be less a thinking of language or meaning, as it is often still taken to be, than a thinking of death.

But the point, for Derrida, would be to get out of what he might call the turnstile or merry-go-round of these consequences,[8] and this escape leads toward other consequences (or perhaps something other than consequences), whereby death can be thought radically as death, and not as dialectically exchangeable with life in the Socratic-transcendental-dialectical set-up: and according to a familiar paradox of deconstructive thought, death is thought *more* radically than in the tradition by being thought of in a sense *less* radically, as neither rending nor repose, neither rip nor R.I.P. Derrida is the death of death. It is on the condition of this "less is more" radicalism that the perhaps optimistically plural title of this conference, "Futures," can be given some... future.

One feature of this curious situation is that the founding philosophical *pathos* of the future-as-death is somewhat modified. It is difficult to sustain at least certain versions of existential earnestness or even excitement about death in the face of the demonstration that death is entailed in every use of a proper name or of the pronoun "I." No doubt Derrida's complaint in "Circumfession" that in "Derridabase" I deprived him of any future is a way of saying that I presented him as a philosopher (and therefore enacted a wish for his death), forgetting that his thinking of death must displace the whole of philosophy with it (and therefore keep him alive to the extent that, as I also—to be fair—tried to argue, enacting a wish for his long life—*il nous enterrera tous, d'ailleurs*—deconstruction is the least philosophical discourse imaginable).

But this deconstructive displacement may seem to replace a thinking of the future as death with a thinking of the future as birth, which runs the risk of generating an at least equal pathos. Derrida may well seem to buy into some such pathos at least in his famous comments about the future's being *monstrous*, especially perhaps at the end of the exergue to the *Grammatology*.[9] For my purposes today, however, the version of this pathos to be found at the end of the "Structure, Sign and Play" essay is more interesting. Here, you will remember, Derrida has invoked "two interpretations of interpretation" in one of the more celebrated half read (rather than half dead: though the two probably go together) paragraphs of his work. No question of choice here, he says, *first* because the category of choice appears thin in this context; *second* because we must first try to think the common ground and the *différance* of that irreducible difference; *and* because (less a third reason, this, than a supplement to the second)

> this is a type of question—let's call it historical still—whose *conception, formation, gestation, labour,* we can today only glimpse. And I say these words with my eyes turned, certainly, toward the operations of childbirth, but turned too toward those who, in a society from which I do not exclude myself, are still turn-

ing them away [so he is turning his eyes toward people who are turning their eyes away from something: thus no one is looking at it] before the still unnamable that is looming [*qui s'annonce*, still: it's not clear to me in the optics of this scene whether the people he has turned his eyes toward have turned theirs away from the still unnamable or from whatever it is that *announces* the unnamable] and which can only do so, as is necessary every time a birth is at work, in the species of the non-species, the formless, mute, infant and terrifying form of monstrosity.[10]

The version from the *Grammatology* made no reference to childbirth, and the emphasis given to childbirth here, in a text written at about the same time, has always seemed rather mysterious to me. Even if there were contingent, perhaps biographical, reasons for this reference to childbirth (though even they would not explain the presence of this reference in the one text and its absence in the other), and even if those same contingent reasons might motivate the linking of childbirth to the terror of the monstrous, it might still seem curious to choose such figures to say something about the radical futurity of the future. However terrifying the prospect of childbirth in general and the reality of the birth of one's own children in particular, childbirth might seem to be part and parcel of the most naturalistic and reassuring temporality imaginable, rather than a sign of the formlessness of the radical future.

The slight oddness of this reference can be brought out by juxtaposing Derrida's childbirth passage with a remark in Kant's *Prolegomena to Any Future Metaphysics That Will Be Able to Come Forward as Science.* In the course of his famous and intensely problematic attempt to distinguish *Grenze* from *Schranke*, bounds from limits as the standard translation has it, Kant stresses a difference between mathematics and natural science on the one hand and metaphysics on the other. The former disciplines know limits but not bounds, in that what cannot be an object of the senses, for example, cannot fall within their grasp, and they are therefore *limited* with respect to such objects, but they do not lead necessarily to the thought of such objects. Metaphysics, on the contrary, cannot but lead us to a thought of bounds, by inevitably transgressing the limits of what can be given in intuition:

But metaphysics leads us towards bounds in the dialectical attempts of pure reason (not undertaken arbitrarily or wantonly, but stimulated thereto by the nature of reason itself). And the transcendental ideas, as they do not admit of evasion and yet are never capable of realization, serve to point out to us actually not only the bounds of the use of pure reason, but also the way to determine them. Such is the end and the use of this natural predisposition of our reason, which has brought forth metaphysics as its favourite child, whose generation [*Erzeugung*], like every other in the world, is not to be ascribed to blind chance but to an original germ [*nicht dem ungefähren Zufalle, sondern einem ursprünglichen Keime zuzuschreiben ist*], wisely organized for great ends [*zu großen Zwecken*]. For metaphysics, in its fundamental features, perhaps more than any other science, is placed in us by nature itself and cannot be considered the production of an arbitrary choice [*das Produkt einer beliebigen Wahl*], or a casual enlargement [*zufällige Erweiterung*: contingent widening] in the progress of experience from which it is quite disparate.[11]

For Derrida in the "Structure, Sign and Play" essay, childbirth is the very figure of what looks as though we could call it a radical contingency of the future; for Kant, it is a figure of the very opposite of that—a wise teleological organization of nature. What are we to make of this apparent divergence in the use of the same figure?

Let us note first of all that Kant's use of this figure of noncontingency does not itself seem to be at all arbitrary or contingent. Childbirth comes along quite naturally here, because it is an essentially teleological figure of teleology itself as the "truth" of metaphysics itself insofar as metaphysics just is the inevitably teleological movement of thought definitive of finite rational beings to the extent that they *are* rational. The dialectic of pure reason, necessarily generated by the fact that the pure principles of possible experience are not themselves given *in* experience and therefore seem to lead beyond it, resolves itself in the third *Critique* into the merely regulative use of the reflexive judgment, as laid out more especially (or so it seems to me) in the antinomy of teleological judgment. The end of Kant's thought, its *telos*, is teleology itself.[12] The image of childbirth here captures this sense in which metaphysics, teleologically produced in us through reason by the agency Kant calls "nature," is *itself* essentially teleological: Kant chooses as a figure of metaphysics just the sort of natural object (i.e., an organism) that in the third *Critique* will call necessarily for teleological judgment (see §65). It might, then, come as no surprise that Derrida should diverge from Kant in his mobilization of this figure, for the infinitesimal and seismic shift that deconstruction marks in the thinking of death I have just alluded to carries with it a similarly infinitesimal and seismic shift in the relation thinking might bear to teleology, the originary complicity of philosophy with its end, *telos* or death being just the type of archeo-teleological determination of which one would be quite justified in thinking that Derrida is most suspicious.

It is, however, entirely in the baffling logic of what I just called the "less is more" radicalism of the deconstructive thinking of death that this apparent shift or displacement with respect to the metaphysical, teleological determination of the future must already be more or less surreptitiously at work *in* that metaphysical determination. I shall be trying to suggest very briefly today that the traces of this ateleological work can be read in what Kant calls judgment. I can attempt to formulate briefly the sort of thing I shall be trying to find Kant saying: for example, that the end of teleology is the end of teleology, or even that the end of the end is the end of the end. I hope the fragment of a reading of Kant will make these formulations seem less gratuitously provocative, and hint at least at a *rapprochement* with what Jacques Derrida's recent work[13] takes the (I think considerable) risk of calling a messianicity without messianism.

Let me begin by recalling some elementary features of Kant's thinking about judgment. Judgment first appears early in the transcendental analytic in the first *Critique* in the context of Kant's insistence that human knowledge is *discursive.* The understanding is a discursive and not intuitive faculty in that it gives rise to knowledge by concepts that it does not *construct,* as is the case with mathematics. *All* the understanding can do with these concepts is judge with them:

Now the only use that the understanding can make of these concepts is to judge by means of them. Since no representation, save when it is an intuition, is in immediate relation to an object, no concept is ever related to an object immediately, but to some other representation of it, be that other representation an intuition or itself a concept. Judgment is thus the mediate knowledge of an object, that is, the representation of a representation of it. In every judgment there is a concept that holds of many representations, and among them of a given representation that is immediately related to an object. . . . Now we can reduce all acts of the understanding to judgments, and the *understanding* may therefore be represented as *a faculty of judgment* [*em Vemögen zu urteilen*]. For, as stated above, the understanding is a faculty of thought. Thought is knowledge by means of concepts.[14]

Thought is knowledge by concepts; we use these concepts discursively, and we therefore use them to judge. But what is proper to the act of judging is the fact of identifying for a concept a *case* of this concept. Judgment always has to do with the case, which gives rise, a little later in the first *Critique*, to a more detailed description of its operation, at the very beginning of the chapter entitled "Transcendental Judgment in General," where the word "judgment" now translates *Urteilskraft*, the word used in the title of the third *Critique*. The understanding being the faculty of rules, judgment is the power of subsuming under those rules, that is, of recognizing cases for them. General logic cannot contain rules for judgment, because (according to a formula that Wittgenstein was also to make famous) we would need a rule to teach the application of rules to cases, and therefore also a rule to teach the application of that rule to its cases, and so on *ad infinitum*.[15] Judgment can be only an innate capacity, a talent or natural gift that cannot be taught, the *Mutterwitz* that no amount of knowledge can ever make up for. (This is why, much later, Kant would say no less famously that philosophy cannot be learned, and why it is possible to become erudite without ever supplying the lack of judgment—this is what justifies Kant's objections to historians of philosophy, especially in the *Prolegomena*, and gives some substance to the sense that erudition is intrinsically *stupid*, stupidity, *Dummheit*, being the term Kant uses to characterize lack of judgment.)

Transcendental judgment, however, appears to have the considerable advantage of being able to give itself its object without exposing itself to the risk that the *Mutterwitz* will let it down. Since transcendental logic is concerned only with the relation of knowledge to a possible object of experience in general (which is why it is transcendental), it can, as Kant says (A135 / B174–5) "specify *a priori* the instance to which the rule is to be applied."

But the comforting aspects of this claim (from which it seems to follow that transcendental logic is one area where stupidity is not a problem, or even that transcendental philosophy would be the natural vocation for those most lacking in judgment, which might of course just be those who are half dead) have, at least by the time of the third *Critique*, been somewhat troubled by a sense that judgment, even of this determinant type, always, and constitutively, bears a difficult relationship to the singular and the contingent, which both constitutes and unsettles the transcendental itself. According to a setup that pervades Kant's thought, the end (*telos*) of transcendental philosophy is the end (*finis*) of transcendental philosophy: or would be that end, were it not for the structure of a generalized teleology without *telos* I shall attempt to point to.[16]

According to the definitive introduction to the third *Critique*, judgment has no place in *doctrine*, in the accomplished system of a metaphysics, but only in *critique*. From the point of view of doctrine, there are only two sorts of concepts (of nature on the one hand, of freedom on the other): in the system of a completed philosophy, judgment, which is *between* these two domains, can be attached to the one or the other, as needed. The introduction to the third *Critique*, having first repeated and justified this division of philosophy into *two*, then draws back to treat of "the domain of philosophy in general [*Vom Gebiete der Philosophie überhaupt*]." This is where we find a famous passage that attempts to trace the frontiers of this domain, containing the objects of a possible application of concepts:

> Insofar as we refer concepts to objects without considering whether or not cognition [*Erkenntnis*] of these objects is possible, they have their field [*ihr Feld*: Pluhar translates as "realm"]; and this field is determined merely by the relation that the object of these concepts has to our cognitive power [*Erkenntnisvermögen*] in general. [So the field would be the place in the "general domain" where there is a still-indeterminate relation between concept and object. Kant does not say if the general domain of philosophy extends still further, but one might imagine that what Kant elsewhere calls "general logic" might occupy those parts of the domain not covered by the field.] The part of this field in which cognition is possible for us is a territory [*Boden*] (*territorium*) for these concepts and the cognitive power we need for such cognition. That part of the territory over which these concepts legislate is the domain [*Gebiet*: the same word Kant used for the encompassing domain of philosophy in general, and this reappearance of the outside in the middle in the context of legislation seems to me to be anything but fortuitous] (*ditio*) of these concepts and the cognitive powers pertaining to them. Hence empirical concepts do have their territory in nature, as the sum total of all objects of sense, but they have no *domain* in it (but only residence [*Aufenthalt*], *domicilium* [this domicile would then appear to be that part of the

territory not occupied by the domain]); for though they are produced according to law, they do not legislate; rather, the rules that are based on them are empirical and hence contingent.[17]

Let's take this distribution as literally as possible. Kant is implicitly inviting us to draw a plan, which we might do as follows:

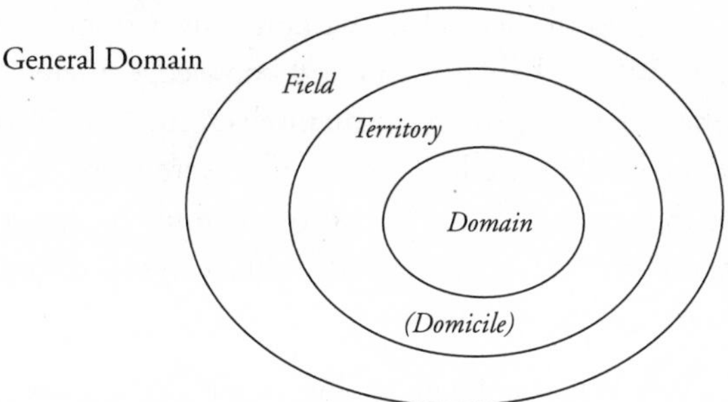

However, we must immediately complicate this, because Kant opens the next paragraph by saying, "Our cognitive power as a whole has two domains, that of the concepts of nature and that of the concept of freedom, because it legislates *a priori* by means of both kinds of concept." But the terrain or territory of these two domains is the same (the terrain of objects of a possible experience), and we must expect that they will be able, and even that they must, share certain objects, which would give the following:

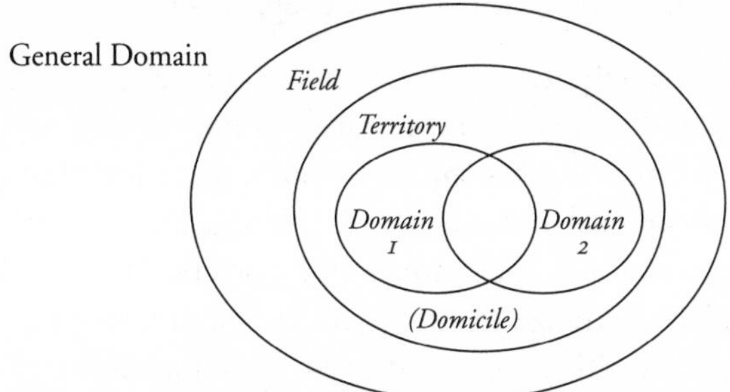

We shall see this topography, which is still quite simple here, gets more and more complicated as Kant advances in his description. The fact that these two legislations bear on domains in the same territory (domains that coincide at least in part, and perhaps totally) gives rise not to interferences at the level of legislation but to a reciprocal limitation (Kant uses the verb *einschranken*) at the level of effects. But these two domains remain two in that their objects are of a different nature, or at least are considered from different perspectives. The domain of nature presents its concepts to intuition, as phenomena, whereas the concept of freedom presents them as things in themselves, without this presentation's taking place in intuition. Where there is theoretical knowledge, there is no thing in itself, and where there are things in themselves, there is no theoretical knowledge. Of such a knowledge (which, if it were to present itself as such, would be the transcendental illusion) one must of course have an Idea, which then takes its place in the field, but without giving rise to a territory, nor, *a fortiori*, to a domain:

Hence there is a field that is unbounded, but that is also inaccessible to our entire cognitive power: the field of the supersensible. [So we were wrong to enclose the field as we did in our diagram, but that leaves the relation between the field and the "general domain" unclear.] In this field we cannot find for ourselves a territory on which to set up a domain of theoretical cognition, whether for the concepts of the understanding or for those of reason. It is a field that we must indeed occupy [*müßen*: necessity here rather than obligation] with Ideas that will assist us in both the theoretical and the practical use of reason; but the only reality we can provide for these ideas, by reference to the laws [arising] from the concept of freedom, is practical reality, which consequently does not in the least expand our theoretical cognition to the supersensible.[18]

Which already complicates the description Kant has given, for where we thought we were dealing with a concentric arrangement of field, territory, and domain, we now see that things are more complicated. Previously, it seemed that theoretical and practical knowledge had each their domain within the territory; now the domain of the practical is, if not identified, at least placed in a strange relation with the (unlimited) field that *surrounds* the territory. To understand what is happening here, we should clearly have to introduce a dynamic element into the representation, allowing practical legislation to happen *from* the field but aiming at the domain within the territory, apparently occupied by theoretical legislation. This is why the celebrated "abyss," the *unübersehbare Kluft*, the cleft over which one cannot see, is not simply a division or accentuated separation between two sides of the same sort, and this is also why the attempt to throw a bridge across it (which would be judgment) is not so easily conceivable as is sometimes thought, unless we think of a one-way bridge:[19]

Hence an immense gulf is fixed between the domain of the concept of nature, the sensible, and the domain of the concept of freedom, the supersensible, so that no transition from the sensible to the supersensible (and hence by means of the theoretical use of reason) is possible, just as if they were two different worlds, the first of which cannot have any influence on the second; and the second *ought to* [*s o l l*, Kant's emphasis] have an influence on the first, i.e., the concept of freedom ought to [*soll* again] actualize in the world of sense the end [*Zweck*] enjoined by its laws. Hence it must [*müßen*] be possible to think of nature as being such that the lawfulness in its form will harmonize with at least the possibility of [achieving] the ends that we are to achieve in nature according to laws of freedom. So there must after all be a ground [*Grund*] *uniting* the supersensible that underlies nature and the supersensible that the concept of freedom contains practically, even though the concept of this ground does not reach cognition of it either theoretically or practically and hence does not have a domain of its own, though it does make possible the transition from our way of thinking in terms of principles of the one to our way or thinking in terms of the principles of the other.[20]

If, then, there is a possibility of transition from one domain to the other, this transition takes place only in one direction (it is impossible to pass from the theoretical to the practical, on pain of transcendental illusion), and it happens, not by throwing a bridge over the abyss, but by passing under, *in a tunnel*, for the *Kluft* may be un-see-over-able, but it has a bottom nonetheless, is cut into the common (sub)soil of the field, a suprasensible subsoil divided between theoretical and practical knowledge. This passage, or its possibility, is not itself of the order of theoretical knowledge. That it be possible to pass from the practical to the theoretical (that legislation according to freedom be compatible with legislation according to nature), that the moral law might have effects that can be registered in the natural-mechanical world, is part of the (being-)law of this law.[21] It is duty's duty to realize itself in the world of nature. The moral law *must be able* (or, if "must" commits us to *müßen*, it *ought to be able*) to realize or actualize itself in the sensory world, following a pre- or archi-moral duty that provides for the pre- or archi-prescriptiveness of prescriptions:[22] duty owes itself the duty of becoming effective. But this primitive *sollen* (which must in fact—in right—precede the distinction between freedom and nature, because it is the principle of their separation as well as of their communication), according to which time owes it to itself to be a *müßen*, according to which the legality of natural legality is such that it must, in its form, lend itself to this realization of moral ends. Only this consequence gives any substance to the archi-duty of duty: for if nature did not *respond* to it, duty could owe itself to itself *ad infinitum* without this duty's being a jot more realizable. The duty of duty, then, *must be* realizable *as it ought to be*, failing which it would not be a duty, and there would be no duty. There ought to be this must, because there must be this ought. This originary connivance between necessity and obligation, nature and freedom, *müßen* and *sollen*, mechanism and ends—it's the law—will make of judgment (which has not yet been named in the Introduction), an essentially teleological judgment.

The sensory world is thus *the end* of duty, or, since duty owes itself to itself from the end, *the end of the end*. What Kant has not yet named as "judgment" will be in some sense the faculty of this doubled end, or of the movement that carries judgment toward its end and ensures that the moral law will find in nature the condition of its possible realization. Nature must needs be such that it can respond to the moral law. Which means that, contrary to what one might think on reading the typic of the second *Critique*, the form of the law, the *Gesetzmässigkeit* that the moral law is supposed to borrow from the laws of nature (the categorical imperative prescribes that I put the maxim of my action through the test of the form of a law of nature), is the form of the moral law that gives its form to natural legality. Nature has a legal form *so as to* be able to respond to the moral law; natural necessity is thus dictated by the moral law, which gives a (suprasensible) foundation to its necessity, but at the same time (digging the tunnel) undermines this foundation. For if natural necessity owes itself to duty, it is no longer quite necessary, nor quite natural. That the (legal) form of nature must accord with the possibility of ends is its end. The end of nature is that the law will find its end in it. Which means that even the archi-determining transcendental judgment of the first *Cri-*

tique is already teleological, for it must presuppose that nature is such that nature will present judgment with cases adapted to the law that the understanding is in a position to prescribe to nature.

It is just this that allows for the possibility of the transcendental position itself. The understanding is legislative for nature in a strong sense: the understanding prescribes itself a nature such that the laws it will pronounce will have at least the *possibility* of finding satisfaction in it. Nature is thus *made for* the judgment that will take its case into account, and this *made for* already gives nature its end as apt to receive moral-practical realizations. Even subsumptive theoretical judgment, then, is determined in return by its apparent other, which returns through the tunnel to pop up in the middle—a foreign legislator.

This is what Kant will say much later, in §76 of the "Critique of Teleological Judgment." Reason demands unity, the unification of the manifold. But the understanding, insofar as it is linked to sensibility and is thus subject to a transcendental logic (for the transcendental is less what goes away from than *what returns to* the singular),[23] can proceed only from the universal to the particular, in which it cannot *not* find the contingent. This contingent must be brought under the law, which is done by postulating a finality of the contingent as such:

> Now, as the particular as such contains something contingent with respect to the general, and yet reason demands unity (i.e., legality) in the combination of even the particular laws of nature (which legality of the contingent is called finality), whereas the deduction of particular laws from the general, as regards what is contingent in them, *a priori* through determination of the concept of the object, is impossible, the concept of the finality of nature in its products becomes for the human faculty of judgment with respect to nature a necessary concept.[24]

Which has as an apparently paradoxical consequence that, to be legal, nature must be fundamentally contingent. If it is to receive the law, nature *must not* be completely necessary. Natural necessity, seen from its end (the law) is that it be contingent. The necessity of necessity is contingency (which calls for teleology). This chance of contingency (the only chance of the law) is not *knowable* as such but is the object of a non-knowledge that calls for what is called judgment. For one to be able to judge *according to the end*, there must be contingency, for only contingency calls for the end as the only chance of its legality. Necessity has no end; it is blind: for the end, this blindness must blind itself again in the contingent.

Nature, then, has a purpose: to be purposive, which it is in contingency only. That there be this purposiveness does not come under theoretical knowledge (for if it were to be demonstrated, contingency would be reduced to natural necessity: this is why Kant keeps on repeating that the principle of judgment—i.e., that you must judge *as if* it were made to be judged—is only subjective, or at least is not objective, while functioning just *as if* it were objective, because without this there would be no "subject"). Nor does it come under practical "knowledge" (no duty here). Rather, it underlies the possibility of these two domains as the presupposition indispensable to their separation. At the end, we know strictly nothing of the end.

This position of judgment, as essentially teleological, is precisely what undermines any clear sense of any *telos* at all for judgment by opening it to an indefinite future in which it seems unlikely that philosophy will ever find peace or repose in the disappearance or doctrinal resolution of its problems. This endless teleology (or thinking of teleology as essentially without *telos*) explains the attraction of thinking of judgment in general along the lines of the so-called "aesthetic" judgment and its purposiveness without purpose or finality without end, or lawfulness without law, as Kant says in §22. This naturally does not mean that all judgment thought in this way is somehow culpably aesthetic, just because this generalized opening of judgment renders quite uncertain the borders of the aesthetic as such. A similar argument can be generated, with no specific reference to the aesthetic at all, from analysis of that most Kantian of motifs, the "guiding thread," the *Leitfaden*, which turns out always to be invoked just where guidance is *not* to be had and any arrival at an end is radically uncertain, or from the question of *orientation* in thought, which turns out to be necessary only where it is impossible to secure.

Which seems to confirm *both* the Derridian and the Kantian readings of the figure of childbirth from which I began. Childbirth is unthinkable without *some* appeal to *something like* a teleology: but what provides the opening for the monstrous is that this teleology has no definable *telos*. This monstrosity[25] inscribed in the notion of childbirth is, however, precisely what prevents philosophy from finding itself in its *telos*, which would be its *finis*, its death. Teleology read in this way is just what holds philosophy short of its end and thus gives it the possibility of a future in spite of itself. It is no accident that the "children" generated by philosophers (*qua* philosophers) should be the books they write.[26] The (half-)death of the philosopher would then never be completed, but would be the (half-)life of philosophy, which half-life lives as a repeated call to reading thrown toward a future in which that reading will never be finished.[27] Derrida's futures are, to that extent, like those of every other philosopher, both absolutely predictable and absolutely uncertain: but those futures will, let me hope here and now, already be marked, in reading, by a gratitude for opening just that futurity to reading, always elsewhere, in Plato and Kant for example, in the past.

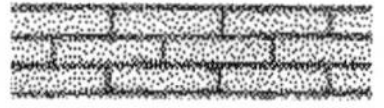

This Contraction

Paul Davies

> Should the highest principle [*Prinzip*] contain the highest paradox in its task? Being a principle [*Satz*] that allows absolutely no peace, that always attracts and repels, that always anew would become unintelligible as soon as one had understood it? That ceaselessly stirs up our activity—without ever exhausting it, without ever becoming familiar? [*Der unsere Tätigkeit unaufhörliche rege machte—ohne sie je zu ermüden, ohne je gewohnt zu werden?*] According to old mystical sayings, God is something like this for the spirits [*die Geister*].
>
> —Novalis, cited by Martin Heidegger, *The Principle of Reason*

> Contradiction. Why just this *one* specter [*Gespenst*]? That is surely very suspicious.
>
> —Ludwig Wittgenstein, *Remarks on the Foundations of Mathematics*

It may be that, despite appearances and some notable claims to the contrary, philosophy has never really denied or even sought to deny the content of the principle of (non)contradiction, formally -(*p*.-*p*), that is, "not (*p* and not *p*)." And this may be so not because there are such things as contradictions lurking as it were in the vicinities of philosophy and thought, always capable, should they not be dealt with effectively, of irrevocable damage—the principle indicating the extent of the damage in such a way that no philosopher, once aware of what a contradiction really is, could ever mean to speak against it. It need not be that the principle first defines and identifies these dangerous things (*p.-p*) and then shows how for the sake of our philosophical well-being they must be treated (that opening regulative "not," -[*p.-p*]). In the end it may simply come down to the principle's necessarily being formulable as a tautology; for to arrive at a tautology and to accept that the tautology has been properly arrived at is surely to accept that here denial makes no sense whatsoever.

The paper moves towards a partial and condensed discussion of one aspect of Heidegger's work that comes or returns to the fore in the writings of the middle to late 1950s, namely, his attempt to detect, in the very idea of metaphysics' being logically grounded, the hint and promise of a thinking that would differ fundamentally from metaphysics. Heidegger believes an inquiry into the logical basis or ground (*Grund*) of metaphysics can demonstrate that that ground does not simply belong to metaphysics and that there is an equivocation here that metaphysics can neither accept nor control. The logico-metaphysical understanding of both the ground of metaphysics and the principle (*Satz*) ostensibly articulating it neither fully determines what is meant by "ground" nor reveals what is essential in the notion of a *Grundsatz.*

In moving towards this discussion of a familiar Heideggerian*ism* or Heideggerian motif, the concern is primarily not with exegesis but with the asking of a quite specific and specifically non-Heideggerian question, albeit one whose significance and relevance will have to be made clear: Why and how does Heidegger, in the 1957 manuscript of his lecture course on Leibniz, *The Principle of Reason* (*Der Satz vom Grund*),[1] subordinate one of Leibniz's two supreme principles to the other, the principle of identity or contradiction to the principle of reason (*Grund*)?[2] It is, I want to suggest, a moment of an unavoidable or almost unavoidable impatience, a moment in this unprecedented and extraordinarily intricate reading of a principle (the principle of reason) when something to do with the principle of contradiction—and so something to do with principles themselves, with what they are and perhaps must be—has to be overlooked, taken as read, let pass as though it were without interest for even the most attentive of readers. And Leibniz did, it seems, fear that people would be unconvinced by what struck him as important in the principle and would see it as unredeemably trivial. Commentators as different as Hegel, Russell, and possibly Heidegger could be taken as showing the fear to be well founded. To put it in succinct if discouraging terms: the topic of this paper is the thought and the status of the thought of what seems *in principle* uninteresting and unremarkable, or, if you will, of what *in principle* seems not to call for thinking.

The first five sections make some general and I'm afraid rather sweeping observations on the context within which the question is to be posed. They outline an argument for our opening hypothesis: to an important degree what is stated in the principle of contradiction has never been denied.

Heidegger's strategies and decisions regarding the principle of contradiction—for example, his insistence, against Leibniz, on distinguishing between it and the principle of identity; his historicizing of the principle; and his reluctance even to employ the words "contradiction" and "paradox" in an account of his own project—seem to follow or to conform to a now-standard post-Hegelian procedure. If it is clear for all sorts of reasons, but especially for Hegelian ones, that no longer can the principle of contradiction be taken simply as stated and its validity be assumed, there is perhaps a sense in which its no longer being taken as stated can now be taken as stated, leaving philosophy with the assumption that the validity and the primacy of the principle have been satisfactorily disproved, otherwise discontinued by being confined to a "classical logic," or merely judged irrelevant, capable only of prompting philosophical indifference. It can sometimes seem as if we have moved from a logical metaphysical certainty that the self-evident truth of the principle meant that nothing more need be said about it to a "post-metaphysical" certainty that, in the wake of the historical, ethical, and logical "displacements" of metaphysics and classical logic, nothing more need be said about the principle that served as one of their mainstays. On the basis of this assumption, the question to Heidegger is not only naive or ill-informed, it is also easily answered.

I

It is in Aristotle's *Metaphysics* that we find the most abiding account of the predicament faced both by the one who would challenge the principle (*archē*) of contradiction and the one who would attempt to meet that challenge; to meet it, initially, in the modest but, for Aristotle, uneducated request that the truth of the principle be demonstrated. It being, Aristotle says, "impossible for there to be a demonstration [*apodeixis*] of everything,"[3] such a request betrays an ignorance of the distinction between those things, statements, or situations that need a demonstration and those that do not. The priority appropriate to the principle is not only logical but also, in a sense, ontological. The *archē*, from the first, concerns beings, what can be said about them and what can be said about what can be said about them. A being cannot both be and not be, and the principle declaring as much is itself a thing, a being, for which a certain sort of (logical) demonstration is inappropriate. Given that it is logically impossible to be genuinely mistaken about this *archē*, it is equally impossible to take people seriously when they dispute it. But given, too, that demonstrating this impossibility is logically impossible, how is one to prevent the dispute from arising, as it were, logically? The fault must lie not with the failure or absence of a particular demonstration but with the disputant. Yet how is one to demonstrate *this*? Aristotle suggests that "a demonstration is forthcoming by way of refutation [*elegtikos*], provided the one who disputes it will say something; and if he says nothing, it is ridiculous to look for a *logon* against someone who has no *logon* insofar as he has none, for such a person is like a plant." If there cannot and need not be a clear-cut proof for what will be called the principle of contradiction, there can nevertheless be a refutation of one who would attempt to deny or to disparage it, as long as the interlocutor speaks, or, rather, as long as he or she becomes an interlocutor; for then it can be pointed out to them that, in speaking, they refute themselves; in speaking, they contradict themselves. To speak here is to give a *logon* (a word, reason, statement) or to propound an argument, in that to speak is to assert something and, in asserting something, to commit oneself to it, at the very least to the extent of one's not being committed to everything or to just anything. Not everything and not just anything follow from what is asserted, whatever it is, and of course it may be anything, whereas everything and just anything supposedly do follow or would follow from a contradiction. It is an *ad hominem* argument, but of a rather strange sort, for one of its effects would actually be to legitimize the logical and philosophical use of *ad hominem* arguments. To the person, but not on the basis of a premise he or she begins by affirming, because what is at issue are precisely the preconditions for such a sharing. To the person, then, but in such a way that should they not speak, it is as if they were not yet a person, indeed not yet human—the usual purchase and purchaser of "speech"—but also not yet even an animal, but a plant, a vegetable. The impossibility of demonstrating everything and the concomitant need to begin without such a demonstration bequeath not only a generous and not unradical acceptance of the necessary contingency of beginning but also a definite, impatient, and so not unviolent requirement that this shall function as the last word on the matter. There is after all, Aristotle insists, a demonstration that further demonstration is not required. Until and unless the disputant respects the *archē*, there is no need to respect the disputant. A condition of speech, here and now, will be that it be bounded by this principle and that the question of these bounds be, in turn, ruled out of bounds.

So much would be at issue here—the ambiguous nature of the responsibilities of speech and of the responsibility to speak, the unfolding of a certain conception of the limits of speech—and so many contemporary concerns would already be under way here that the present paper will doubtless seem concerned only with what is least contemporary because surely already settled, and certainly with what is least interesting, namely, contradiction and its principle, that part of Aristotle's text, for example, to which Leibniz would effectively return us when he describes a proof as a reduction to what itself needs no proof. If Leibniz's writings prevaricate about how this absence of the need for a proof is to be understood—is it a question of innateness, of logical intuition, or just of the practical impossibility of proofs to infinity?—Leibniz handles it by treating truths as necessary truths, as reductions to identities, where the axiom of identity (*A* is *A*, or, if *A* then *A*) already states and so is already identical with the principle of contradiction (*A* is not not *A*, or, if *A* then not not *A*). If demonstration will henceforth continue to consist in the reduction to the scene first enacted in Aristotle's *Metaphysics*, it is a scene now implicitly formalized as the axiomatic, self-grounding, and logical basis of metaphysics. Leibniz calls the principle governing this description of demonstration *the principle of identity or of contradiction.* It is one of his two supreme principles, the other being the principle of (sufficient) reason; and not to accept it, to challenge it in any way whatsoever, will now count as *prima facie* evidence of illogicality, of being in principle incapable of philosophizing.

II

The principle of (sufficient) reason states: *nihil est sine ratione* (nothing is without reason; *Nichts ist ohne grund*). To understand the principle, Heidegger says, is to understand it "without further ado" (*ohne weiteres*) as immediately "illuminating" (*PR*, 3 / *SG*, 14). No effort is required to grasp it because understanding (*Verstand*) is a reason-seeking operation and so is itself, from the first, animated by the insight or law expressed in the principle. But what happens when we apply the principle to itself, when we inquire into its reason or ground? Either we immediately and without further ado see that some reason or ground must ground or justify the principle, or we immediately and without further ado see that the illumination emanating from the principle must exempt the principle from self-application. Either the principle applies to itself or it does not. If it does apply to itself, then the immediacy with which we first grasped it needs to be qualified and mediated in turn by the question of its reason or ground. An answer to this further question, if available, would presumably be a more or equally fundamental principle, a principle either grounding the principle of ground or explaining why and how the principle grounds itself. If it does not apply to itself, then what the principle says is not true, for there is at least one thing that does not satisfy the demand made by the principle. It seems as if either the principle of reason is not properly a fundamental principle (a *Grundsatz*) or the principle of reason is false. Heidegger's lecture course endeavors to liberate the principle of reason from this double bind: to let it resound as both properly fundamental and groundless; to let its being groundless provide an insight into what might now have to be meant by a "fundamental thinking." To read the principle in such a way that we move from regarding it as the logical and methodological protector of the development of "scientific philosophy" to hearing in it something of another thinking. The principle is no longer to be restricted to the causal "because" and the reason-giving "because." It needs to be extended even to the "because"

Heidegger finds in Angelus Silesius's line "The rose is without why; it blooms because it blooms" (*Die ros ist ohn warum; sie blühet, weil sie blühet*). Indeed, in Silesius's unusual coupling of "because" and "without" Heidegger sees at first a contradiction of the principle (*PR*, 35 / *SG*, 67) and then finally a key to a new appreciation of it. What seems, immediately and straightforwardly, to go without saying does not go without saying: the self-evident is not self-evident. But this state of affairs is to be remedied neither by a final, unequivocal saying (even a saying of "without") nor by the formulating of a new principle and a new self-evidence. Heidegger's lecture invites us to listen to a series of variations in and on the words *Satz* and *Grundsatz*. It encourages us to wonder whether, in the future, a genuinely principled philosophy might not have to relinquish the assumption that there are genuinely unambiguous laws of thought. To hear another possibility in the equivocating of what has worked and continues to work so well as the unequivocal basis of "calculative thinking." (The Heideggerian steps are well known; although, as we shall see, in *The Principle of Reason* Heidegger goes to great lengths to undermine the tendency to summarize or narrativize them. There is thus intentionally much in the lecture course that does not tally with any Heideggerian*ism.*)

For Heidegger's purposes, the principle of reason must be held apart from that other principle judged by Leibniz to be its equal: the principle of identity or contradiction. And this for two reasons: (a) "'Nothing without ground'—itself groundless—is a contradiction." The principle of contradiction would, it seems, simply rule out the very phrase and predicament Heidegger's course takes as its subject.[4] (b) If demonstration involves reduction to an identity, then any question to the principle of reason must touch on its relation and possible reduction to an identity. The principle of identity must be capable of resolving the matter. For Heidegger, this importing of the principle(s) of identity and contradiction is "thoughtless," a judgment that feeds into the supposedly Hegelian or post-Hegelian assumption that easily answers the question this paper wants to ask. Either (a) the principle of contradiction is false and so can never be proved, there being in fact "true contradictions," such as perhaps "'Nothing without ground'—itself groundless"; or (b) all talk of contradiction and identity here can be shown to be derivative: to continue to tie philosophy to the issue of whether the *principle* of identity or contradiction is true, provable, or primary is both to remain indebted to the secure "what goes without saying" that is being called into question and to preclude philosophy from any thoughtful access to its own history, language, and future possibilities. Having thus been either disproved or dislodged, the principle of identity or contradiction need detain the philosopher no longer. Rejecting the principle credibly rests on accepting one or the other of these assertions. We need to unpack them.

III

The most explicit and the least apologetic advocate of "true contradictions" must be the philosophical logician Graham Priest: "I know of no historical defence of the law of non-contradiction since Aristotle worth mentioning. Is this because Aristotle's arguments were conclusive? Hardly."[5] Priest would give short shrift to the view that even if there is no "conclusive argument" for the principle of contradiction, there is nevertheless a conclusive argument that not every *logon* requires one. He would do so in part because one accepts the logical possibility of contradiction from the beginning, as soon as one considers that from any two states of affairs (*a*, *b*) there will logically be four possibilities (*a*, *b*, neither *a* nor *b*, both *a* and *b*). Thus for "*p* is true" (or *p*) and "*p* is false" (or -*p*), we can logically distinguish *p*, -*p*, neither *p* nor -*p*, and both *p* and -*p*. Standard logic might, in its liberal or more benevolent moments, permit the third of these (neither *p* nor -*p*) to stand alongside the first two (*p*, -*p*); but it will never allow the fourth (both *p* and -*p*). Priest wonders why. He argues that there are moments when the consistency secured for logic by this refusal must break down. Logic must concede the possibility and plausibility of paraconsistency. "Dialetheism" asserts that valid arguments sometimes entail contradictions, that is, conclusions that are both true and false. "True contradiction" is shorthand for the unavoidability and the necessity of such statements. Sometimes "*p*.-*p*" is wholly justified. It is what philosophy, logic, and mathematics sometimes have to assert; and at such times, no other formulation and no further analysis can stand in for such an assertion. But when? And how does one know when one has arrived at such a moment?

In order to formalize his true contradictions, Priest must first dismiss the promiscuous entailment clause (*ex contradictione quodlibet*) that traditionally accompanies the logical definition of contradiction. Not everything and not just anything follows from a true contradiction. How then do we distinguish between a true contradiction and a false or only seemingly unresolvable one, say between the liar paradox and 6 + 6 = 17? An appearance of the latter, unlike an appearance of the former, tells us that we have gone wrong. But, again, how does the former tell us that it is unresolvable? Is there not a problem with simply stipulating that this contradiction will never be resolved? What, logically, could really prevent my continuing to try to resolve it, my continuing to try to show that it can be transcribed or recontextualized so that what it says is either true or false, or perhaps neither true nor false. One answer here, of course, and the one that occupies most of Priest's time, concerns the technical achievement of demonstrating that the acceptance of true contradictions need no longer be deemed illogical or alogical. There is a way of formalizing, containing, and generating statements that are both true and false and so a way, logically, of living with them. The rules here are so exacting and so concerned to restrict the number of contradictions permitted to stand as candidates for dialethic status that the reader must wonder whether a better way of designating that status can't be found. The problems in this regard are legion. For example, what does the existence of "true contradictions" do to the very meaning of "to know"? Normally and necessarily, as Priest would concede, for any false proposition p I can never know that p. But it looks as if for a true contradiction (and so a true *and false* proposition p), I can know that p. Does the "contradiction" or the paraconsistency extend from the true and false proposition to the knowing of it, so that I both do and do not know it? This hardly seems feasible. Priest wants us to know that there are true propositions and thus wants us to know, in a given instance, that a true and false proposition p is true (and false). And "to know" here means what it always means. But can it? Or how can it? The logical apparatus needed for damage control is extensive, and it works by forever refining the difference between "true contradictions" and the rest. It is hard to see what is gained for philosophy and for a philosophical understanding of paradoxes by this particular act of renaming. But our comments are aimed not so much at this aspect of Priest's project, its technical ingenuity, as they are at its philosophical inspiration. Priest admits the rarity of true contradictions; indeed he seems to accept an *ad hominem* or transcendental argument to the effect that almost all of the contradictions we discover or construct are not dialethic. Yet there is one area where this is not so and where contradictions are both inevitable and inevitably dialethic.

If philosophy has traditionally ruled against the validity of "*p.-p*," it has nevertheless persistently found itself raising the issue and requiring the concept of a limit, which issue and which concept can be shown to entail just this fourth option (neither "*p*" nor "*-p*" nor "neither *p* nor *-p*" but "*p.-p*"). The limit in one of its manifestations can be thought only by not being thought, by being thought *as* what cannot be thought, and can be expressed logically and philosophically by not being expressed, by being expressed *as* what cannot be expressed. These various philosophical and logical introductions of a limit concept invoke what necessarily limits the domain of the principle of contradiction and so invoke what can be thought or expressed only in the form of a thought or an expression not subject to the principle. True contradictions are contradictions at or on limits. Thus their description has much in common with Hegel's response to Kant's attempt to give to transcendental or critical philosophy the task of delimiting metaphysics. Without an awareness of its proper limits, reason and its metaphysical productions were doomed to contradictions (antinomies). For Kant, only a critical remarking of those antinomies could resolve them. Resolving the theoretical antinomies in the first *Critique* involved the critical realization of the limits that reason must set itself, limits that follow from the distinction between a description of what is in terms of how it is in itself and a description of what is in relation to reason. About the former there is nothing we can reasonably say and nothing we can know. Hegel points out that this nothing, this limit to knowledge beyond which lies that unknowable in-itself about which reason must, on pain of contradiction, neither ask nor speculate, does not need to be presented as a threat to reason, as something before which reason waves the principle of contradiction as though it read "thus far and no further." The unknowable in-itself is known as such and in-itself when it is grasped in just these very terms. Consequently, however, the idea of transcendental or critical philosophy as a noncontradictory process of contradiction resolution comes under review. Philosophy in its insistence on the theoretical employment of the principle of contradiction as the principle of the *avoidance* of contradiction is unable to accept that to run up against a limit is to have already transgressed that limit. The unknowable is known as the unknowable; there is nothing else to it that resists or evades knowledge, no transcendent metaphysical inquiry to which reason finds itself tempted but from which it must be protected. Reason, for Hegel, thus advances in a way Kant (at least Hegel's Kant) could not recognize. It does not do so by transcendentally remarking and thereby avoiding contradiction; in fact quite the opposite. Hegel is Priest's heroic exception to the philosophical tradition's principled anti-dialetheism. He is heralded as the only philosopher to have offered a thorough critique of Aristotle's attempts either to demonstrate or to explain why we need not demonstrate the principle of contradiction.

The problem here is one of nuance, but it will take us straight to the heart of the matter. Is it so obviously the case that for Hegel there are true contradictions in Priest's sense? That is to say, is it so obvious that the move is from Aristotle and "-(*p*.-*p*)" to Hegel and "*p*.-*p*"? There are at least three ways in which one might gloss the principle of contradiction presented as "-(*p*.-*p*)":

(a) "*p*.-*p*" must be avoided.
(b) "*p*.-*p*" indicates an error.
(c) "*p*.-*p*" must be overcome.

Note that even Aristotle and the classical logicians acknowledge a straightforward sense in which there are contradictions. Logical and rhetorical *reductios* depend upon them. If the disputant in the *Metaphysics* accepts the philosopher's invitation to speak, he will find himself involved in one. Contradictions can be produced and discovered; but to name a production or discovery as "a contradiction" is to imply something about the process of production or discovery itself. Even if one does not accept the wording of (b), perhaps any interpretation of the principle of contradiction must acknowledge that when a contradiction occurs, it must be taken as an indication or symptom. It calls for action, evasive or otherwise, for further thought or interpretation. Thus (a) and (c) can be supplemented, respectively, by the claims that "*p*.-*p* indicates that *p*.-*p* must be avoided" and that "*p.-p* indicates that *p.-p* must be overcome." Surely for Hegel as much as for anyone, thinking must experience contradictions as a problem and a challenge. The Hegelian objection to transcendental philosophy in this regard is that the means by which it would protect thought from contradiction bespeaks an inability to engage with it. In other words, a thinking that would genuinely uphold the principle of contradiction must not simply pay lip service to it but rather must face up to contradictions and derive from their formal unresolvability a means of overcoming them. The process may well be endless, but as a philosophical process it still accords with the idea that a particular contradiction must be purged of its capacity to paralyze thought. For speculative and dialectical philosophy, the process is to be seen as already conveying the hope of reconciliation. If contradictions are unavoidable and in this sense "real," and if without them there could be no genuinely philosophical thought, that thought in its Hegelian guise as much as any other sets itself the task of contradiction resolution. Hegel, rigorously opposed to any realist view of contradictions and also to the view that would give the principle concerning them a purely apotropaic function—as in (a) above, and he would of course judge such views to be themselves contradictory—thus nonetheless comes to endorse a version of the principle such as (c). If Hegel's attack on the pre-Hegelian endeavor to control or avoid contradiction—to control contradiction by avoiding it—shows how thought thrives on contradiction, this final "contradiction" is to be read as shorthand for "the overcoming of contradiction." When, in the *Science of Logic*, Hegel says, "everything is inherently contradictory," he is describing the dynamic and dialectical life of the concept and of thought.

Were the contradictions Hegel identifies fully dialethic in Priest's sense, that is, contradictions whose presence denies the principle of contradiction, there would be no dialectical remarking of them. There is, in this respect, a tension between the dialectic and the dialethic; and a thinking defined by the former cannot be conflated with a thinking committed to the possibility of the latter. Whatever else it does, the Hegelian negative negates and overcomes contradiction. The difference between the dialectical and the transcendental (or critical) treatments of contradiction does not come down to one of denying or accepting the principle of contradiction. Whereas for Priest the contradictions that arise at the limits of experience, thought, and language are necessarily dialethic and ought to be recognized as such, for Hegel they denote rather the impoverished and incomplete nature of our thinking. For Hegel, we might say, there are not really any "limit concepts." The thinking that recognizes a limit contradiction must recognize it as the contradiction that limits a certain type or shape (*Gestalt*) of thinking. This moment of recognition introduces a difference between the thinking capable of recognizing and so of overcoming the contradiction and the thinking that remains historically and logically limited by the contradiction. And although ultimately even *this* difference entails a contradiction and so must also be overcome, that "final" overcoming does not render thought *truly* contradictory. Doubtless we have not begun to do justice to the subtleties of Hegel's engagement with contradiction, but at the very least it should be clear that he is not quite Priest's ally.

IV

Of central concern for writers and philosophers such as Blanchot, Levinas, and Derrida are the repercussions of what they see as the successes of Hegelianism, the successes that might be said to constitute the topic and the task of Hegel's project. The speculative retrieval of what matters historically and logically—the achievement of Hegelian *Erinnerung*—leaves a question, itself barely legitimate, as to the sense of what does not matter, of what cannot be recuperated, recalled, or retold. Thus Blanchot, for example, is drawn to the strange way in which art, in its continuing beyond its historical apotheosis, can carry no philosophical interest or significance. It is this continuing failure to matter that interests Blanchot. Something happens and continues to happen, but in doing so can add nothing to what has happened; its continuing production is a nonproduction. For Levinas, we may suggest that the ethical relation at the center of his work is an obligation precisely to what does not matter historically, to the one whose story, deferred until it can be properly told and judged from the perspective of history, is always already silenced, historically absent. Derrida, noting the formal similarities here, explicitly reads Hegel in terms of an unthematizable remainder. Each of these three thinkers seems committed to a certain post-Hegelian (or non-Hegelian, or not quite Hegelian) treatment of contradiction. Derrida names it when he describes Blanchot's writing as performing "a disarticulation of the logic of identity and contradiction." He refers to the "sign of the contradiction without contradiction" in Blanchot, and again to a "nondialectizable contradiction."[6] The disarticulation of contradiction leaves us, it seems, not with no contradiction but with one no longer capable of serving either a pre-Hegelian or a Hegelian function. In "Pas," Derrida suggests that the "without" in "contradiction without contradiction" must be read by way of its own unsettling nonproductivity as a "without without without" (*sans sans sans*).[7] Whereas for Hegel, the thinking that acknowledged a contradiction found, in that acknowledgment, the means to negate and overcome that contradiction, Levinas, Blanchot, and Derrida, among others, are drawn to what is not negated and so to what needs must be described in terms of a faltering or weakening of negation. What does this weakening do to and for contradiction? How does the disarticulation of contradiction stand in relation to the principle of contradiction?

To do justice to a difference that, by definition, evades or falls short of the dialectic between "identity" and "nonidentity" (the dialectic between tautology and contradiction), another vocabulary is introduced: "diachrony," "différance," "difference and repetition," and so on. Indebted to Hegel for the thought of an identity always already constituted by difference,[8] these writers and philosophers would attempt to wrest the thought of difference away from any logical or dialectical dependence on identity, and so from the relation with identity that produces or confronts those difficulties traditionally named "contradictions." Contradictions would be seen to rely on the *hama* and *kata ta auto,* that is, on the absolute coincidence of the affirmation and the negation (at the same time and in the same respect) that has characterized them since Aristotle. If identity is constituted by difference, this "being constituted by" permits of no speculative retrieval of an identity between identity and difference. "Contradiction" and "paradox" denote ways of attempting to tame a difference or an impossibility that ought to be thought otherwise. But surely if contradiction has traditionally been associated with the coinciding of opposites, then to point out, perhaps by way of a deconstruction or disarticulation of identity and the present, that such absolute coincidences can never occur is also to point out that there can be, in principle, no contradictions.

For example, consider the manner in which Levinas proposes the distinction between the saying and the said (*le dire* and *le dit*). One of its side effects is the way it enables the self-refuting, self-contradicting statement to continue signifying over and above its formal and thematic demise. Levinas refers to the skeptical thesis that, when refuted, returns and returns to refute itself endlessly. That endlessness is the very feature Levinas wants to applaud as attesting to what in philosophy tells of another commitment. The self-refuting thesis is not a paradox, but the persons who propose it do thereby contradict themselves. Levinas's idea of the saying of the said permits us to say that what counts in the proposal of the thesis is not, however, silenced by the fact of this contradiction. If Levinas wants his description of the saying of the said to follow the becoming paradoxical or enigmatic of what would, on first view, simply be a self-contradiction, how are we to take this notion of enigma and paradox? Is it to be distinguished from contradiction—as is perhaps Deleuze's conception of the impossible and the paradoxical?[9] If so, then to the extent that it is not a contradiction, the principle stands, and to the extent that it is a contradiction, the new or specific designation must emphasize how—unlike all other contradictions—it resists the application of the principle. Thus we seem to have dialetheism, or at least a view whose judgment on the principle amounts to that of dialetheism. Either way, it is worth noting that Levinas's hyperbolic reintroduction of time (of diachrony) ensures that what goes without saying here ("without saying" in both its colloquial English and its Levinasian meanings) is contradiction itself. Not all saids are contradictory. It is just that a contradictory said, in this case the self-refuting skeptical thesis, makes the point so well. Nor is there properly a contradiction between saying and said. Nor is the saying to be analyzed pragmatically; it is not that the saying of the skeptical thesis uses the semantic content of the thesis as a means of conveying something else, a second or further said. The skeptical thesis serves Levinas's purposes because it is both this thesis and, in being presented as this thesis, a contradiction; that is, if it continues signifying, it cannot do so simply because of its content, but it must do so partly or almost completely because of its content. Yet, whatever the subtleties, notice that regarding contradiction itself there is nothing to be said, or, rather, it suffices to acknowledge that here there is only the said and perhaps that the logicians have said it. How are Levinas's readers to grasp the idea of the saying of the said without supposing that they are thereby escaping the full force of the said contradiction *as* a contradiction? If contradiction as such goes without saying, then the introduction of saying is a foolproof way of avoiding contradiction. When the phenomenon, in being described, turns into enigma, into something other than a phenomenon—when, in appearing, the phenomenon turns into what does not appear—then some Levinasian account of that turning, if it does not do it justice, at least presents it as implicating ethics rather than logic. And why is this not also a matter of contradiction resolution or avoidance? Whatever else it does, the saying of the said both implicitly upholds the principle of contradiction in its most straightforward and strictest Aristotelian version, insofar as the principle is a principle of the avoidance of contradiction, and allows Levinas's text to avoid any question concerning the principle and its logic.

Derrida's writing of the term *différance* supposedly preempts just this sort of summary of his texts. Indeed it would not be difficult to show that several of Derrida's comments on Levinas illustrate Levinas's continued indebtedness to a logic and a language from which he would like to imagine his philosophy has broken. *Différance* then would help to sustain a philosophical writing that, aware of the impossibility of a break with a philosophy or metaphysics where "contradiction" and "paradox" designate the sites of a perpetual problem, is nevertheless committed to a different way of thinking of, remarking, and perhaps naming those sites. Thus, almost from the first, Derrida prefers to speak of "force" and "desire" rather than "contradiction." Wherever thinking encounters a contradiction that lingers and that acquires, in its lingering, a coherence as a contradiction, what that thinking encounters can also be understood as "expressing the force of a desire." What a contradiction expresses is not itself to be named a contradiction and so is not itself something that can be avoided or overcome, or held to indicate an error. What has traditionally been called a contradiction is to be regarded as a symptom whose diagnosis demands another type of naming, one not so implicated in the metaphysics of (co)presence and phono-logo-centrism. With his talk of "force," as with the "undecidability" that follows from it, Derrida suggests both that the name "contradiction" remains too much the property of Hegelianism, too bound up with the sense of an eventual reconciliation or resolution, and that what is at issue in writing and thinking of *différance* is nothing that can be "subsumed by the generality of *logical* contradiction." Force, undecidability, *différance*: a matter neither of a direct polemical challenge to a traditional way of diagnosing contradictions nor a clear-cut move beyond such diagnosis. These interventions of Derrida's, if they do not simply replace "contradiction" or "paradox," can, however, be cited as reasons for reluctance to use those words. But there is a fine line between a remarking of contradiction that warrants such reluctance and a thinking that assumes that contradictions and paradoxes, newly remarked, are henceforth avoided and avoidable. One has to stay very close to the principle if one does not want to be read as simply upholding it.

To return for a moment to Priest, and to Derrida's place in Priest's survey of the history of philosophy. Derrida's *différance* is considered in a section of Priest's book concerned with various philosophical theories of meaning each of which can be said to challenge the idea of semantic determinacy. "All such theories," Priest writes, "end in contradictions at the limit of expression." And "all render some important states of affairs ineffable (while managing to express them). And in all cases the states of affairs in question are ones that are, in some sense, about notions that make expression in language itself possible: the unity of the proposition (Frege, early Wittgenstein), reference (Quine), truth (Davidson . . .), rule-following (Wittgenstein), *différance* (Derrida)."[10] For a reader familiar with Derrida's texts, especially the "Différance" essay, it will be clear that in some respects Derrida's project is not dissimilar to Priest's. Thus *différance*, too, is to mark what it is in the thought of limits (limits of language and reason, limit as origin and end) that necessarily escapes thematization by a logic and metaphysics committed to a whole network of principles governing truth and presentation. Derrida's work, then, would not only serve as one more example of a philosophical inquiry destined to failure and to the production of contradictions but would itself comment on the general implications of such failure and on what calls for principled philosophical inquiry in the first place. This second-order questioning, however, as Derrida acknowledges, gives him neither the right nor the means to produce texts that can exempt themselves from the formal difficulties, the contradictions, befalling the texts and arguments he would examine. The contradictions cannot be simply pointed out and then recalled in a survey of a philosophical tradition because the pointing out must itself be bound to the very problems of thought it would take as its object. This would be one feature of Derrida's work distinguishing it from the work of most, perhaps all, of the others in Priest's list and also from Priest's list itself. But no matter how ingeniously Derrida's own texts show themselves to be both vulnerable to the necessity and the impossibility of self-reference and able to keep a minimal distance from the tradition in which self-reference and the paradoxes associated with it can be summarized and labeled accordingly, nothing prevents Priest's point from being made over and over again. Logically, Derrida runs up against a limit, and in speaking so as not to speak of it, or in writing it under erasure—however we choose to describe it, he can be aligned with all the other philosophers whose inquiries condemn them to the same non-end. At this juncture one might concede the formal similarity and so the extent to which Derrida must remain within a self-referential dilemma, but then add that Derrida's remarking of that dilemma is not only logical but also pragmatic, ethical, and political. It concerns the vulnerability of a discourse that must (logically and ethically) take responsibility for its incompleteness, not only the yet-to-be-discovered incompleteness that manifests itself in an inability to conclude, but also the incompleteness of and at the beginning, the impossibility of a justification for starting where one does, here where one must justify oneself. Derrida is increasingly interested in outlining a responsibility for what, according to any ethico-political system, it is unreasonable to demand responsibility for. In shifting the emphasis in this fashion, however, it is important to avoid the trap of a certain Levinasianism and the appeal, as though in place of argument, to ethics, not to logic. It is interesting to note how this allusion to something more or other than logic seems to repeat Aristotle's move in his not quite (or not simply) logical demonstration, the silencing *elegtikos.* It is even more interesting to see how Derrida's relatively recent return to a phenomenological or quasi-phenomenological description of this anarchic responsibility cites the "disarticulation of contradiction" and attempts to utilize it.

It is the proximity of the Hegelian conception of contradiction to that of reconciliation that leads Derrida to distrust the term. But although what distinguishes Derrida's treatment of contradiction from Priest's might be described as his view that, for Hegel, contradictions are resolvable and are thus not exactly "true" in the dialethic sense, this does not mean that Derrida himself can be seen as championing the idea of true contradictions. It is not that Hegel does not go as far, with respect to contradiction, as Priest thinks he does, but rather that going as far as Priest thinks Hegel and he want to go is, on Derrida's terms, not possible. On this point Derrida's project is perhaps more conservative than Priest's, certainly less sure that the principle of contradiction has ever been, or can ever be, challenged by either a new logic or a rewritten history of traditional logic.

Consider the difference between Derrida and Priest here as one of contrasting narratives.

Priest	*Derrida*
1. The principle of contradiction from Aristotle onwards.	1. Contradiction before Hegel.
2. Hegel's challenge to the principle.	2. Hegel's attack on the pre-Hegelian endeavor to control or avoid contradiction, an attack which shows how thought thrives on (the overcoming of) contradiction.
3. Logic after Hegel, not necessarily indebted to Hegel for there are other arguments for "*p.-p*".	3(i). A reading of contradiction as expressing the force of a desire. 3(ii). A disarticulation of contradiction which seeks to indicate the faltering of the advance of Hegelian reconciliation.

Hegel plays a necessary role in the third stage of both the Priest and the Derrida "narratives," but it is only in the latter that the role is necessarily played by him. Hegel's critical treatment of contradiction and of the status and place of the logical principles in their Leibnizian determination is thereby necessarily endorsed by Derrida. Nevertheless the move from stage 2 to stage 3 involves a subtle qualifying of this endorsement and proposes a slightly different take on Hegel's successful complicating of the notions of identity and contradiction. Derrida's 3(i) is consistent both with dialetheism (and so with Hegel as read and narrated by Priest) and with Hegelianism (as read and narrated by me). "Step" 3(ii) would undermine that consistency but in such a way that both it and 3(i) cannot escape being judged as pre-Hegelian and as still committed to the principle of contradiction. So be it. Such judgments miss Derrida's sense for what, in always leaving one just this side of reconciliation, also prevents a simple celebration of traditional (pre-Hegelian) "contradiction" and "paradox." Neither with it nor beyond it, the narrative itself cannot be sustained, and 3(ii) ensures that this third stage cannot really be a stage at all. If we never reach an end or Hegelian conclusion, we also never arrive at a concluding (dialethic) contradiction. The disarticulation of contradiction is thus neither Hegelian nor dialethic, and the thinking that would acknowledge or attempt to work with it will always be vulnerable to a Hegelian or dialethic paraphrase. If the reasons given for no longer simply endorsing the pre-Hegelian (Leibnizian) principle of identity or contradiction are Hegelian (or perhaps dialethic) ones, then the concern of 3(ii) is either with the Hegelian (or perhaps dialethic) remarking of the principle or with a restating of the principle: -(*p*.-*p*) states that "*p*.-*p*" must be disarticulated.

Derrida's philosophy is often broached in terms of its relation to limits and logic. It is often associated with other anti-epistemological arguments in which, as one such commentator puts it, what are at stake are "the limits of logic and other discursive and disciplinary boundaries." Such arguments "follow classical assumptions and arguments to their limits in order to derive their logical consequences, which lead to contradictions from within the classical theories themselves"; and the theories making use of these arguments "are not constrained (or are not constrained in the same way) by the classical principles and limits that they problematize."[11] Notice how close this applied Derridianism comes to dialetheism; indeed they appear virtually interchangeable. Why not accept the term? Derrida would not hesitate to admit to the extraordinary repercussions of having to adopt a difficult theory or argument even if it entailed changing the whole of our logical and metaphysical vocabulary or at least the manner in which it is to be used and cited. Think of the proliferation of "both . . . and . . . " and "neither . . . nor . . . " clauses in Derrida's work, not only "both *p* and -*p*" and "neither *p* nor -*p*" but also "both 'both *p* and -*p*' and 'neither *p* and -*p*'" and "neither 'both *p* and -*p*' nor 'neither *p* nor -*p*,'" and so on. Derridianism might fit more comfortably with dialetheism than did Hegelianism. But if we know that neither Arkady Plotnitsky (the commentator quoted above) nor Derrida would be happy with the appellation, is it not because dialetheism remains within the purview of traditional logic and metaphysics, a thinking bound to principles—however complex the new understanding of at least one of them now must be? Logic, in exceptional circumstances, can be shown to embrace paraconsistency, and the logical and philosophical task of the paraconsistent logician is also either one of protecting classical logic from this exception or one of showing the extent to which it needs no special protection. On this summary, either Derrida endorses true contradictions or he so breaks with that thinking for which the principle of contradiction is a principle that its "disarticulation" is to be the last word on the subject. In other words: insofar as Derrida does not break with a formal logical-metaphysical project, his conclusions are compatible with those of dialetheism; insofar as the conclusions are incompatible, Derrida does break with any such project. But Derrida, unlike his commentator, might also be unhappy with this anti-epistemological application. The disarticulation of contradiction and contradiction without contradiction are not to be so easily accommodated, yet are perhaps to be accommodated as what can never be easily accommodated. With the repeated emphasis on this intriguing difficulty—the difficulty of this disarticulation—and on what prevents it from hardening into another (radical) logical thesis, there remains necessarily the always less intriguing difficulty of this contradiction. It has to be contradiction's own difficulty that resonates in the halting disarticulation that confronts it. Without such a resonance, that disarticulation and that other "without" would be everywhere silent and illegible. The reader has to realize that its ostensible weakening by way of disarticulation cannot, by definition, be the last word. Thus the middle *sans* in "*sans sans sans*" must, in its turn, be read so as not to produce a contradiction. The weakening of the negative goes all the way down. One of its consequences can be illustrated by recalling the three meanings of "freeplay" and "undecidability" that Derrida distinguishes in the afterword to *Limited Inc.* First, a sense that "determines in a manner that is still too antidialectical, hence too dialectical, that which resists binarity, or even triplicity." Second, a sense that "defines, still within the order of the calculable, the limits of decidability, of calculability, of formalizable completeness." And third, a sense that "remains heterogeneous both to the dialectic and to the calculable. In accordance with what is only ostensibly a paradox, this particular undecidable opens the field of decision or of decidability."[12] The first sense acknowledges an undecidability always recuperable by a Hegelianism. The second sense acknowledges an undecidability always compatible with and so recuperable by a dialetheism. And the third sense, this particular undecidable, clearly in this context—and perhaps always—the impetus for Derridian deconstruction? There is a tantalizing ambiguity as to how we are to interpret "in accordance with what is only ostensibly a paradox." There are two mutually exclusive—that is, contradictory—interpretations; for either it says that we, like the traditional philosophical logician, are to realize that the contradictory assertion(s), the paradox, to which we seem to be committed can be shown not to be contradictory, or it says that we are not to use the word "paradox" here at all, for what is at issue has nothing to do with a traditional philosophical logic. For many of his readers and commentators, it is this latter interpretation that is to take precedence. It alone permits the third sense of undecidability—this particular undecidable—both to resist the Hegelian or dialethic paraphrase and to assert something radically and logically *new*. On our reading, however, the former interpretation cannot be logically or methodologically excluded. Decision, the moment of decidability, is not the avoiding or overcoming or even disarticulating of a contradiction or paradox. And this is not because, on Derrida's description, decision and decidability must somehow be deemed to have challenged or broken with the principle of identity or contradiction. In none of its meanings does undecidability entail that contradiction is sustained in decision or calculation. The disarticulation of contradiction is not primarily an ingenious means of theorizing and utilizing contradictions after Hegel and after a Hegelian or non-Hegelian subversion of the principle. "Disarticulation" so qualifies the noun that, in principle, no such theory or subversion is possible. It may not be Derrida's topic, or indeed an issue of much interest to him, but the principle stands. Yet why choose here between the two interpretations of "what is only ostensibly a paradox"? Why not continue and conclude here, too, with "both . . . and . . . " or "both 'both . . . and . . .' and 'neither . . . nor . . . '"? Because I know of nowhere in Derrida's work where such formulations are allowed to stand as conclusions. Their employment, however "playful" or "perverse," is always to be qualified or justified as though they were only ostensibly dialethic. *This* undecidable that "opens up the field of decision" is not a contradiction.[13]

V

And so it may be that, despite appearances and despite some notable claims to the contrary, philosophy has never really denied the principle of contradiction. On at least one interpretation of that instructive, regulative, or stipulative opening "not"—"not (*p* and not *p*)," -(*p*.-*p*)—it may be that no serious philosopher has ever even claimed to deny it, that it is in principle impervious to any denial. Yet to contend as much is to run the risk of being charged with dogmatism, with adherence to an incipient transcendental argument; for how is the contention to be supported if not, ultimately, by the claim that to deny the principle of contradiction is simply to fail to meet the conditions required for "philosophy" as such, for what it is to be a "serious philosopher"? If there is a speech act that can be accurately classified as a denial of the principle of contradiction (for example, "I deny -[*p*.-*p*]"), then, presuming the correctness of the contention that the principle of contradiction cannot be denied, the performance of the speech act—inevitably destined to failure—can tell us something only about the behavior or the state of mind of the speaker. We would have to treat it as a symptom rather than as a meaningful contribution to a philosophical conversation. For various current debates, this enforced symptomatology can be regarded only as unjustifiably exclusionary and as untenable for (variously) logical, ethical, or historical reasons. Indeed the "philosophy" such symptomatology would protect and define—and protect by defining—could perhaps be challenged most effectively in the name and with the voice of the one it would begin by silencing, the one who says or who says he says "*p*.-*p*." It would begin by taking seriously what philosophy, ostensibly by definition, claims to be unable to take seriously—*this* denial, the denial of *this* principle—and it might conclude by treating the principled refusal to admit the possibility of anyone's denying the principle of contradiction as the real symptom in the affair, the thing that really requires historical or genealogical investigation. Thus even if philosophy has never denied or claimed to deny the principle, saying so may prove to be inherently difficult. But this particular way of countering and utilizing a transcendental argument to generate or to invoke the figure of the "excluded" cannot count against the principle itself or, at least, against what in this principle makes it a principle.

If, on the one hand, the "excluded" is presented as stating "*p* and not *p*," then what matters in the presentation is the fact that the contradiction is being used to undermine the authority of the philosopher. The stubborn refusal to accept the principle is treated as a symptom both by the philosopher in the dispute and by the observer of the dispute who would enjoy or celebrate the philosopher's frustration and the disputant's perseverance. The observer's (or metaphilosopher's) symptomotology might appear or imagine itself to be more charitable than the philosopher's, but neither of them thinks that what the disputant is saying—"*p* and not *p*"—is *true.* What matters in the observer's use of the scene is the effect the refusal of philosophy has on the philosopher. The observer requires the philosopher to be unable to accept the content of the disputant's speech. Accordingly the observer requires that the philosopher and the observer uphold the principle of contradiction. (Note that if the observer thinks he or she has good Priest-type reasons for defending the disputant—that is, the "*p*.-*p*" in question just is one of Priest's true contradictions—then there is no need to "observe" the encounter. There are good reasons for engaging in the conversation and for trying to get the philosopher to accept exactly what the disputant is saying. Of course we have doubted whether there can be such a move, but, as far as the objection we are considering here is concerned, what counts is not just the philosopher's happening to be unable to accept the contradiction but his or her being, in principle, incapable of doing so.)

If, on the other hand, drawing on the "disarticulation of contradiction," we envisage the disputant as saying something other than "*p* and not *p*," this particular problem is not going to arise at all. The disarticulation of contradiction, this weakening of negation, might lead us to imagine the Aristotelian scene a little differently. What if it were Melville's Bartleby who were being asked to speak? What if, when ordered to speak and so to enact the performative contradiction the philosopher knows such speaking must produce, the disputant were to say "I would prefer not to," that is, if he were to speak but not quite activate the contradiction and thereby reinforce its principle. Bartleby's strange way of not quite refusing to go along with things seems to be a way of continuing both to go along and not to go along. If it is nonparticipation, it is not strong enough to be judged so. Its effect on the other characters in Melville's story, the manner in which it insinuates itself into their own words and actions, might be described in terms of a refusal or resistance that does not quite reach the point of being something anyone could recognize *as* a refusal or resistance; and some might see here a useful allegory or analogy for literature's refusal of philosophy, a refusal that philosophy cannot recognize as a refusal. But if what is intriguing in Bartleby's assertion is the blend of affirmation and negation that never quite results in "yes" or "no," this does not mean either that the sentence is both true and false or that it is neither true nor false. It is or may be true just to the extent that Bartleby would prefer not to do whatever it is he is being invited to do. There is much that is interesting here, much that is important for an account of (literary and nonliterary) speech acts, but as we have already noted, to attend to this sort of "excluded" or problematic utterance is not to attend to a contradiction. Indeed if the attention such intervening noninterventions merit seems due to their being almost "paradoxes"—almost "contradictions"—then that "almost," as much as the "paradox" and "contradiction" it qualifies, is indebted to the principle that instantiates them. What matters is that Bartleby's words do not take the form of a contradiction. In terms of the disarticulation of contradiction, the one thing the systematically excluded has never said and could never say is "*p* and not *p*."

VI

"Some people get stirred up because, after the reference in my inaugural address 'What Is Metaphysics?' (1929), I keep on raising the question of logic." (*Man regt sich sogar darüber auf, daß ich seit dem Hinweis in der Antrittsrede 'Was ist Metaphysik?'* [1929] *imer wieder die Frage nach der 'Logik' vorbringe.*)[14] Which could mean either that logicians, horrified then, remain so now, or that those not horrified then do not quite see the need for endlessly repeating the step away from logic implicit in Heidegger's announcement about the derivative nature of negation and in his claim, following this announcement, that "the idea of logic disintegrates in the turbulence of a more original thinking."[15] But it is surely a step away.

Famously, "What Is Metaphysics?" sets the tone: "The proposition that contradiction is to be avoided [*der Satz vom zu vermeidenden Widerspruch*] is the commonly cited ground rule of all thought [*die gemeinhin beigezogene Grundregel des Denkens überhaupt*]." "But are we allowed to tamper with the rule of 'logic'? [*Aber läßt sich die Herrschaft der 'Logik' antasten?*]" "We assert that the Nothing is more original than the 'not' and negation. [*Wir behaupten: das Nichts ist ürsprünglicher als das Nicht und die Verneinung.*]"[16] The nothing, linked in the lecture to an anxiety that robs us of speech, a fundamental mood preventing participation in each and any conversation, usefully returns us to Aristotle's *Metaphysics*. Note the crucial performativity of the "We assert" (*Wir behaupten*). This assertion against logic would speak of and to what resists ontical articulation and thematization. It deliberately has the force and the provocation of Aristotle's disputant.

A principle tells us how we are to go on. It tells us how we are to proceed. A paradox tells us that we must do something we cannot do, namely go on, go on to affirm what cannot be, most commonly to assert a proposition and its contrary. Most commonly, most catastrophically, a paradox will demand that we assert something that is both true and not true. "Paradox" is perhaps the best name for the catastrophes that can befall and have befallen principles, those moments when what must be taken as read cannot be taken as read; moments when what by definition need not be thought further, indeed cannot be thought further, must be thought further; moments when one must go on but cannot go on.

The idea that what some think should be the most settled and the most settling of entities (principles) can come to be seen as what is most unsettling for thinking is conveyed in the passage from Novalis cited by Heidegger in *The Principle of Reason* and used above as the first of our epigraphs: "Should the highest principle contain the highest paradox in its task?" Yet having cited the word "paradox," Heidegger will not return to it in the lecture course. But are there not places where it might usefully be returned to? Why, for instance, does Heidegger, when he considers whether the principle of reason (*nihil est sine ratione*, *Nichts ist ohne Grund*, nothing is without reason [ground]) addresses itself and so says of itself either that it, too, has a reason (a ground) or that it alone, among all that is, is groundless—why does Heidegger say nothing of the matter of self-referentiality, nothing of the paradoxes of self-reference and self-predication, again nothing of paradox itself?[17] Is the word simply quoted as a rhetorical gesture despite its seemingly accurate and straightforward naming of the issue at hand? How can a formulation such as "Nothing without reason—this, which is something, is without reason" (*PR*, 17 / *SG*, 35), how can this repetition or doubling of "without"—a word whose importance for this course must not be understated—" 'without reason' without reason," how can all of this not bring to mind, in the impending paradoxicality of the question, the question of paradox? If "paradox" obliges us to begin to read what has to be taken as read, namely the very principles governing our reading and thinking, then does it not name exactly what Heidegger is trying to do in this lecture course with the principle of reason?

These are no doubt bad questions, the sort to be expected perhaps from the nervous (and nervously hostile) newcomer to Heidegger's work, who, feeling that something ought to be said, confronts the bewildering intensity of the way in which Heidegger lingers with and over these four words, *Nichts ist ohne Grund.* And they must seem bad reasons for other than Heideggerian reasons as well, because it is not obvious that the principle itself as formulated either yields or moves toward a contradiction. It could simply be false. But of course for Heidegger the question of its possible falsity does not arise; what is to be considered is its *success.* Heidegger begins with the immediate success of Leibniz's formula, an immediacy Heidegger will not undermine but will certainly interrogate with a view to its historicity. One question, if not exactly the first then almost the first, will be precisely how this principle, so self-evident, so instantly accepted and put to work, remained unformulated for so long. Thus its validity has from the first gone without saying, and Heidegger is concerned with pondering a moment of originality, of composition, where what is composed immediately goes without saying, is immediately taken at face value. So if the principle of reason is considered in this sense as valid—that is, as what is everywhere taken as valid—the question of its self-application does not arise. And arising as it does, it can hardly be said to warrant our questions concerning paradox, because such questions can be shown to depend upon the principle of reason's being derivative, and so upon its not being the principle of principles. As we said earlier, were there to be for Leibniz a proof of the principle of reason, it would be in terms of the principle of identity or contradiction. It would involve the reduction of the principle of reason to an identity and thus to something it would be contradictory not to uphold. In such a case the principle of reason would apply to itself but in so doing would indicate the logical priority of the principle of identity or contradiction. And here there would be no paradox as such. But, given that Heidegger wants to claim the priority of the principle of reason and wants to read it as the principle of principles, the principle that brings us to the question of what a principle is as a principle, is it not a matter of insisting upon paradox? Not if the figure and the predicament that we know as "paradox" itself depends upon the principle of contradiction: not if the principle of contradiction is the condition of the possibility of something's being identified as a paradox. Here, then, is the thesis, and if true, it would explain Heidegger's (and perhaps Derrida's) reluctance to use the term. "Contradiction" and "paradox" are problems only for those engaged on certain specifiable projects, projects that would fall under the heading of what Heidegger calls "logistics."

In "On the Essence of Truth" Heidegger twice refers to the appearance of paradox (*den Anschein des Paradoxen*), to an apparent paradox. Unlike Derrida's "only ostensibly a paradox," Heidegger's reference does not assert that there is really no paradox here but rather explains why a certain way of writing, a certain type of sentence or discourse, is to be avoided, namely, because it has the air of paradox about it. What is to be avoided is this word, this figure. One is being instructed not to apply this term to the sorts of difficulties Heidegger is describing because the term itself militates against what is most thought-provoking in those difficulties. It returns them to the domain of a traditional logic. Later, the implications of this instruction will reveal themselves in a discussion of both the effect of the principle of contradiction on our thought of language and the view of language presupposed by the principle. Thus the following from *What Is Called Thinking?*: "To be possible, the proposition must from the start avoid self-contradiction. This is why the law, that contradiction must be avoided, is considered a basic tenet of the proposition. Only because thinking is defined as *logos*, as an utterance, can the statement about contradiction perform its role as a law of thought."[18] To read the principle not only and no longer as a law of thought is to begin to uncover what is derivative in that philosophy of language for which the proposition is the exemplary linguistic entity.

In this connection, consider Heidegger's lifelong attempt to wrest "logic" from "logistics," where this title is said to conceal the transformation of logic into the question of the essence of language. His continuing to raise the question of logic has everything to do with this retrieval or rediscovery of the logos in logic. The development of logistics arises from a change in the way philosophy broaches the question of language, but it also, for Heidegger, reveals an inability to think through the consequences of this change. Logistics is the axiomatic securing of calculative thinking. On the one hand, we have: calculative thinking, logistics, philosophical logic (including everything that goes by the name of the philosophy of language), and any propositional logic (including Hegel's). And on the other hand? A thinking of language *as* language, a thinking at least dependent upon the claim that everything done in the name of philosophical logic entails thinking language as something other than language, presenting language as a means of communication or expression, as an instrument. However it is presented, it is a matter of its being necessarily subservient to laws, the clarification of which requires that language be thought primarily in terms of this subservience and so as analogous to other realms or phenomena where one advances by appealing to what precedes or underlies them. If "language" names what is always, in principle, a possible object of study, and if such study proceeds by identifying and classifying linguistic entities or the parts of language, then a decision has already been made as to its nature or essence.

If Heidegger can sometimes seem uninterested either in justifying such claims or indeed in even advancing them as explicitly or as crudely as this, what does he do? In seeking a thinking of language as language, he offers a series of meditations upon language in which one encounters the tautology "language is language" as thought-provoking, as though the essence of language might come to language by way of tautology. Heidegger often moves away from a focus on the sentence or proposition, as when we are instructed to follow the movement of a lecture rather than to treat it as the context within which a particular sentence or proposition comes to have an expressive or thetic function. "Die Sprache spricht" is not a sentence propounding an argument or thesis, a sentence that the text in which it appears would either justify or defend. Rather it serves a thinking that would wish to withhold such assertions. The texts do not permit us to add to the content of the tautology, thus transforming it into something nontautological. They attempt to bring us to a point in our thinking about language where we cease to expect there to be anything more that can or need be said. Many of Heidegger's later writings touch on tautologies or incline towards them. Consider the frequent verbalizing of the noun: the world worlds (*die Welt weltet*), time times (*die Zeit zeitet*), language speaks (*die Sprache spricht*), nothing nothings (*das Nichts nichtet*). Although not themselves tautologies, they along with so many of Heidegger's controversial etymologies return us to what in the word, the name, verbalizes the name so as to say the same of the same, to let the name unfold in and on its own terms. Heidegger also evokes a renewed saying of the same, tautology, as a means of moving against and away from Hegel and the speculative proposition, that is, as a means of distinguishing his later thinking and the (poetic) thinking that thinking announces from Hegelian thought.

If one reason for eschewing talk of paradox and contradiction takes us to the crux of Heidegger's reflections on language, another takes us to Heidegger's rethinking of the history of philosophy (metaphysics), a history in which the principle of contradiction is encountered as an event. In the 1939 lecture course on Nietzsche and "the will to power as knowledge and metaphysics," Heidegger examines Nietzsche's attempt to ask about the presuppositions of the principle of contradiction. He applauds Nietzsche for recognizing that the principle asserts something about beings and about the being of beings but argues that Nietzsche fails to grasp what is most significant in the retrieving of a law of thought as a law of being. The law in its Aristotelian version says explicitly and knowingly, "the essence of beings consists in the constant absence of contradiction."[19] Nietzsche correctly detects the imperative within the principle, the manner in which it demands that before a being is accepted as true and so as the being it is, the criteria for what is to count as true and the conditions for its acceptance must be established. This is what the principle does. But for Heidegger, Nietzsche overlooks the historicity of this demand and of the principle's being given as a demand in this way by Aristotle. When Nietzsche asks for the presuppositions of the principle of contradiction he is not asking for something unknown or unavailable to Aristotle. The question is already Aristotle's. The introduction of the principle already tries to answer it and, in answering it, to function as a genuine *archē*. Nietzsche argues both that not being able to contradict is an incapacity rather than a truth and that the absence of contradictions cannot be a thesis about what there is but rather must be an instruction as to how existence is to be defined and as to what is to be counted as existing. But, for Heidegger, this is not really to argue against Aristotle. Nietzsche's interpretation of the principle and the demand it would make on thinking belongs to the thinking that has traditionally sought to meet that demand. To treat the principle merely as a demand on thought, as though its efficacy or its power has always depended on its passing itself off as a truth or law of nature rather than as an instruction, is still to presuppose the meaning of that "truth" and of the (natural) beings over which it holds sway. To treat the principle as a law of thought, however complex the accompanying analysis, is to fail to appreciate how the principle might occur historically as such a law and as this demand. Heidegger imagines the moment:

Something present and permanently necessary gets lost as such if its presence and its presentness are disregarded by the perspective on another point in time, if its perspective is disregarded by the perspective on something impermanent. If this happens the result is that the same thing is affirmed and denied of a being. Man is thoroughly capable of something like this. He can contradict himself. But if man maintains himself in a contradiction, what is impossible does not of course consist in the fact that yes and no are thrown together, but that man excludes himself from representing beings as such and forgets *what* he really wanted to grasp in his yes and no. Through contradictory assertions which man can freely make about the same thing, he displaces himself from his essence into nonessence; he dissolves his relation to beings as such. [*Durch widersprechende Behauptungen, die der Mensch ungehindert über dasselbe vorbringen kann, setzt er sich aus seinem Wesen in das Unwesen; er löst den Bezug zum Seienden als solchen.*] This fall into the nonessence of himself is uncanny in that it always seems harmless, in that business and pleasure go on just as before, in that it doesn't seem so important at all what and how one thinks: until one day the catastrophe is there. [*Dieser Abfall in das Unwesen seiner selbst hat darin sein Umheimliches, daß er sich stets wie eine Harmlosigkeit ausnimmt, daß dabei die Geschäfte und das Vergnügen genauso weitergehen wie zuvor, daß es überhaupt nicht so sehr ins Gewicht fällt, was und wie man denkt; bis eines Tages die Katastrophe da ist*].[20]

This is not an easy passage. We restrict ourselves to one question. When is the catastrophe there? It is as though the catastrophe befalls not Aristotle but the disputant. As though a more nuanced account of the "demonstration" in the *Metaphysics* would take Aristotle's difficulty in imagining the disputant as human to denote the extraordinary effect of the principle on the human disputant. It is not the paradox that is catastrophic but rather the principle itself when read as a principle of being.

Heidegger reads the principle of contradiction first as a principle of being, and later as a saying of being. Can we not say that "paradox," the word and its always temptingly easy application, commits us to not reading the principle?

VII

At the beginning of *Being and Time*, Heidegger reflected on the three main presuppositions that kept the question of the meaning of being at bay: first, "being is the most universal concept"; second, "being is indefinable"; and third, "being is self-evident." Regarding this third presupposition, Heidegger continued: "Whenever one cognizes anything or makes an assertion, whenever one comports oneself towards beings, even towards oneself, some use is made of 'being'; and this expression is held to be intelligible 'without further ado' ['*ohne weiteres*']."[21] In the context of his fundamental ontology, Heidegger will consider these presuppositions not as reasons for abandoning any attempt at a new theory of being but as theoretically vague and undeveloped features of a pretheoretical relation to being. Thus the sense of being that passes without further ado is to be retrieved in a positive description of the vague everyday understanding of being that characterizes being-in-the-world. The existential analytic of that being-in-the-world thus brings to the fore the complexity of what does factically pass without further ado. In theory and in everyday existence, being passes "without further ado"; but the simplistic interpretation of that self-evidence as it is presupposed in the former cannot begin to comprehend or to analyze its meaning in the latter. Hence, in part, Heidegger's project. Thirty years later Heidegger would reflect on another instance of an unthought self-evidence, the *ohne weiteres*, which, letting the principle of reason function as a principle, keeps at bay an investigation into what this principle says of itself and of what a principle is. But here it is not a matter of a description or analysis of factical life, the pretheoretical engagement only dimly perceived in the theoretical overview. There is here no existential analytic and no fundamental ontology. It may be that without such a logical, methodological, and chronological contextualizing, what passes without further ado cannot and ought not lose entirely its simple and theoretical import: what passes without further ado—unlike the meaning of being in *Being and Time* and unlike the principle of reason as it is read and rehearsed in the lecture course—*passes*, unremarked and unremarkably, without further ado.

It is, it seems, a question of transition, from philosophical logic and the philosophy of language to a thinking of language as language, from principles understood as what protects thinking from the catastrophic paradox to an encounter with principles in their historicity as catastrophic. *The Principle of Reason* is concerned with teaching and following a certain transition or alteration, but it is also an investigation into the very idea of such a move. In a strange way *The Principle of Reason* constantly invites the reader or listener to the thought that the step we thematize as having been taken—be it earlier in the lecture course or earlier in Heidegger's work—just to the extent that we do thematize it and do tell ourselves a story about how we got where we are, has not been taken and so remains to be taken. It points to what I have elsewhere called the doubling of the "not yet" in Heidegger.

Heidegger will read Leibniz, the thinker of the calculus, of calculability, with an ear for what, in the principles or rather the principle of principles underpinning that thought, cannot be calculated, an exception that would not be a logical exception, less an exception to the rule than the exception in and of the rule, the exceptionality of the exceptional rule, the principle of principles, the principle of reason. Now of course this principle is not, for Leibniz, *the* principle of principles. It is one of the two supreme principles. Importantly, its role for Leibniz is also transitional, permitting the logical step from mathematical reason (the domain of the principle of identity or contradiction) to the reason of natural philosophy, metaphysics, and ontology. Heidegger, in effectively arguing for the primacy of the principle of this transition, forces both the principle and the idea of such a transition back on itself, to think the principle (*Satz*), the essence of the principle and the principle of principles, as itself a transition, a step or leap (*Satz*).

With the proviso that what follows be seen as no more than extracts from a commentary on *The Principle of Reason*, we can isolate a few overdetermined if understated moments in the reading of a principle:

(i) At the very center of the lecture course, at the point where the sixth lecture turns into the seventh, we find one of the oddest and most convoluted qualifications in all of Heidegger's work. The passage in question interrupts what the reader is surely predisposed to see as a quintessentially Heideggerian move, the move we expect Heidegger to make and the inference we expect him to draw. It occurs just prior to the step, the leap (*Satz*, not *Schritt*) from one way of hearing or reading the principle (*Satz*) to another way of reading or hearing the principle. Everything is in place. Heidegger has introduced Silesius's thought-provoking "The rose is without why; it blooms because it blooms" and has implied that what is said there about this being (the rose) will be appreciated thoughtfully only once the principle of reason is treated no longer as a statement about reason but as a statement about beings. Heidegger has thus distinguished between two tonalities, two ways in which the principle of reason is to be read:

The principle of reason reads: *"Nihil est sine ratione."* We hear this now often enough almost to the point of tedium. We should now tune in to how, in this sentence which speaks in a hollow unison, two different tonalities vibrate. [*Der Satz vom Grund lautet: Nihl est sine ratione. Nichts ist ohne Grund. Wir hören dies nun schon oft genug, fast bis zum Überdruß. Doch wir sollen jetzt vernehmen, wie in diesem gleichtönend hingesagten. Satz zwei verschiedene Tonarten schwingen.*] We can say: "*Nihil* est *sine* ratione." In the affirmative form this means: *everything has* a reason. Yet we can also set the pitch in this way: "Nihil *est* sine *ratione.*" In the affirmative form, this means: every *being* (*as a being*) has a *reason.* (*PR*, 39–40 / *SG*, 75)

In one tonality, the stress falls on the "nothing" and the "without": *Nihil* est *sine* ratione. Here is the principle in its traditional sounding, heard "now often enough almost to the point of tedium." In the other tonality the stress falls differently: Nihil *est* sine *ratione*; every being has a reason. From a principle of reason to a principle of being: the second tonality permits us to detect the true subject of the principle. Heidegger envisages the listeners' response to such a declaration: "Why wasn't this obvious content of the principle mentioned at the very first?" (*PR*, 44 / *SG*, 82). It is one of the tasks of the sixth lecture to justify this reticence and to show why the ordinary way of seeing that the principle concerns beings might miss what is vital in it. The problem lies in the very notion of a supreme or fundamental principle (*Grundsatz*) or *Prinzip*, namely that feature that permits it to stand as "something underivable [Unableitbares], the sort of thing which puts a check on thinking" (*PR*, 45 / *SG*, 83–84). As something underivable, the principle immediately goes without saying; its validity is assumed without further ado. Whether one immediately hears it as a principle about reason or a principle about beings, one hears it as a principle. Heidegger proposes that we remain for a while with the insight that "the principle *of* reason does not immediately speak *about* reason, rather about beings" (ibid.), in other words, that we do not take a step from one immediacy to another. To remain with this insight, Heidegger says, "is a dangerous step [*ein gefährlicher Schritt*]," for it brings us into a very different and critical relation with the (fundamental) principle. "Here all the steps of the discussion yet to come can still run awry despite our seeing what the principle of reason speaks about [*hier trotz der Sicht auf das, worüber der Satz vom Grund aussagt, noch alle folgenden Schritte der Eröterung in die Irre laufen können*]" (*PR*, 45 / *SG*, 84). Having issued this warning, Heidegger recalls an occasion on which he did not heed it. He refers back to his 1929 monograph *On the Essence of Reasons* (*Vom Wesen des Grundes*) and to its step from the principle to what is not defined in it, from reason to beings. It is not that such a step or the arguments warranting it are incorrect. It is precisely their correctness that led us astray, in some way betraying an immediacy that still called for thinking. Of that essay, Heidegger remarks: "This view of the apparent content of the principle [of reason] does not attain an insight into what lies closest at hand. Instead it allows itself to be compelled to take a step that is almost unavoidable [*fast unvermeidlich*]. Thus we can portray this step as an inference [*Den Schritt konnen wir in einer Schlussfolge also darstellen*]" (*PR*, 45 / *SG*, 84). In the seventh lecture Heidegger alludes to what is "virtually unavoidable [*zunächst unvermeidliche*]" (*PR*, 51 / *SG*, 93).

Heidegger is preparing his audience for a step, but before taking it we find not only this recollection of an almost unavoidable step (inference) but also the brief and now well-known remarks on metaphor (*Übertragung*). Metaphor as well is to be defined by and restricted to that securing of a movement, that thematizing of transition, characteristic of metaphysics. Metaphor is the figure that denotes the always already representable nature of transference. The theory of metaphor, or the theory metaphor endorses, always ensures a backdrop to any transference of meaning, a guaranteed intelligibility. The step to be undertaken in the course is thus a step from one sort of stepping (be it inference or the advancing of arguments and philosophical theses in the form of propositions, sentences, or metaphors) to another sort of stepping, one marked by the polysemic play of and on *Satz*.

Heidegger is referring back to *On the Essence of Reasons*, looking back in a way that interrupts a not-unfamiliar (Heideggerian) transition. If anything, this paper seeks, perhaps against the pull of Heidegger's seminar (at least against the pull of a certain Heideggerianism that would simply assume the possibility of this leap, this alteration in and of *Satz*), to stay this side of the leap from principle and sentence to what befalls the word on the other side. In this respect, *The Principle of Reason* holds out a fascinating prospect of a systematic undermining of a whole series of "steps beyond and away" characteristic of the confidence with which a Heideggerianism might wish to address metaphysics and the tradition. But if *The Principle of Reason* can be described as unfolding in this fashion, why, first, does Heidegger later feel compelled to add, "We can no longer hold back the question: why wasn't the change in tonality immediately introduced at the beginning of the entire lecture course?" (*PR*, 52 / *SG*, 95). And why, second, is it not enough to settle this matter, that is, to justify the first part of the course, by something like the summary from one step to another? Not a transition, this move toward a leap, but detours (sometimes summarizable; Heidegger recounts five main points). Nevertheless, however finely held apart from progression, from inference, either inference or a pre-leap must get us to the leap itself, if anything does, and once there, if we are ever there, no retrospective justification, no description of the detours we and the course have taken, can ever quite suffice.

Note then that in the reference back to *On the Essence of Reasons*, in this self-quotation, Heidegger alludes to a time and a text where something like the step we readers and listeners are about to take was explicitly taken. There was an earlier diagnostic and thematic treatment of the principle that allowed something to be said about the nature of ground and principle. The step we are about to take must be neither conceived nor taken as that one was. We were once led astray by Heideggerian self-evidence.

The course, it seems, cannot justify itself and its development by thematizing itself, even as a development from the thematizable to the unthematizable. It cannot tell or tell on itself even as a development from the tellable to the untellable. Quite literally, Heidegger, the course, can say neither what it is doing nor where it is going, and certainly not when it has succeeded in doing it, succeeded in getting there. Perhaps this impossibility is a part of its success, but it cannot be said to be. This at least would be a prefatory hypothesis to a commentary on the course. Note that according to it, nothing can be avoided by confessing to an earlier almost unavoidable erring or inferring. Indeed there might be a worry about the ambiguity of the "almost" in "almost unavoidable" (*fast unvermeidlich*), and the worry is a logical worry. For the "almost" allows us a way of avoiding the step, the logical step, the inference, yet here the "almost" can also attest to the "almost" nature of inference itself, that is, to its capacity to lead astray unless it be secured. Secured by what? Precisely by principles. Inferences are not necessarily valid, and a "valid inference" is always defined relative to a particular set of axioms. Inferences do not in and of themselves carry the full force of the logical "must." *Either* an inference is almost unavoidable because it is logical (and logic just is almost unavoidable, about as close to unavoidable as you can get; and now, because of that "almost," there is a way for us to proceed logically away from logic—for if an inference were unavoidable we could not have avoided it, but because it is almost unavoidable we can), *or* an inference is almost unavoidable because it is not logical enough, so that we need not be bound to it.

(ii) Here it is no more than a matter of citing a sentence of Leibniz's cited by Heidegger in the third lecture: "In one of his later pieces Leibniz writes: There are two supreme principles for all proofs, *Principium nempe contradictionis . . . et principium reddendae rationis*" (*PR*, 22 / *SG*, 44). For Heidegger, what is vital here is the characterization of the principle of reason as a principle pertaining to the rendering of reasons and so to the demand that reasons be rendered. In the latter part of the course, a reflection on this rendering will result in the double reading of "reckoning" and "calculating," the climax of Heidegger's demonstration that at the very heart of *Logistik* another sense or possibility can be thought. I am drawn, however, to the simple *nempe* (the "of course"), which interrupts the straightforward naming of the principle of contradiction and reminds us that its place as a supreme principle is especially obvious, as though of the two principles it is the introduction of the second, the principle of reason, which needs to be clarified. The English translator puts it well: "the principle—it goes without saying—of contradiction." And for Leibniz, of course, once instated, the principle does go without saying, for were it to be gainsaid there would be no securing of either the inferences (the steps) of logic or the demonstrations upon which geometry depends. The principle of reason is the means by which Leibniz conceives of a move beyond mathematics, but the principle serving mathematics will always be presumed by that move and will always accompany it. Heidegger's claim that when the principle of reason is described in terms of the rendering of reasons something is said about the very essence of principles as such requires that this *nempe* be dismissed. There is no "of course" about it and no need, in citing it, either to mention or to challenge it explicitly. That it does not go without saying can, it seems, go without saying. It should be obvious that there is no obviousness about it. The principle of contradiction is derivative. This step at least, the step that will lead to Heidegger's extraordinary analysis of the principle and its groundless ground, this step away from the utterly prosaic self-evidence of the principle of identity or contradiction, must surely have been taken.

(iii) Again from the third lecture:

The constant appeal to the principle of contradiction may be the most illuminating thing in the world for the sciences. But whoever knows the history of the principle of contradiction must concede that the interpretation of its content remains questionable. Over and above that, for the last one hundred and fifty years there has been Hegel's *Science of Logic.* It shows that contradiction and conflict are not reasons against something's being real. Rather, contradiction is the inner life of the reality of the real. This interpretation of the essence and effect of contradiction is the centerpiece of Hegel's metaphysics. Ever since Hegel's *Logic* it is no longer immediately certain that where a contradiction is present what contradicts itself cannot be real. So within the context of our considerations of the fundamental principle of reason in many respects it remains an overhasty procedure if, without hesitation and without reflection, we appeal to the fundamental principle of contradiction and say that the principle of reason is without reason, that this contradicts itself and therefore is impossible. Of course [*Freilich*]—but what are we supposed to make of this state of affairs: the principle of reason without reason? (*PR*, 18 / *SG*, 38)

"Of course" the thing that interests Heidegger here is a contradiction, but calling it that gets us nowhere precisely because the principle that would insist that thinking avoid or resolve contradiction has been, since Hegel, disputed.

We have scarcely begun to indicate here in the first of our moments just how intricately the lecture course plays with and on the thought of transition and how it deliberately withholds any thematizing of the step to be taken and of the step to which we would be taken, a feature of the course that makes those instances of summary, self-reference, and reintroduction especially difficult. One effect of all this is to problematize various versions of the steps, say, from the thought of the principle as a principle to the thought of the principle as a saying of being or from metaphysics to poetic thinking, steps that a more orthodox Heideggerian interpretation might assume have been taken. So construed, the course can be read quite easily alongside the "disarticulation" (with its *pas au-delà* and *sans sans sans*) we referred to earlier. It serves as a template for the sorts of readings in which Derrida will be interested: it is an exemplary and influential moment. The return to Leibniz and to the question of the principle in its provoking of the Hegelian treatment of each also links this talk of stepping to the problem of conceiving of and narrating the move away from Hegel. The stages might be represented as follows:

1. The principle of contradiction.
2. Hegel's challenge to the principle.
3. A re-reading of the principle of reason that is no longer tethered to the principle of contradiction, there now being only one supreme principle.

For Heidegger, as for Derrida, the third stage, in its multiple hesitations and its complicating of the very notion of transition or step, undermines the narrative itself. (One may even feel that what Heidegger is striving to detect in the principle of sufficient reason just is what Derrida calls "this particular undecidable.") Heidegger's lecture on Hegel and the principle of identity belongs to the same period as *The Principle of Reason*, and a course on Hegel's *Science of Logic* belongs to the same year. It is to Hegel that Heidegger turns to consider identity and contradiction; he turns to Leibniz for sufficient reason and principles as such. Heidegger is engaged in an examination of Leibniz and the principle of principles that would be both indebted to the Hegelian reading and yet also concerned with what in Leibniz and the principle resists that reading. But again is there anything here that is not clear or justified?

Indebted to Hegel's account of contradiction, Heidegger must nonetheless limit its scope and efficacy. But is it not a little strange to present that account as though it pertained solely to one of Leibniz's principles? Does Hegel's argument not implicate each of the principles and, indeed, the essence of the principle itself? Applied to the principle of identity or of contradiction, it would not, if successful, have the effect of reinstating another principle as the principle of principles, but would demand that thinking renegotiate the very question of its relationship to the principles it has inherited or assumed. In the *Encyclopaedia Logic*, Hegel is anxious that Leibniz's principle of reason be read in such a way that it does not fall back into tautology, a situation he fears will result if the notion of "ground" is not made clearer. But neither the principle nor Leibniz's application of it (or comments about it) can satisfactorily clarify the notion of "ground"; and the relentless operation of the *reductio*, the prevalence of the principle of identity or contradiction, continues to hold sway. Thus Hegel can later say, "The philosophy of Leibniz represents contradiction in its complete development."[22] Regarding Heidegger's appropriation of a Hegelian argument, then, we would need to ask what prevents him either from applying that argument to the principle of reason as well, or from wholeheartedly endorsing Hegel's statement that the principle as a principle can say nothing about ground. The statement, in its Hegelian intonation at least, encourages us to look elsewhere, certainly not to linger with this contradiction: the principle of ground without ground.

Following the lecture course on Hegel that centers on the principle of identity, Heidegger, as we have said in passing, will attempt to revitalize the tautology in contrast to Hegel's revitalizing of the simple predicative proposition. It is noticeable that Heidegger, unlike Hegel and unlike Leibniz, always distinguishes between the principles of identity and of contradiction. It is the former, Heidegger says, that counts as Leibniz's supreme principle. Note that were this the case, Heidegger ought not to pass so quickly over the *nempe* that announces the principle of contradiction. And Leibniz frequently emphasizes the point, writing of "the principle of contradiction or, what amounts to the same thing, the principle identity." It is just this "amounting to the same thing" that organizes Hegel's fragmented Leibniz interpretation and that leads him to want to protect what is speculatively retrievable in the principles of reason, identity, and contradiction, excluded middle, and so on, from the absolutely empty formal identity statement $A = A$.

(iv) Heidegger's argument against the principle of contradiction is Hegel's argument for the inherently contradictory nature of principles themselves when conceived as laws of thought. This is perhaps puzzling enough. But what of Heidegger's argument against the principle he describes as being fundamental for Leibniz, the principle of identity? How can the principle of identity, now *contra* Leibniz and Hegel severed from the principle of contradiction, be subordinated to the principle of reason? An answer is given at the beginning of the course on Leibniz. It is a matter of admitting that the meaning of "identity" is itself controversial. "One often formulates this principle as A = A. But equality is something other than identity [*Aber Gleichheit ist etwas anderes als Identität*]. What identity really means is by no means universally and unanimously determined" (*PR*, 8 / *SG*, 21). It can be understood in a variety of ways, one of which would take it to be synonymous with "the same"(*das Selbe*), where "the same" serves as the basis (the ground or reason) for two or more things being called identical or being deemed to belong together. Thus one definition of identity would ground it in the principle of reason. Interestingly, the indeterminacy of identity, which leads one from its association with equality to its association with sameness, seemingly precludes "equality" from being one of the other ways in which "identity" might be understood. And by the eleventh lecture, in his reading of the principle of reason as a saying of the sameness of being and ground (reason), Heidegger can at least establish one clear meaning of identity that can be safely discarded:

> "The same" does not mean the empty oneness of the one and the other, nor does it mean the oneness of something with itself. "The same" in the sense of this oneness is the indifference of an empty, endlessly repeatable identity: A as A, B as B. [*Das Selbe nicht das leere Einerlei von einem und Anderem, auch nicht das Einerlei von etwas mit ihm selbst. Das Selbe im Sinne dieses Einerlei ist das Gleichgültige der leeren, endlos wiederholbaren Identität: A als A, B als B.*] (*PR*, 89 / *SG*, 152)

By the close of the course, then, a particular notion and meaning of identity will be statable and dismissable. Such a dismissal will have been hinted at in the first lecture and apparently performed by the eleventh. The notion is the one we find in Leibniz's "absolute identical proposition," the one we find in the name "the principle of identity." In the first lecture this principle loses its primacy because of the indeterminacy of "identity." By the end of the course, it seems, we will have stepped away from a now determined identity statement. Much more argument and exposition is needed here, but I suspect such efforts would show that there is no moment in the lecture course when that determination either takes place or could take place.

One of the steps Heidegger's work attempts to prepare us for is that from logistics to a thinking of language as language. The tautology would be one of the ingredients of this latter thinking, but it would need to be absolutely distinguished from the quondam identity statement one finds presented in Leibniz and criticized by Hegel. But how can this distinction be made absolute? Can even the step away from the principle of identity or contradiction be taken unequivocally? Or might not the problematizing of the "step" already be under way here.

In its Hegelian treatment, Leibniz's principle of reason is always in danger of the sophistry that "never gets further than mere grounds." This danger exists because the empty identity statement holds a significance it can neither justify nor sustain. The principle of reason, Leibniz's transition from mathematics to philosophy—or, perhaps, from (formal) logic to ontology—is caught on the horns of a dilemma. It cannot produce a genuine philosophy and so is no real step at all because of the respect it feels is owed to and demanded by the principle of identity or contradiction; and it cannot construe that principle in a manner permitting any other step away from its logic. Thus, as Hegel writes in the *Encyclopaedia Logic*:

> When people speak of a sufficient ground, the predicate is either otiose, or else it is one which transcends the category of ground as such. The predicate "sufficient" is otiose and tautological if it is supposed to express only the capacity to ground something, since a ground only is a ground to the extent that it possesses this capacity. If a soldier runs away from a battle in order to save his life, he acts in such a way that is contrary to his duty, of course; but it cannot be maintained that the ground which has determined him to act in this way was insufficient, for if it was he would have stayed at his post.[23]

What is needed is the revitalizing of the principle of reason by way of a speculative and genuinely transitional retrieval. Philosophy can achieve this, in part, by distinguishing between the now philosophically insignificant identity statement and the philosophically interesting claim that identity presupposes difference; at bottom, a difference of identity, the speculative identity of identity and difference. For Heidegger as well, a treatment of the principle of reason should show, first, how the principle has served the logico-calculative thinking of a philosophy still dominated by a relation to mathematics and by its thematization of that relation;

and second, how the principle, heard in a different register, can work against that dominance, indeed how it can say something about the essence of calculation and calculability. For both Hegel and Heidegger what is at stake is a new and genuine transition, for the former possible and realizable, for the latter always bound to a faltering "not yet" upon which the new thinking of transition, if it is to be both new and thoughtful, must depend. In each case the step (in)to this other stepping takes the form of a step away from what is said to be obviously redundant, a saying of the same that is not yet the vital saying of the same, a saying of the same that must everywhere and always go without saying. In Hegel's hands, even its form is vacuous and to be avoided. In Heidegger's hands, the matter is more complicated.

(v) Heidegger subordinates the principle of contradiction by way of an allusion to Hegel's achievement, the principle of identity by way of a distinction between interesting and noninteresting senses of identity, the latter already implicating the principle of reason. However subtle the development of the lecture course, these moments strike us as noteworthy because, in a course that mentions every sense of every step, rehearsing a principle as just such a step, they seem to go unremarked. But if everything would prompt us to assert—with Hegel—the derivative nature of contradiction and—with Heidegger—the derivative nature of identity, there must still be a question about the discarded and unlamented equality statement, that sense of identity we must no longer recognize as being of philosophical interest.

Beginnings, principles, and grounds are never simple. It may be that an overconfident assumption of the principles of identity and of contradiction have prevented a philosophical appreciation of this fact. Hegel, Heidegger, Derrida, and others would remind philosophy of this oversight and would, in various ways, dent this confidence. Formally, the principle of contradiction is a tautology: -(*p*.-*p*). One way of challenging the dominance both of the principle and of the principled foundationalist philosophy that its confident assertion might encourage is to show just how many ways there are of glossing that opening "Not." None of the glosses we considered earlier ("*p*.-*p*" must be avoided, indicates an error, must be overcome, must be disarticulated) is a tautology. Hegel, Heidegger, and Derrida at times support just this sort of complicating of the issue. Nevertheless, if beginnings, principles, and grounds are never simple, it does not follow that there is nothing simple in them; and it may be that alongside or supplementing the complex interpretations there needs to be a reflection that returns the principle to tautology. More than anyone, Heidegger conceives of a path of thinking that tends toward simplicity; but it is a simplicity that, although expressed tautologically, is not to be conflated with the empty simplicity of the formal tautological identity statement. There is nothing of *logistics* in this thinking; nothing in the principle of identity or contradiction that might sustain this thinking. And yet: "Some people get stirred up because, after the reference in my inaugural address 'What Is Metaphysics?' (1929), I keep on raising the question of logic." To keep on raising the question of logic is perhaps to suggest that one never arrives at a thinking of language as language that renders "the question of logic" a question having nothing to do with philosophical logic, with logistics. Note that in the significance accorded tautologies, the later Heidegger would appear to have a thought in common with the early-twentieth-century logicians, namely that such logical constructions (precisely not inferences, not steps) can show us something about the essence of language. Can anything in the new and not-yet-guaranteed thinking of language as language guarantee either the criteria establishing that the saying of the same here is wholly removed from that of the logicians, or the truth and intelligibility of the story that thinking might want to tell of the central step away from logic?

VIII

How, then, to conclude?

Earlier I noted both the fascination with what remains unthought and insignificant in Hegelianism and the attempt to write and to think for the sake of this systematically excluded remainder, the paradoxical and paradoxically post-Hegelian attempt to address the "always already" that is always and already absent from any "category" or "a priori."

In this paper I have tried to show how, in the matter of logic and the principle of contradiction or identity, and in our Hegelian or post-

Hegelian discussions of them, there is also something left behind, deemed uninteresting because, here, uninterestingly true. What is left behind in and of a principle once one has retrieved from it what is of speculative, ontological, poetic, or ethical importance is simply what need not be remarked speculatively, ontologically, poetically, or ethically; what instead goes without saying and what, should we insist upon addressing it, can be greeted only by an irritated and unphilosophical "of course." But is that not what "principle" means, at least a crucial part of what "principle" means? Leibniz writes this uninterestingly true but indispensable component of the principle—the principle of the principle—as the empty identity statement "$A = A$," which, for him, also states "A = not not A." It is what generates the *nempe* in the naming of the two supreme principles, and it is also, to return to the beginning, what makes it impossible for philosophy in whatever guise, or indeed for anyone, to speak from the position of Aristotle's disputant; to speak, that is, as though with the voice and from the place of contradiction. One can never speak against what in the principle of contradiction makes it a principle and makes it *this* principle. Even the principle of (sufficient) reason, which does seem to invite or to succumb to such an interrogation, does so only by always also hinting back at this principled invulnerability. The vulnerability of the principle of reason (and so, for Heidegger, of the principle of principles), its "paradox," what makes it essentially thought provoking, can only be thought, read, and identified as such in a gesture that leaves unthought and takes as read the truistic and trivial identity that precedes it.

Recalling another contemporary topic, we might end by noting that in addition to the anarchic, preoriginary "yes" to the other that we find in Levinas, the unknown that we find in Blanchot, and the undecidability of affirmation that we find in Derrida, it is as though there were a further "yes." A "yes" to what is most mundane and obvious, a "yes" to an essentially uninteresting *archē*, a "yes" to what, rather than being heard "now often enough almost to the point of tedium," is always tediously unheard or almost heard, never quite heard, when a principle resounds *as* a principle. These prefixes or qualifications—"un-," "almost," "never quite"—carry none of the significance (or, better, the significant insignificance) of what resists the descriptive, analytical, or thematizing operations of philosophy. What they help to denote is anarchically non-anarchical. However one imagines or radicalizes the attentiveness to it, it is a "yes" to what in principles need never be attended to and so to what in principle must thereby always hold. Might such a "yes" not also have been partly Aristotle's point? And also Leibniz's? Of course.

History of the Lie

PROLEGOMENA

Jacques Derrida

Before I even begin, before even a preface or an epigraph, allow me to make two confessions or two concessions. Both of them have to do with the fable and the phantasm, that is to say, with the spectral (in Greek, *phantasma* also means specter or phantom). The fabulous and the phantasmatic have a feature in common: *stricto sensu* and in the classical sense of these terms, they do not pertain to either the true or the false, the veracious or the mendacious. They are related, rather, to an irreducible species of the simulacrum or of virtuality. To be sure, they are not truths or true statements as such, but neither are they errors or deceptions, false witnesses or perjuries.

The first conceded confession touches on the proposed title: "History of the Lie." By a slight displacement, by slipping one word in beneath another, it seems to mimic the famous subtitle of a text that some years ago very much interested me. In *The Twilight of the Idols*, Nietzsche gives the subtitle "History of an Error" ("Geschichte eines Irrtums") to a sort of narrative in six episodes that, on a single page, recounts in effect, and no less, the history of the "true world" (*die Wahre Welt*). The title of this fictive narrative announces the narration of a pure fabrication: "How the 'True World' Finally Became a Fable" ("Wie die 'wahre Welt' endlich zur Fabel wurde"). It is not, then, a fable that is going to be told, but rather the story of how a fable fabricated itself, so to speak. The teller is going to proceed *as if* a true story were possible on the subject of the history of this fabrication, a fabrication that produces, precisely, nothing other than the idea of a true world—which risks hijacking the supposed truth of the narration: "How the 'True World' Finally Became a Fable." "History of an Error" is only a subtitle. This fabulous narration about a fabulation, about the truth as fabrication, is a *coup de théâtre*. It puts onstage some characters who will remain more or less present, like specters, in the wings: first Plato, who says, according to Nietzsche, "I Plato, I *am* the truth"; then the Christian promise in the form of a woman; then the Kantian imperative, "the pale Koenigsbergian idea"; then the positivistic cock's crow; and finally the Zarathustrian midday. We will call upon all these specters again, but we will also call on another, whom Nietzsche does not name: Saint Augustine. It is true that the latter, in his two great treatises on lying (*De mendacio* and *Contra mendacium*), is always in dialogue with Saint Paul, Nietzsche's intimate acquaintance and the privileged target of his ferocity.

Although the memory of this fabulous text will remain with us, the history of the lie cannot be the history of an error, not even an error in the constitution of the true, in the very history of the truth as such. In Nietzsche's polemical and ironic text, in the vein of this fable about fabulation, the truth, the idea of a "true world," would be an "error."

The lie, however, in principle and in its classical determination, is not the error. One can be in error or mistaken without trying to deceive and therefore without lying. It is true, however, that lying, deceiving, and being mistaken are all three included in the category of the pseudological. In Greek, *pseudos* can mean lie as well as falsehood, cunning, or mistake, and deception or fraud as well as poetic invention, which increases the possible misunderstanding about what is meant by "misunderstanding"—and it does not simplify the interpretation of a "refutative" dialogue as dense and sharp as the *Hippias Minor* (*e peri tou pseudous, anatreptikos*). It is also true that Nietzsche seems to suspect Platonism or Christianity, Kantianism and positivism of having *lied* when they tried to get us to believe in a "true world." To lie is not to be mistaken or make an error. One does not lie simply by saying what is false, as long as one believes in good faith in the truth of what one believes or assents to in one's opinions. Saint Augustine recalls this fact at the opening of his *De mendacio*, where he proposes, moreover, a distinction between belief and opinion that could still have great pertinence for us today, in a new way.[1] To lie is to want to deceive the other, sometimes even by saying what is true. One can speak falsely without lying, but one can also say what is true with the aim of deceiving someone, in other words, while lying. But one does not lie if one believes what one says, even if it is false. By declaring, "the person who utters a falsehood does not lie if he believes or, at least, is of the opinion that what he says is true," Saint Augustine seems to exclude the lie to oneself. Here is a question that will stay with us from here on out: is it possible to lie to oneself, and does every kind of self-deception, every ruse with oneself, deserve to be called a lie?

It is difficult to believe that the lie has a history. Who would dare to tell the history of the lie? And who could promise to tell it as a true story? Even supposing, *concesso non dato*, that the lie has a history, one would still have to be able to tell it without lying. And without giving in too quickly, too easily to a conventionally dialectical schema whereby the history of error, as history and work of the negative, would be made to contribute to the process of truth, to the verification of the truth in view of absolute knowledge. If there is a history of the lie, that is, of the false witness, and if it touches on some radicality of evil named lie or perjury, then, on the one hand, it cannot let itself be reappropriated by a history of error or of the truth. On the other hand, although the lie supposes, or so it seems, the deliberate invention of a fiction, nevertheless not all fiction or fable amounts to lying—and neither does literature. One may already imagine countless fictive histories of the lie, countless inventive discourses, devoted to simulacrum, to fable, and to the production of new forms on the subject of the lie, which nevertheless would not be deceitful histories, that is (if we may rely on the most classical and dominant concept of the lie), which are not perjuries and false witnesses.

Why invoke here a classical and dominant concept of the lie? Is there, practically and theoretically, a prevalent concept of the lie in our culture? And why recall right away the features of this concept? I am going to formalize these features, in my own fashion, which I hope is true, correct, and adequate—for the thing is not so simple, and if I am wrong, it would not be a lie unless I did it on purpose. But it will be difficult, I will even venture to say impossible, to prove that I did it on purpose, a fact I underscore because it brings me already to one of my theses, namely: for structural reasons, it will always be impossible to prove, in the strict sense, that someone has lied even if one can prove that he or she did not tell the truth. One will never be able to prove anything against the person who says, "I was wrong but I did not mean to deceive; I am in good faith," or, alleging the always possible difference between the said, the saying, and the meaning-to-say, the effects of language, rhetoric, and context, "I said that, but that is not what I meant to say, in good faith, in my heart of hearts; that was not my intention; there has been a misunderstanding."

Here, then, is a definition of the traditional definition of the lie, such as I believe I must formulate it here. In its prevalent and recognized form, the lie is not a fact or a state; it is an intentional act, a lying. There is not the lie, but rather this saying or this meaning-to-say that is called lying: to lie would be to address to another (for one lies only to the other; one cannot lie to oneself, unless it is to oneself as another) a statement or more than one statement, a series of statements (constative or performative) that the liar knows, consciously, in explicit, thematic, current consciousness, form assertions that are totally or partially false; one must insist right away on this plurality and on this complexity, even on this heterogeneity. These intentional acts are destined for the other, an other or others, with the aim of deceiving them, with the aim of *making* them *believe* (here the notion of belief is irreducible even if it remains obscure) what is said, there where the liar, for his or her part, is supposed, by an explicit commitment, an oath, or an implicit promise, to tell the whole truth and only the truth. What matters here, in the first and last place, is the intention. Saint Augustine also underscored this point: there is no lie, whatever one may say, without the intention, the desire, or the explicit will to deceive (*fallendi cupiditas, voluntas fallendi*).[2] This intention, which defines veracity and lying in the order of *saying* or the act of saying, remains independent of the truth or falsity of the content, of what is *said*. The lie pertains to saying, and to the meaning-to-say, not to the said: "He who does not know that what he says is false does not lie if he thinks it is true, but he does lie who tells the truth when he thinks it is false, because persons must be judged according to their deliberate intention."[3]

This definition appears at once obvious and complex. We will need each of its elements for our analysis. If I have insisted on the fact that this definition of the lie delimits a prevalent concept in our culture, it is to improve the chances of the hypothesis that such a concept—determined by a culture, a religious or moral tradition, perhaps more than one legacy, a multiplicity of languages, and so forth—that such a concept, then, itself had a history. Here, however, is a first and then a second complication: if the, apparently, most common concept of the lie, if good sense concerning the lie, has a history, then that concept is caught up in a becoming that risks always relativizing its authority and value. But (here is the second complication) we also have to distinguish between the history of the concept of the lie and a history of the lie itself, a history and a culture that affect the practice of the lie, the manners, motivations, techniques, means, and effects of the lie. Within a single culture, and there where a stable concept of the lie would reign without division, the social experience, the interpretation, the operation of lying can change. This "lying" can give rise to another historicity, an internal historicity of the lie. Assuming that we have at our disposal, in our so-called Western tradition (Jewish, Greek, Christian, Roman, Islamic), a dominant, unified, stabilized, and therefore reliable concept of the lie, it would not be enough to grant it an intrinsically theoretical historicity, namely, that which would distinguish it from other concepts in other histories and other cultures; one would also have to examine the hypothesis of a practical, social, political, technical historicity that would have transformed it, or even marked it with ruptures within our tradition.

It is to this latter hypothesis that I would like to grant some provisional privilege here. But will it ever be possible to distinguish among the following three things, namely: (1) a history (*Historie*) of the concept of the lie; (2) a history (*Geschichte*) of the lie, made up of all the events that have happened *to* the lie or *by way of* the lie; and, finally, (3) a true history that orders the narrative (*Historie, historia rerum gestarum*) of these lies or of the lie in general? How is one to dissociate or alternate these three tasks? We must not ever overlook this difficulty.

Still before getting to the epigraphs, before even beginning to begin, I must make a second confession. You would have every right to distrust it, as you would with any confession. By reason of all sorts of limits, in particular the strictly assigned limits of time, I will not say everything, not even the essential part of what I may think about a history of the lie. That I do not say the whole truth about a history of the lie will not surprise anyone. But I will not say even the whole truth of what I myself, today, am able to think or to testify to concerning a history of the lie and the manner, altogether different, in which, according to me, it would be necessary to listen to or to tell this history. I will not say, therefore, the whole truth of what I think. My testimony will be lacunary. Am I guilty of this? Does this mean that I will have lied to you? I leave this question suspended, I turn it over to you, at least until the discussion period and doubtless beyond that.

By way of epigraph, two fragmentary quotations will now have to watch over these prolegomena. We will first hear from two thinkers whose memory we must honor here. Their memory inhabits this institution.

Far from being content to tell a certain history, each of these two fragments reflects in its glow a paradoxical and strange *historicity*.

Historicity of the lie, to begin with. That politics is a privileged space of lying is well known, as Hannah Arendt recalls more than once:

> Lies have always been regarded as necessary and justifiable tools not only of the politician's or the demagogue's but also of the statesman's trade. Why is that so? And what does it mean for the nature and the dignity of the political realm, on one side, and the dignity of truth and truthfulness, on the other?[4]

This is how "Truth and Politics" begins, the first English version of which appeared in 1967 in the *New Yorker* magazine and was a response to a journalistic polemic that had followed the publication of *Eichmann in Jerusalem*. As we all know, Arendt, in her own way, had taken on the mission of journalist at the Eichmann trial. She then denounced numerous lies and falsifications concerning her of which the press, in particular, had been guilty. This is the context she recalls in the first note to "Truth and Politics." She thereby points to an effect of the media, and she does it in a well-known magazine, the *New Yorker*. I underscore without delay the dimension of the media, the places of publication, and the magazine titles, both New York and international publications, for reasons that will continue, I hope, to become clear. It was in the *New York Review of Books* of the period (for this magazine also has a history, and Arendt wrote frequently for it) that she published some years later, in 1971, "Lying in Politics: Reflections on the Pentagon Papers." As for the "Pentagon Papers," the secret documents that then secretary of defense Robert McNamara commissioned on American policy in Vietnam from the Second World War to 1968, they themselves had been published, as you also know, by another newspaper, at once a New York paper and an international paper, the *New York Times.* Speaking of what was "in the mind of those who compiled the Pentagon Papers for the *New York Times,*" Arendt specifies:

> The famous credibility gap, which has been with us for six long years, has suddenly opened up into an abyss. The quicksand of lying statements of all sorts, deceptions as well as *self-deceptions* [I emphasize "self-deceptions," which will be one of our problems later on: Is "self-deception" possible? Is it a rigorous and pertinent concept for what interests us here, that is, the history of the lie? In strictest terms, does one ever lie to oneself?—J.D.], is apt to engulf any reader who wishes to probe this material, which, unhappily, he must recognize as the infrastructure of nearly a decade of United States foreign and domestic policy.[5]

If history, especially political history, is full of lies, as everyone knows, how could the lie *itself* have a history? How could the lie—which is such a common experience, whose structure is apparently so simple, whose possibility is as universal as it is timeless—have a history that is intrinsic and essential to it? Yet here is Arendt, once again in "Truth and Politics," who draws our attention to a mutation in the history of the lie. This mutation would be at work in the history of both the *concept* and the *practice* of lying. It is only in our modernity that, according to Arendt, the lie has attained its absolute limit and become complete and final. Ascension and triumph of the lie: whereas Oscar Wilde had complained, in days gone by, of what he called—and this was the title of a famous text—"the decay of lying" in the arts and letters, Arendt, on the contrary, diagnoses in the political arena a hyperbolic growth of the lie, its passage to the extreme, in short, the absolute lie. This is not absolute knowledge as the end of history, but history as absolute lie. How are we to understand this?

> Such completeness and potential finality, which were unknown to former times, are the dangers that arise out of the modern manipulation of facts. Even in the free world, where the government has not monopolized the power to decide and tell what factually is or is not, gigantic interest organizations have generalized a

kind of *raison d'état* frame of mind such as was formerly restricted to the handling of foreign affairs and, in its worst excesses, to situations of clear and present danger. And national propaganda on the government level has learned more than a few tricks from business practices and Madison Avenue methods. (TP, 255)

It would be tempting but somewhat facile to oppose, like two ends of history, the negative concept of this evil, the absolute lie, to the positivity of absolute knowledge, whether in the major mode (Hegel) or the minor mode (Fukuyama). One should doubtless be suspicious and somewhat uneasy about this notion of the absolute lie given what it still supposes of absolute knowledge, in an element that remains that of reflexive self-consciousness. By definition, the liar knows the truth, if not the whole truth at least the truth of what he thinks; he knows what he *means to say*; he knows the difference between what he thinks and what he says; he knows that he is lying. This essential link between knowing, knowledge, self-consciousness, and lying was already professed and played with by Socrates in that other major text in our tradition on the subject of lying, the *Hippias Minor* (*e peri tou pseudous*). If it must operate in consciousness and in its concept, then the absolute lie that Arendt speaks of risks being once again the other face of absolute knowledge.

Elsewhere in the same article, two examples taken from European politics restage "lies" of the modern type. The actors in this restaging are de Gaulle and Adenauer. The former claimed, and almost succeeded in making people believe, that "France belongs among the victors of the last war"; the latter "that the barbarism of National Socialism had affected only a relatively small percentage of the country" (TP, 252). These examples are framed by formulas that oppose once again the *traditional* political lie to the *modern* rewriting of history and insist on a new status of the image:

We must now turn our attention to the relatively recent phenomenon of mass manipulation of fact and opinion as it has become evident in the rewriting of history, in image-making, and in actual government policy. The traditional political lie, so prominent in the history of diplomacy and statecraft, used to concern either true secrets—data that had never been made public—or intentions, which anyhow do not possess the same degree of reliability as accomplished facts. . . . In contrast, the modern political lies deal efficiently with things that are not secrets at all but are known to practically everybody. This is obvious in the case of rewriting contemporary history under the eyes of those who witnessed it, but it is equally true in image-making of all sorts . . . for an image, unlike an old-fashioned portrait, is supposed not to flatter reality but to offer a full-fledged substitute for it. And this substitute, because of modern techniques and the mass media, is, of course, much more in the public eye than the original ever was. (TP, 252)

Because the image-substitute no longer refers to an original, not even to a flattering representation of an original, but replaces it advantageously, thereby trading its status of representative for that of replacement, the process of the modern lie is no longer a dissimulation that comes along to veil the truth. Rather, argues Arendt, it is the destruction of reality or of the original archive: "In other words, the difference between the traditional lie and the modern lie will more often than not amount to the difference between hiding and destroying" (*TP*, 255).

We will have occasion to return at length to the logic of these propositions. Are the word and the concept of "lie" still appropriate, given precisely their conceptual history, to designate the phenomena of our political, techno-mediatic, testimonial modernity to which Arendt will have so early and so lucidly drawn our attention—and often because she had herself experienced it most painfully, in particular when she was a reporter during the Eichmann trial?

Here now is the other epigraph. The historicity that it also names would be that of a certain *sacredness* or *sanctity*. This sacrosanctity (*Heiligkeit*) is constitutive—in Kant's view, for example, as well as in an Augustinian tradition that Kant does not explicitly claim—of the duty or the unconditional imperative not to lie. The duty one has to tell the truth is a sacred imperative. Reiner Schürmann notes in *Heidegger on Being and Acting: From Principles to Anarchy*, in the course of a reading of Heidegger:

Since the notion of the *sacred* belongs in the context of the original, it keeps historical connotations: the sacred is "the trace of the fugitive gods," leading toward their possible return (says Heidegger in *Holzwege*, pp. 250ff.). On the other hand, *awe* and *piety*, since they accompany the phenomenon of the originary, direct thinking toward that event, presencing, which is not at all historical.[6]

I

I will now try to begin—and without lying, believe me—by telling a few stories. In an apparently narrative mode, that of a classical historian or chronicler, I will propose a few specific examples on the basis of which we will try to progress in a reflective fashion, by analogy with what Kant might have said about "reflective judgment." We will thus proceed from the particular to the general, so as to *reflect* rather than *determine*, and to reflect in view of a principle that experience cannot provide. If I refer already, at least by analogy, to the great and canonical Kantian distinction between determinant judgment and reflective judgment, it is for three reasons: *first*, this distinction gives rise, in the *Critique of Judgment*, to antinomies and to a dialectic that are doubtless not foreign to those in which we will soon find ourselves entangled; *second*, Hannah Arendt, once again in "Truth and Politics," recalls at length the virtue Kant accords to the example, and she quotes, moreover, the *Critique of Judgment*; *finally and especially*, Kant is also the author of a brief, dense, difficult essay, written in polemical response to a French *philosophe*, Benjamin Constant, which constitutes in my view one of the most radical and powerful attempts in the history of the West, after Saint Augustine, to think, determine, reflect the lie, but also to proscribe or prohibit any lie. Unconditionally. I am referring to that short text, famous yet rarely read and not well known, entitled "On a Supposed Right to Lie Because of Philanthropic Concerns" ("Uber ein vermeintes Recht aus Menschensliebe zu lügen," 1797). Arendt frequently cites Kant in the article to which I have just referred and elsewhere, but she never mentions this essay even though it is so necessary and at the same time formidable, even irreducible to the profound logic of what she wants to demonstrate. Without going as far as would be necessary in the reading of this text, one may already take rigorous account of how Kant defines the lie and the imperative of *veracity* or *veridicity* (for the contrary of the lie is neither truth nor reality but veracity or veridicity, truth-saying, meaning-to-say-the-true, *Wahrhaftigkeit*). The Kantian definition of the lie or the duty of veracity is so formal, imperative, and unconditional that it appears to exclude any historical consideration, any consideration of conditions or historical hypotheses. Without the casuistic concern for all the difficult and troubling cases that Augustine analyzes, most often based on biblical examples, Kant seems to exclude any historical content when he defines veracity (*Wahrhaftigkeit*; *veracitas*) as an absolute formal duty: "Veracity in statements that cannot be avoided," he says, "is the formal duty [*formale Pflicht*] of man to everyone, however great the disadvantage that may arise therefrom for him or for any other."[7]

Although this text is expressly juridical and not ethical; although it deals, as its title indicates, with the "right to lie" (*Recht . . . zu lügen*); although it speaks of *duty of right* (*Rechtsuflicht*) and not of *ethical duty*, which could appear at first more propitious for, or less incompatible with, a historical viewpoint, Kant seems all the same to exclude from his definition of the lie all the historicity that, by contrast, Arendt introduces into the very essence, into the event and the performance of the lie. This is because Kant's viewpoint, if it is in fact that of right, remains purely and formally juridical; it corresponds to the concern with the formal conditions of right, the social contract, and the pure source of right. He writes:

> Hence a lie defined merely as an intentionally untruthful declaration to another man does not require the additional condition that it must do harm to another, as jurists require in their definition (*mendacium est falsiloquium in praeiudicium alterius*). For a lie always harms another; if not some other human being, then it necessarily does harm to humanity in general, inasmuch as it vitiates the source of right [it makes it useless: *die Rechtsquelle unbrauchbar macht*].[8]

Kant no doubt means to define in the lie what is *a priori* bad in itself, in its immanence, whatever may be its motivations or its consequences; but he is concerned above all with the very source of human law and of sociality in general, namely, an immanent necessity to tell the truth, whatever may be the expected effects or the external and historical contexts. If the lie is not unconditionally banned, then humanity's social bond is ruined in its very principle. In this pure immanence there resides the *sacredness* or *saintliness* of the rational commandment to tell the truth, to mean-to-say what is true. A moment ago, Reiner Schürmann was saying that sacredness was historical. In another sense, and in this case, it seems that for Kant this is not so, not at least in the common sense. But the hypothesis remains that sacredness is historical in another sense as origin and condition of a history and of a human sociality in general. In any case, Kant writes: "To be truthful [*wahrhaft*] [loyal, sincere, honest, in good faith: *ehrlich*] in all declarations is, therefore, a sacred [*heiliges*] and unconditional [*unbedingt gebietendes*] commanding law of reason [*Vernunftgebot*] that admits of no expediency whatsoever."[9]

I come finally to the promised examples and to my chronicles of two worlds. I select them in fact from the closest proximity to our two European continents, Europe and America (between Paris and New York) and from our newspapers, the *New York Times* and the Paris edition of the *International Herald Tribune.* A few months ago, soon after his election, when he had already announced his irrevocable decision that France would resume its nuclear tests in the Pacific, President Jacques Chirac, you recall, solemnly recognized, on the anniversary of the infamous Vel d'Hiv raid, the responsibility, which is to say, the culpability, of the French State under the Occupation in the deportation of tens of thousands of Jews, in the institution of laws applying only to Jews (the *statut des Juifs*), and in numerous initiatives taken over and above those ordered by the Nazi occupier. This culpability, this active participation in what is today judged to be a "crime against humanity," has now been recognized. Irreversibly. It is now admitted by a state as such; its admission is signed and sealed by a head of state elected by universal suffrage. It is publicly declared, in the name of the French State, before the figure or in the face of international law, in a theatrical act widely publicized throughout the world by the written press, by radio and television (I am underscoring once again this relation between the *res publica* and the media because it, along with this mutation of the status of the image, is one of our themes). The truth proclaimed by President Chirac has from now on the status, that is, both the stability and the authority, of a public, national, and international truth.

Yet this truth concerning a certain history has itself a history. It will have been legitimated, accredited, established as such only more than 50 years after the facts in question. Six presidents of the French republic (Auriol, Coty, de Gaulle, Pompidou, Giscard d'Estaing, Mitterrand) had deemed it until now neither *possible, opportune, necessary,* nor even *correct* or *just* to stabilize it as a truth of this type. Not one of them believed he was obliged to commit France, the French nation, the French republic, with a kind of signature that would have come to assume responsibility for this truth: France guilty of a crime against humanity. (One could cite numerous such examples and such situations today, from Japan to the United States or to Israel, which concern past violence or acts of repression, notorious war crimes or more recently uncovered ones, the justified or unjustified use of atomic bombs in Hiroshima and Nagasaki—as you know, despite the testimony of many historians, President Clinton persists in the official view that the decision to bomb Hiroshima and Nagasaki was justifiable—not to mention what may still happen regarding the politics of Japan in Asia during the war, the Algerian war, the Gulf war, ex-Yugoslavia, Rwanda, Chechnya, and so forth. And since I have just mentioned Japan in parentheses, it so happens that, as I was preparing this lecture, then Japanese prime minister Tomiichi Murayama made a declaration whose every word and whole pragmatic structure would have to be evaluated. Without committing the Japanese state at its head and in the permanence of its imperial identity, in the person of the Emperor, a prime minister speaks. Before what he calls significantly "these irrefutable facts of history" and an "error in our history," Murayama expresses in his own name—a name that says more than his own name but in no way commits the name of the Emperor—his "heartfelt apology" and his mourning; this mourning is at once personal and vaguely, very confusedly, that of the nation and the State. What is a state mourning, when it grieves for the deaths of those that are neither heads of state nor even fellow citizens? How is one to think a remorse or the excuses of a state now that international law has defined crimes against humanity? This is a swarm of questions that could not have been posed in these terms some 50 years ago. I quote Murayama's letter of declaration: "I regard, in a spirit of humility, these irrefutable facts of history, and express here once again my feelings of deep remorse and state my heartfelt apology." And then, having evoked "colonial" repression—which ought to give other former empires some ideas—the Japanese prime minister adds: "Allow me also to express my feelings of profound mourning for all victims, both at home and abroad, of that history." This confession is also the responsibility of a task; it makes a commitment for the future: "Our task is to convey to the younger generation the horrors of war, so that we never repeat the errors in our history."[10] The language of fault and confession are allied, so as to attenuate the effect, with the heterogeneous language of error; here then one can, probably for the first time in history, dissociate the concept of the State or the nation from what had always characterized it, in a constitutive and structural fashion, namely, good conscience. However confused this event may be, and however impure its motivation remains, however calculated and conjunctural the strategy, there is here a progress in the history of humanity and its international law, of its science and its conscience. Kant perhaps would have seen in it one of those events that are a "sign," a sign that, like the French Revolution, for example, and despite the failure or the limitation, reminds, demonstrates, and heralds [*signum rememorativum, demonstrativum, prognosticum*], attests thereby to a "tendency" and the possibility of a "progress" in humanity. All of this remains incomplete, for Japan, France, or Germany, but it is better than nothing. Whereas the Soviet Union or Yugoslavia, which no longer exist, are protected from any guilty conscience and any public recognition of past crimes, the United States has a whole future before it. I close this parenthesis and return home.)

That for more than a half century, no head of the French State deemed it possible, opportune, necessary, correct, or just to constitute as truth an immense French guilt, to recognize it as truth, all of this leads one to think that the value of truth in this case, that is, veracity, the value of a statement concerning real facts (for truth is not reality), but above all a statement in conformity with what one thinks, might depend on a political interpretation concerning values, which are moreover heterogeneous (possibility, opportunity, necessity, correctness, or justice). To these values truth or veracity would therefore in principle be subordinate. This is an enormous problem, as you know, doubtless a classical one, but it is a problem for which we must try today to find some historical, political, techno-mediatic specificity. Among former presidents, de Gaulle himself, to whom Chirac nevertheless says he owes his whole political inspiration, never dreamed of declaring the culpability of the French State under the Occupation, even though or perhaps because the culpability of the "French State" (this was moreover the official name of France under Vichy, the Republic having been abolished and renamed "État français") was in his eyes that of a nonlegitimate if not illegal state. We can also take the case of Vincent Auriol, that other president of the Republic who did not deem it possible, necessary, opportune, correct, or just to recognize what Chirac has just recognized (and to recognize it for conjunctural reasons that are no doubt more complex than the simple, unconditional obedience to the sacred commandment of which Kant speaks). Of 80 French parliamentary representatives, Vincent Auriol was one of the very few who refused to vote full powers (*les pleins pouvoirs*) to Pétain on July 10, 1940. He therefore knew, alas, that the interruption of the Republic and the transition to this État français guilty of the Status and deportation of Jews was a legal act engaging the responsibility of a government of France. The discontinuity of the interruption was itself inscribed in the legal continuity of the Republic in the État français. It is the French Republic that, by way of its legally elected representatives, resigned its own status. Such at least is the truth in its formal and juridical legality. But where is the truth of the thing itself here, if there is one? François Mitterrand, on several occasions and until the end of his last term, also refused to recognize the official culpability of the État français. He explicitly alleged that the said État français had been installed through usurpation by interrupting the history of the French republic, the only political or moral person that had to account for its actions and that, at the time, found itself either gagged or in illegal resistance. The French republic, today, had nothing, according to him, to "confess"; it did not have to assume the memory and culpability of a period in which it had been put out of action. The French nation, as such and in its continuity, had no obligation to accuse itself of crimes against humanity committed unjustly in its name. Mitterrand refused such a recognition even as he inaugurated the public and solemn commemorations of the Vel d'Hiv raid, and even when there were many who, over the course of many years, through letters and official petitions—with which I am very familiar for having signed them—urged him to do what, happily, President Chirac has just done. I will cite one other typical position on this problem, that of Jean-Pierre Chevènement, former cabinet minister under Mitterrand, a very independent Socialist, opposed to the model of Europe now being constituted, worried about national sovereignty and honor, who resigned his post as minister of defense during the Gulf War. In Jean-Pierre Chevènement's opinion, although Chirac did well to recognize the incontestable culpability of the État français, the consequences of this "veracity" and the terms in which it was elaborated run grave risks, for example that of legitimating in return Pétainism and encouraging all the forces that today seek to accredit the idea according to which "Pétain is France."[11] This was also most likely the viewpoint of General de Gaulle himself and perhaps, in a less determined fashion, that of the presidents who succeeded him. In a word, truth and veracity are certainly necessary, but they must not be put into operation in just any fashion, at just any price. *Toute vérité n'est pas bonne à dire*, as the French proverb puts it; that is, it is not always good to tell the truth, which means the imperative is not as sacred and unconditional as Kant wished. One would have to take account of hypothetical imperatives, pragmatic opportunity, the moment, the forms of the statement, rhetoric, the addressee, and so forth. To distinguish between the legality of the Vichy government and the popular will that resigned in the face of it, moreover, Chevènement has to go back much further in time, at least five years, in order to determine real responsibilities. By right, the properly historical analysis would be infinite, and with such an analysis the distinction between lie and veracity risks losing the strict outline of its borders.

Here then is a first series of questions: By not declaring officially what is now a state's historical truth, were former presidents, from de Gaulle to Mitterrand, lying or dissimulating? Does one have the right to say that? Could they, in their turn, accuse Chirac of "lying"? Are any of them lying? Who lied and who told the truth? Can one speak here of lie? Is that a pertinent concept? And if it is pertinent, what would be the criterion of the lie? What would be the history of this lie? And especially, a still different question, what would be the history of the *concept of the lie* that would support such questions? If there were some lie here and if it were pertinent to determine this or that to be a lie, who would be its subject and who the addressee or the victim? I will naturally come back to the formation and formulation of this first series of questions, but, still in a preliminary mode, I would like to underscore *two original features* in this example.

On the one hand, there is in fact a historical novelty in this situation, in this pragmatics of the opposition veracity/lie, if not in the essence of the lie. At issue here is a veracity or a *lie of state* determinable as such, on a stage of international law that did not exist before the Second World War. These hypotheses are posed today with reference to juridical concepts, such as "crime against humanity," that are inventions and thus "performatives" unknown to humanity before this, as juridical concepts implying international jurisdictions, contracts, and interstate charters, institutions and courts of justice that are in principle universal. If all of this is historical through and through, it is because the problematic of the lie or of the confession, the imperative of veracity on the subject of something like a "crime against humanity," had no sense, either for individuals or for the state, before the definition of this juridical concept in Article 6c of the statutes of the International Military Tribunal at Nuremberg, and in particular, as concerns France, unless I am mistaken, before these crimes were declared "imprescriptible" by a law dated December 26, 1964.

On the other hand, the objects in question, those on the subject of which a verdict is to be reached, are not natural realities "in themselves." They depend on interpretations, but also on performative interpretations. I am not speaking here of the act of performative language by which, confessing some culpability, a head of state produces an event and provokes a reinterpretation of what his predecessors have said on the issue. Rather I mean to underscore above all the performativity at work in the very *objects* of these declarations: the legitimacy of a so-called sovereign state, the position of a boundary, the identification or attestation of a responsibility are performative acts. When performatives succeed, they produce a truth whose power sometimes imposes itself forever: the location of a boundary, the installation of a state are always acts of performative violence that, if the conditions of the international community permit it, create the law, whether durably or not, where there was no law or no longer any law, no longer a strong enough law. In creating the law, this performative violence—which is neither legal nor illegal—creates what is then held to be legal truth, the dominant and juridically incontestable public truth. Where today is the "truth" concerning boundaries in ex-Yugoslavia, in all its divided "enclaves" that are enclaved in other enclaves, or in Chechnya, or in Israel? Who tells the truth and who lies in these areas? For the better and for the worse, this performative dimension *makes the truth,* as Augustine says. It therefore imprints its irreducibly historical dimension on both veracity and the lie. This original "performative" dimension is not taken thematically into account, it seems to me, by either Kant or Arendt. I will try to show that, despite everything dividing or opposing them from another point of view, they share this misrecognition, or at least this insufficient explication, just as they both neglect the symptomatic or unconscious dimension of these phenomena. Such phenomena cannot be approached without, at the very least, the combination of a "logic of the unconscious" and a theory of the "performative." This does not mean that the *current* and currently elaborated discourse of psychoanalysis or of speech-act theory is sufficient to the task. It means even less that there is a ready articulation between them—or between them and a discourse on politics or the economy of tele-technological knowledge and power. We are defining here a task and the conditions of an analysis on the scale of these phenomena of "our time."

The rewriting of history, lie, falsification, negation, and disavowal: all these questions point toward stakes that, because they are so easily recognizable, I did not think it useful to insist upon. For lack of time, I will do no more here than evoke or situate, in the immediate vicinity of a new problematic of the truth of state, those searing figures that are revisionism and negationism. You know that these figures are endlessly proliferating; they are reborn from the very ashes they would like at the same time to conjure away and insult. How is one to fight them, which is to say first of all refute them, dispute them, recall them to the very truth of their negationist and disavowed relentlessness? How to prove by bearing witness? What is the best response, at once the most just, the most correct, the most critical, and the most reliable? Will this perversion be resisted by establishing by law a truth of state? Or rather, on the contrary, by reinitiating—interminably if necessary, as I believe it will be—the discussion, the recalling of evidence and witnesses, the work and discipline of memory, the indisputable demonstration of an archive? An infinite task, no doubt, which must be begun over and over again; but is that not the distinctive feature of a task, whatever it may be? No state, no law of state, no reason of state will ever be able to take its measure. This means not that the state has to renounce its right or its law but that one must remain vigilant to make sure it does not do disservice to the cause of a truth that, when left to itself, always risks being perverted into dogmatism or orthodoxy.

II

So as to illustrate just how formidable this performative power can be in our tele-techno-mediatic modernity, here now is another, apparently minor sequence in the same story. I said that the media would occupy a central place in this analysis. The *New York Times* wanted to report on Chirac's recent declaration. Concerned with truth and competence (let us assume that to be the case), it turned responsibility for the article over to a professor. The idea of competence is associated in our culture with the university and with university professors. Professors know and say what is true; that is what everyone presumes. This professor, who was presumed to know, teaches in a great New York university. He even passes for an expert in matters of French modernity, at the crossroads of philosophy, ideology, politics, and literature. He is the author, as the *New York Times* recalls, of a book entitled *Past Imperfect: French Intellectuals, 1944–1956*. And so, on July 19, 1995, the *New York Times* published an article with the title "French War Stories," by Mr. Tony Judt, a professor at New York University. Before concluding that—I quote—"It is well that Mr. Chirac has told the truth about the French past," the author of *Past Imperfect* had denounced as shameful the behavior of French intellectuals who, for a half-century, had been in his opinion too little concerned with this truth and with its public recognition. He notes first of all that Sartre and Foucault had been on this subject—I quote—"curiously silent." And he chalks this up to their sympathy for Marxism. This explanation is somewhat amusing, especially in the case of Foucault, when one knows that the majority of the latter's most durable and best-known "political commitments" were anything but Marxist and sometimes were even expressly anti-Marxist. I will quote what Professor Judt then writes only in order to proliferate, by way of introduction, the examples of faults that will always be difficult to determine. There will always be several possibilities among which one must hesitate to choose. Exactly what is it a matter of here? Incompetence? Lack of lucidity or analytic acuity? Good faith ignorance? Accidental error? Twilight bad faith falling somewhere between the lie and thoughtlessness? Compulsion and logic of the unconscious? An outright false witness, perjury, lie? These categories are no doubt irreducible to each other, but what is one to think of the very frequent situations in which, *in fact, in truth*, they contaminate one another and no longer lend themselves to a rigorous delimitation? And what if this contagion marked the very space of so many public discourses, notably in the media? Here then is what Professor Judt says in order to account for the silence, which in his view is guilty, of Sartre and Foucault:

> Intellectuals, so prominent in post-war France, might have been expected to force the issue. Yet people like Jean-Paul Sartre and Michel Foucault were curiously silent. One reason was their near-obsession with Communism. While proclaiming the need to "engage," to take a stand, two generations of intellectuals avoided any ethical issue that could not advance or, in some cases, retard the Marxist cause.

These declarations may appear merely a little confused and vague, especially where it is a question of the "Marxist cause" for Foucault. But Professor Judt does not stop there. After the subtitle, "Shame of the Intellectuals" (a subtitle for which he must at least share responsibility with the newspaper, as we are unfortunately so often obliged to do whenever we think we have to write for the newspapers), the professor-journalist denounces intellectuals who have come *after* Sartre and who maintained, according to Mr. Judt, a guilty silence in the face of Vichy France's guilt and its "crimes against humanity":

> No one stood up to cry "J'accuse!" at high functionaries, as Émile Zola did during the Dreyfus affair. When Simone de Beauvoir, Roland Barthes and Jacques Derrida entered the public arena, it usually involved a crisis far away—in Madagascar, Vietnam or Cambodia. Even today, politically engaged writers call for action in Bosnia but intervene sporadically in debates about the French past.

Even if I am ready to concede a share of truth in this accusation, I must declare that in the main it filled me with indignation, and not only—please believe this—because it also concerns me personally and because along with others I am the object of a veritable calumny. This is not the first time that newspapers bearing the name of New York in their title have said whatever they please and lied outright about me, sometimes for months at a time and over several issues. If I was particularly shocked, however, by this *contre-vérité*, as one calls it in French, it is not only for this reason, nor simply because, like others, I am among those who care about what M. Judt calls the "French past." It is especially because, with others, I have more than once made my concern known publicly, on this subject and others (Algeria, for example), and because along with others I had signed an open letter to President Mitterrand asking him to recognize what Chirac has just recognized. Upon reading the *New York Times* and feeling discouraged in advance, which is, alas, too often the case, I had already given up any notion of answering and correcting this countertruth, which had become accepted as truth through the conjoined force of the presumed authority of an academic expert and a newspaper with a massive and international distribution (both American and European, for the same article was reprinted verbatim three days later in the European edition of the *International Herald Tribune*). Fortunately, four days later, the countertruth was denounced in the same newspaper by another American professor whom I do not know but to whose competence and honesty I wish to pay grateful tribute: Kevin Anderson, who teaches at a more modest rank in a less celebrated university (he is associate professor of sociology at Northern Illinois University). The *New York Times* was thus obliged to publish a letter "to the editor" from Kevin Anderson, under the title "French Intellectuals Wanted Truth Told." Such letters are always printed in an unobtrusive and sometimes unlocatable place, whereas the effect of truth, or rather of countertruth, of the first article "properly speaking" remains ineffaceable for millions of readers, and especially for European readers of the *International Herald Tribune* who will have never read the letter in question. Kevin Anderson criticizes the whole political analysis of Professor Judt (permit me to refer you to it), and he specifies in particular that:

> On June 15, 1992, a petition signed by more than 200 mainly leftist intellectuals, including Mr. Derrida, Régis Debray, Cornelius Castoriadis, Mr. Lacouture and Nathalie Sarraute, noted that the French occupation government in 1942 acted "on its own authority, and without being asked to do so by the German occupier." It called on Mr. Mitterrand to "recognize and proclaim that the French state of Vichy was responsible for persecutions and crimes against the Jews of France."

To my knowledge—but I don't know everything, and it is not too late—Professor Judt has not yet acknowledged publicly that he did not tell the truth. You will have noticed that, in speaking of the *contre-vérité* of his article, I never said that Professor Judt lied. Everything that is false cannot be imputed to a lie. The lie is not an error. Plato and Augustine both insisted on this. If the concept of the lie has some resistant specificity, it must be rigorously distinguished from the error, from ignorance, from prejudgment, from faulty reasoning, from failure in the realm of knowledge, and even—and this is where things are soon going to get complicated for us—from failure in the realm of action, practice, or technique. If the lie is neither the failure of knowledge and know-how, nor error; if it implies ill will or bad faith in the order of moral reason, that is, the order not of practice but of pure practical reason; if it addresses belief rather than knowledge, then the project of a history of the lie should not resemble in the least what could be called, following Nietzsche in *The Twilight of the Idols*, the history of an error (*Geschichte eines Irrtums*).

No doubt, one ought to keep a sense of proportion. But how to calculate proportion when the capitalistico-techno-mediatic power of an international newspaper can produce effects of truth or countertruth worldwide, which are sometimes tenacious and ineffaceable, concerning the most serious subjects in the history of humanity, going far beyond the modest persons implicated in the recent example I have just given? Keeping everything in proportion, then, I would say that the history I have just recited would be neither the history of an error nor the history of a lie. In order to lie, in the strict and classical sense of this concept, one must know what the truth is and distort it intentionally. Thus, one must not lie to oneself. I am convinced that if Professor Judt had had a clear and distinct knowledge, if he had had a current consciousness of the fact that the intellectuals he accuses had signed that letter to Mitterrand, he would not have written what he wrote. I think it is reasonable to give him this much credit: he did not lie. Not really. He did not mean clearly and deliberately to deceive his reader and to take advantage of that reader's confidence or belief. Yet, is it simply, in all innocence, an error on his part or a simple lack of information? I do not believe that either. If Professor Judt did not seek to know more or enough about the subject, it is also because he was in a hurry to reach a conclusion and therefore to produce a "truth effect" confirming at all cost his general theses on French intellectuals and politics, with which one may be familiar from his other writings—and which I am not alone in finding somewhat simplistic. We could show this if that were the subject of our lecture and if we were given the time. What I want to underscore here is that this countertruth does not belong to the category of either lie or ignorance or error, doubtless not even to the category of self-deception that Hannah Arendt talks about. It is not reducible to any of the categories bequeathed to us by traditional thinking about the lie, from Plato and Augustine up to Kant and even up to Arendt, despite all the differences that separate all these thinkers from each other. For here is the hypothesis that I wish to submit for your discussion: the concept of lying to oneself, of self-deception, for which Arendt has an essential need so as to mark the specificity of the modern lie as absolute lie, is also a concept that is irreducible to what is called in all classical rigor a lie. But what I am calling here too quickly the classical rigor of the concept of lie also has a history, to which we are heirs and which in any case occupies a dominant place in our heritage and in our common language. Self-deception is not "bad faith," either in the ordinary sense or in the sense Sartre gives to it. It requires therefore another logic, other words; it requires that one take into account both some mediatic techno-performativity and a logic of the *phantasma* (which is to say, of the spectral) or of a symptomatology of the unconscious toward which the work of Arendt signals but which it never deploys as such, it seems to me. There are several signs in "Truth and Politics" that this concept of lying to oneself plays a determining role in the Arendtian analysis of the modern lie. To be sure, Arendt finds material to illustrate this lie to oneself in anecdotes or discourses from other centuries. We have known for a long time, she notes, that it is difficult to lie to others without lying to oneself; and "the more successful a liar is, the more likely it is that he will fall prey to his own fabrications" (TP, 254). But it is especially to modernity that she assigns this possibility, from which she draws a very paradoxical consequence on the subject of democracy itself, as if this ideal regime were also the one in which deception were properly destined to become "self-deception." Arendt acknowledges therefore an "undeniable strength" to the arguments of "conservative critics of mass democracy":

Politically, the point is that the modern art of self-deception is likely to transform an outside matter into an inside issue, so that an international or inter-group conflict boomerangs onto the scene of domestic politics. The self-deceptions practiced on both sides in the period of the Cold War are too many to enumerate, but obviously they are a case in point. Conservative critics of mass democracy have frequently outlined the dangers that this form of government brings to international affairs—without, however, mentioning the dangers peculiar to monarchies and oligarchies. The strength of their arguments lies in the undeniable fact that under fully democratic conditions deception without self-deception is well-nigh impossible. (TP, 255–56)

I leave suspended the capital but far too difficult question of what can be understood here by "fully democratic conditions."

III

I do not know if she read it or knew it, but we have an obligation to the truth to say that these Arendtian theses fall directly in line with an article by Alexandre Koyré. Also published in New York, the article appeared in a 1943 issue of *Renaissance*, journal of the École Libre des Hautes Études, with the title "Réflexions sur le mensonge" and was republished in June 1945 in the *Contemporary Jewish Record*, with the title "The Political Function of the Modern Lie." This text has also just been republished by the Collège International de Philosophie.[12] It begins as follows: "Never has there been so much lying as in our day. Never has lying been so shameless, so systematic, so unceasing." All the Arendtian themes are already in this article, in particular that of the lie to oneself ("That man has always lied, to himself and to others, is indisputable") and of the modern lie:

> Right now we want to concern ourselves with the contemporary lie, and even more strictly, with the contemporary political lie. We remain convinced that in this sphere, *quo nihil antiquius*, the present epoch, or more exactly, its totalitarian regimes, has created some mighty innovations. . . . Modern man—*genus totalitarian*—bathes in the lie, breathes the lie, is in thrall to the lie every moment of his existence.[13]

But Koyré also poses a question that unfortunately he does not pursue, at least not in the direction that would seem to me necessary today. He wonders in fact, which Arendt did not do, whether one still has—I quote—"the right to speak here of 'lie.'"

We cannot follow closely here the answer he outlines to this question.

Allowing myself to refer you to it, I will do no more than point out schematically, in the strategy of his answer, the stakes and the principal vein of a philosophical but also ethical, juridical, and political difficulty. What can be done with his response by anyone attempting to write a history of the lie and a genealogy of the concept of the lie, as well as of that sacred veracity, that *Heiligkeit* of the safe, the saintly, the healthy, or the safe and sound [*l'indemne*], that will always have linked the ethical to the religious?

In Koyré's strategy, to whose necessity and force I first want to pay tribute, I would be tempted to recognize at once a *limit* and an *opening.*

A. *The limit,* first of all. Koyré seems to suspect in fact *any* question concerning the right to use the word "lie." He insinuates at least that such a question, as question, may be the first sign of a totalitarian perversion. He is not wrong, not simply wrong. The risk does in fact exist, and it remains a terrible one. One may wonder, however, whether this risk ought not to be treated otherwise and each time by taking into account—without any relativism—singular and novel historical situations, and especially by introducing into the analysis of these situations concepts that seem to be structurally excluded by both Koyré and Arendt, and before them by Kant, for essential reasons.

Koyré first of all rightly recalls that the notion of "lie" presupposes that of veracity, of which it is the contrary or the negation, just as the notion of the false supposes that of the true.[14] He then adds a pertinent and grave warning, a warning that must never be overlooked, especially in politics, but that should not, all the same, halt us in our pursuit of a deconstructive genealogy of the concept of lie and therefore of veracity. How to proceed with such a genealogy—so necessary for memory or critical lucidity, but also for all the responsibilities that remain to be taken today and tomorrow—in such a way that it does not consist all the same in merely ruining or discrediting what it analyzes? How to conduct the deconstructive history of the opposition of veracity and lie without discrediting this opposition and without opening the door to all the perversions against which Koyré and Arendt will always have been right to warn us?

Here then is Koyré's warning. That it was written in 1943 must be kept in mind, both because of what was happening then and what has happened since, what is developing today when his diagnoses concerning totalitarian practices of the period (for us it was yesterday) could be largely extended to certain current practices of the so-called democracies in the age of a certain capitalistico-techno-mediatic hegemony:

> The official philosophies of the totalitarian regimes unanimously brand as nonsensical the idea that there exists a single objective truth valid for everybody. The criterion of "truth," they say, is not agreement with reality [later on, Koyré will recall that there is a theory of the lie in *Mein Kampf* and that the readers of this book did not understand that they themselves were being spoken of], but agreement with the spirit of a race or nation or class—that is, racial, national or utilitarian. Pushing to their limits the biological, pragmatist, activist theories of truth, the official philosophies of the totalitarian regimes deny the inherent value of thought. For them thought is not a light but a weapon: its function, they say, is not to discover reality as it is, but to change and transform it with the purpose of leading us towards what is not. Such being the case, myth is better than science, and rhetoric that works on the passions preferable to proof that appeals to the intellect.[15]

To avoid any misunderstanding, I repeat and underscore that what Koyré is saying here seems to me true, correct, necessary. One must first of all subscribe to it. An unfailing vigilance will always be necessary so as to be on guard against the danger he exposes. And yet, as you heard, what he condemns goes well beyond biologism and the official philosophies of totalitarianism: he denounces all of what he calls "pragmatist" and "activist" interpretations of the truth, which is potentially quite a lot. This suspicion can touch on everything that exceeds, in more than one direction, the determination of truth as objectivity or as the theme of a constative utterance, or even as adequation; at the limit, it touches on any consideration of performative utterances. In other words, the same suspicion would be aimed at any problematic that delimits, questions, and *a fortiori* deconstructs the authority of the truth as objectivity, or—and this would be yet something different—as adequation or even as revelation (*aletheia*). The same suspicion would be aimed at any problematic that takes into account, for example in the area of the political or rhetorico-techno-mediatic *res publica*, the possibility of institutive and performative speech (be it only that act called *testimony*, which always implies a performative promise or oath). A problematic of this sort, which is so necessary—*for the best and for the worst*—would therefore risk seeing itself disqualified or paralyzed in advance.

I underscore here two equally necessary precautions. *On the one hand*, I am not saying this in order to dismiss the suspicion that Koyré formulates: once again, this suspicion is indispensable and legitimate; it must watch over these new problematics, however urgent they may be. *On the other hand*, it is true that these same new problematics (of a pragmatico-deconstructive type) can in fact serve contradictory interests. This double possibility must remain open, as both a chance and a threat, for otherwise we would no longer be dealing with anything but the irresponsible operation of a programmatic machine. Ethical, juridical, or political responsibility, if there is any, consists in deciding on the strategic orientation to give to this problematic, which remains an interpretive and active problematic, in any case a performative one, for which truth is not, any more than reality, an object given in advance that it would be a matter of simply reflecting adequately. It is a problematic of testimony, as opposed to proof, that seems to me to be necessary but that I cannot develop here. (I specify also very quickly, since I do not have the time to say more, that I am using the word "performative" here a little facilely, setting aside many questions that I have formulated elsewhere on the opposition performative/constative, on the paradoxes and especially the limits of its pertinence and its purity. Austin having been the first to put us on guard against this alleged "purity,"[16] it is certainly not against him that I would attempt at top speed to restore it or reestablish its credit.)

B. Such would be a *limit* on Koyré's remarks in this article. I believe one encounters it again in Arendt. But Koyré also sketches a *step beyond this limit*. It is this direction that I would have liked to pursue. Koyré suggests that, far from going *beyond* the distinction between truth and lie, totalitarian regimes and their analogues of all sorts have in fact a vital need for this oppositional and traditional distinction. This is because they lie from within this tradition, which they therefore have every reason to want to maintain intact and in its most dogmatic form so as to operate the deception. The only difference is that they grant primacy to the lie within the old metaphysical axiomatics, thus contenting themselves with a simple reversal of the hierarchy, a reversal that Nietzsche says, at the end of "History of an Error" (and elsewhere), must not satisfy us.

We will cite Koyré again at some length:

In their publications (even in those they call scientific), in their discussions, and of course in their propaganda, the representatives of totalitarian regimes are scarcely hampered by objective truth. More puissant than God Almighty, they change the past as well as the present according to their whim. [It is by this rewriting of the historical past that they even exceed God, who, for his part, would be powerless to change the past: in 1943, during the Vichy regime, in a note that today could be extended infinitely, Koyré evokes "the historical teaching of totalitarian regimes" and even the "new history manuals of French schools"]. One might conclude, as many have, that totalitarian regimes function outside the sphere of truth and lie.

We do not believe, however, that this is at all the case. The distinction between truth and lie, the fictitious and the real, remains altogether valid within totalitarian conceptions and regimes. Only their place and their role have been reversed: totalitarian regimes are founded on the *primacy of the lie.*[17]

At the time he wrote, Koyré had no difficulty illustrating this "primacy of the lie" in a totalitarian system (whether proclaimed or not), which more than any other needs a belief in the stable and metaphysically assured opposition between veracity and lie; and we would have no trouble illustrating this today, whether we look nearby or far away. By definition the liar is someone who says that he says the truth (this is a law of structure and has no history), but the more a political machine lies, the more it makes the love of truth into the watchword of its rhetoric. "I hate lies" is a famous declaration by Marshall Pétain. Koyré recalls it. For my part, I would have liked to comment on that other slogan from the Vichy period and its reactionary ideology of the return to the earth, as the surest locus of family and patriotic values: *La terre ne ment pas*, "The earth does not lie."

Among the perspectives opened up in these several pages by Koyré, one would have to privilege two of them, it seems to me, and leave suspended there a serious question.

1. The first opening concerns the paradoxical perversion that consists in second-degree lying: "the old Machiavellian technique," says Koyré, an art of which Hitler was a master and which consisted of saying the truth while knowing he would not be taken seriously by the uninitiated. The result is a sort of conspiracy "in broad daylight," which Arendt will also often speak of as the modern lie: to tell the truth in view of deceiving those who believe they ought not believe it. Koyré is not the first to identify this ruse, any more than was Freud before him, but Koyré

does indicate a concern with interpreting it as a modern political technique in the age of mass communications and totalitarianism.

2. The second perspective opens onto a *theory of the secret.* This is in fact the fundamental and most insistent theme of the article: it is not the secret of a secret society, but of a "society with a secret" whose structure permits a conspiracy "in broad daylight" that is not a contradiction in terms.

3. It is the very original deployment of this theory of the modern political secret that might inspire a worry, about which I will say just a few words. Koyré seems to consider that any secret is in principle a threat for the *res publica,* indeed for the democratic space. This is understandable and in overall conformity with a certain essence of *politeia* as absolute phenomenality. But I wonder if we do not see here signs of the inverse perversion of politicism, an absolutization of the political, a limitless extension of the region of the political. By refusing any right to secrecy, the political agency summons everyone to behave first of all and in every regard as a responsible citizen before the law of the *polis.* Is there not here, in the name of a certain type of objective and phenomenal truth, another germ of totalitarianism with a democratic face? I could not read without a certain indignant amazement one of Koyré's notes that, by way of illustrating how one acquires training in secrecy, cryptic codes, and lying, launched a scatter-shot accusation at Spartans, Indians, Jesuits, and Marranos: "We cite at random the training in lying that was received by the young Spartan and the young Indian; the mentality of the marrano or of the Jesuit."[18]

If one were to insist on an unconditional right to the secret against this phenomenalism and this integral politicism, and if such an absolute secret had to remain inaccessible and invulnerable, then it would concern less the political secret than, in the metonymic and generalized figure of the Marrano, the right to secrecy as right to resistance against and beyond the order of the political, or even of the theologico-political in general; and in politics, it could inspire, as one of its figures, the right to what the United States names with that very fine phrase for the most respectable of traditions, in the case of *force majeure,* there where the *raison d'état* does not dispense the last word in ethics: "civil disobedience."

For lack of time, I must hasten these prolegomena toward their conclusion—and return to Hannah Arendt. Is a history of the lie possible, as such? I am less certain of it than ever. But supposing that one were still to attempt such a history, then one would have to take into account the whole oeuvre of Arendt and more precisely, in the two essays I have cited, a *double square* of motifs, of which one set seems propitious and the other unfavorable for such a project.

In conclusion, then, a program and two squares of four telegrams.

In the first place, several motifs seem propitious for such a history of the lie.

1. The concern, clearly expressed, to remove such a history from "moral denunciation."[19] Somewhat like Nietzsche, in a fashion that is both analogous and different, Arendt wanted to treat these questions "in an extra-moral sense."

2. The consideration not only of the development of the media but also of a new mediatic structure that has transformed the status of the iconic substitute, of the image,[20] and of public space (a thematics absent from Koyré's remarks).

3. The clearly marked intention to *delimit the order of the political,* to surround it with theoretical, practical, social, and institutional boundaries (which are in principle very strict, even if, as one can easily imagine, they remain difficult to draw, for noncontingent reasons). This is undertaken in two directions: *on the one hand,* by setting out that man, in his "singularity," in the "philosophical truth" of his solitary individuality, is "unpolitical by nature" (TP, 246);[21] *on the other hand,* by assigning to the order of the judiciary and the university, which is virtually independent of the political, new missions and capital responsibilities in this delimitation of the political lie (TP, 260–61).

4. Finally, although the word is not used and there is not a sufficient or determining development, a problematic is sketched of the *performativity* of the lie whose structure and event would be linked in an essential fashion to the concept of action and more precisely of political action.[22] Hannah Arendt often recalls that the liar is a "man of action," and I would even add: par excellence. Between lying and acting, acting in politics, manifesting one's own freedom through action, transforming facts, anticipating the future, there is something like an essential affinity. The imagination is, according to Arendt, the common root of the "ability to lie" and the "capacity to act." The capacity to produce some image: pro-

ductive imagination as experience of time, Kant or Hegel would have said. The lie is the future, one may venture to say beyond the letter of Arendt's text but without betraying her intention in this context. To tell the truth is, on the contrary, to say what is or what will have been, and it would be to prefer instead the past. Even if she insists on marking its limits, Arendt speaks of "the undeniable affinity of the lie with action, with changing the world—in short, with politics." The liar, says Arendt, needs no accommodation to appear on the political scene; he has the great advantage that he always is, so to speak, already in the midst of it. He is an actor by nature; he says what is not so because he wants things to be different from what they are—that is, he wants to change the world. In other words, our ability to lie—but not necessarily to tell the truth—belongs among the few obvious, demonstrable data that confirm human freedom (TP, 250).

Even if such utterances require some modalization and need to be placed more prudently under a certain index of possibility (a translation that we do not now have the time to undertake now), it goes without saying that not only do we have here, as illuminated by Arendt, the very idea of a history of the lie but, more radically, the thesis according to which there would be no history in general, and no political history in particular, without at least the possibility of lying, that is, of freedom and of action. And also of imagination and of time, of imagination as time.

In what way does the Arendtian discourse close or risk closing what it opens up in this manner? This is what I would like to evoke in conclusion, or at least so as to have done with these modest prolegomena.

For, on the other hand, *four motifs* seem to me to have played an inhibiting, if not prohibiting, role in the attempt to take such a history seriously.

1. The absence of a veritable problematic of testimony, witnessing, or bearing witness. Arendt is not interested in the history of this concept, as that which strictly distinguishes testimony from the proof or the archive, even if in fact and not by chance an equivocation always blurs the limits between these radically heterogeneous possibilities. The distinction between "factual truth" and "rational truth," which forms the backbone of this whole discourse, appears to be insufficient here. Arendt herself acknowledges that she is using it only provisionally and for con-

venience (TP, 239). She names testimony more than once (TP, 238, 243), but no more than with the lie, faith, or good faith, does she make it the veritable theme of an eidetic analysis. Nor does Koyré for that matter. Both of them proceed as if they knew what "lying" meant.

2. This is not unrelated to the concept of "lying to oneself" or "internal self-deception" (LP, 35), which plays a determining role in all these demonstrations by Arendt. Now, such a concept remains confused, in the "psychology" it implies. It is also logically incompatible with the rigor of any classical concept of the lie. To lie will always mean to deceive the other *intentionally* and *consciously* and while *knowing* what it is that one is *deliberately* hiding, therefore while not lying to oneself. The *self*, if at least this word has a sense, excludes the self-lie. Any other experience, therefore, calls for another name and no doubt arises (we are going quickly here) from another zone or another structure, from intersubjectivity or the relation to the other, to the other in oneself, in an ipseity more originary than the ego (whether individual or collective), an enclaved ipseity, a divisible or split ipseity. I will not say that psychoanalysis or the analytic of *Dasein* (two discourses that are no longer ordered principally around a theory of the ego or the self) are alone capable of taking the measure of the phenomena that Arendt calls lying to oneself and self-deception; nevertheless, Arendt, like Koyré, at the point at which both of them speak necessarily of lying to oneself in politics, apparently does everything to avoid the least allusion to Freud and to Heidegger on these problems. Is this fortuitous? Is it fortuitous that they do not even mention the Marxist concept of *ideology*, if only to re-elaborate it? Despite its fundamental obscurity, despite the philosophical or theoretical limits of the discourses that have sometimes deployed it, the concept of ideology all the same marks a *site*, the *place* of what we are seeking to determine here. Even if this determination remains a sort of negative topology, it is very valuable and takes us farther, beyond consciousness and knowledge, in the direction of a locus of nontruth that is neither that of error, ignorance, or illusion nor that of the lie or of lying to oneself. Ideology, in the Marxist sense, has nothing to do with any of these.

3. What seems to compromise if not the project of such a history of the lie, at least its irreducible specificity, is an indestructible *optimism*.

Such an optimism is not to be accounted for by psychology. It does not reflect primarily a personal disposition, a habitus, a being-in-the-world, or even a project of Hannah Arendt's. After all, to speak of our age as the age of the absolute lie, to seek to acquire the means to analyze it with relentless lucidity, hardly shows optimism. "Optimistic" rather is the conceptual and problematic apparatus that is here put in place or accredited. What is at stake is the determination of the political lie but also, above all, of the truth in general. The latter must always win out and end up being revealed because, as Arendt repeats frequently, in its structure it is assured stability, irreversibility; it indefinitely outlives lies, fictions, and images.[23] This classical determination of the truth as indefinite survival of the "stable" (*bebaion* is Plato's and Aristotle's term)[24] seems to call for a great number of "deconstructive" questions (and not only in the Heideggerian style). By excluding even the possibility that a lie might survive indefinitely, it not only goes against experience itself but also makes of history, as history of the lie, the epidermic and epiphenomenal accident of a *parousia* of truth. Now, a specific history of the lie itself should pass, at least, by way of the history of the Christianization (with Paul, with certain Church Fathers, with Augustine and his *De mendacio*, and so forth) of the Greek thematics of *pseudos* (at the same time the false, the fictive, and the deceptive, which does not simplify things or which simplifies them too much), of the *eidolon*; and of the spectral *phantasma*, of rhetoric, of sophistics and the politically useful lie, according to Plato's *Republic*,[25] of the useful, curative, or preventive lie as *pharmakon*. This radical Christianization is found, in the secularized state so to speak and in the age of Enlightenment, in the Kantian doctrine that condemns the lie as absolute decline, "human nature's capital vice," "negation of human dignity"; "the man who does not believe what he says is less than a thing," says Kant in his "Doctrine of Virtue."[26] One would be tempted to reply: Unless he does not cease thereby being less than a thing in order to become something and even someone, already something like a man.

4. That is why, finally, one may always worry about the secondarization, relativization, or accidentalization, even the banalization, of a theory or a history of the lie, once it is still dominated by the Arendtian certainty of a final victory and a certain survival of the truth (and not merely of veracity) over the lie, even if one accepts its teleology as merely

a just regulating idea in politics, or in the history of the human socius in general. For me, it is a matter here not of opposing to this risk the Judeo-Christiano-Kantian hypothesis of the lie as radical evil and sign of the originary corruption of human existence but underscoring that without at least the *possibility* of this radical perversion and of its infinite survival, and, notably, if one does not take into account *technical* mutations in the history and the structure of the simulacrum or the iconic substitute, one will always fail to think the lie itself, the possibility of its history, the possibility of a history that intrinsically involves it, and doubtless the possibility of a history, period.

However, to hasten the conclusion, one has to admit that nothing and no one will ever be able to prove, precisely—what is properly called "to prove," in the strict sense of knowledge, theoretical demonstration, and determinant judgment—the existence and the necessity of such a history as history of the lie.

One can only say what it could or should be, the history of the lie—if there is any.

Translated by Peggy Kamuf

Out of the Blue

SECRECY, RADICAL EVIL, AND THE CRYPT OF FAITH

Peter Fenves

Everything acts in secret. This declaration could be said to be the disclosure of philosophy, the disclosure of the possibility of discovery in general. When it is disclosed that everything acts in secret—or, to quote a sentence from Heraclitus, *physis kryptesthai philei*[1]—then there is something like philosophy as the *philia* to which the secret of "natural" secrecy is confided. The *philia* of philosophy could even be said to consist not in a love for secrecy, nor in a love for the exposure of secrecy, but in a love for the exposure of the love of secrecy; and this love would reach its end, if not its destination, with the disclosure of the impossibility of discovery in general. This paradoxical discovery could be interpreted in two divergent ways: on the one hand, the disclosure of the impossibility of discovery in general could mean that nothing—or nothing of *philosophical* import, nothing other than "natural" things—is hidden; on the other, it could mean that whatever escapes generality—one of whose names is "being"—conceals itself. These two interpretations of the paradoxical disclosure of the impossibility of disclosure in general lay out the vanishing points for philosophy at the end of its love for the exposure of the love of secrecy: points into which philosophy itself, as an independent and self-assured discipline, itself vanishes.

This, then, is the hypothesis: everything acts in secret, and by disclosing that everything acts in this way, philosophy discloses itself. But this hypothesis immediately meets a strong philological objection: an injustice is done to Heraclitus's fragment when it is rendered so inaccurately as "everything acts in secret." The apparently more appropriate translation "nature loves to hide itself" is not much better, however, since each word of the sentence *physis kryptesthai philei* harbors its own secrets—secrets that more than one philosopher has attempted to wrest, not now from nature, or *physis*, but from the one who, as author of this sentence, was renowned for his obscurity. By saying that everything that comes to light loves to obscure itself, "The Obscure" obscures himself. The Heraclitean sentence cannot fail to speak of its own obscurity at the same time that it speaks of everything else: both *physis* and its disclosure in speech are drawn into secrecy.

And so nothing about this declaration can be clear. If nothing can be clear, however, nothing can be obscure. As an apophantic sentence, "everything acts in secret" promises to reveal something; but since it reveals nothing other than the universality of concealment, its revelation is self-defeating. Applied to itself, it appears to give the lie to itself. But it only *appears* to do so: self-defeat does not equal self-refutation, and the sentence defies any straightforward treatment according to the tortuous paradigm of the so-called "Cretan liar's paradox." Still less can it be consigned to the sphere of "performative contradictions," for its subject matter is nothing less than the concealing character of performativity. The "essence" of every performance lies in secrecy, which means that everything recognizable under the category of "speech act" may hide the fact that it is something else altogether—*a limine*, a nonaction: an omission or a passion. This possibility makes every performance precarious: none can secure its right to be recognized as a performance. The impossibility of any action's being fully and finally recognizable *as* an action, however, grants it the possibility of being an utterly new action, which is to say, the possibility of being an action in the eminent sense: the beginning of something new.

No one has traced the imbrications of possibility, impossibility, disclosure, and secrecy with more tenacity and daring than Jacques Derrida. The following paper is dedicated to him for this reason—and for many others as well. It is dedicated to Derrida in three senses: the last section of the paper pays attention to one motif that traverses his philosophical work; the first section adopts one mode in which he has taught us to disclose the surface secrets—or aporias—of a philosophical text; and the whole is dedicated to Derrida "himself." Or to be less grand, and less sure that the reflexive "himself" captures anyone in particular, it is dedicated to the one who could address us all, himself included, as "Marranos that we are, Marranos in any case, whether we want to be or not, whether we know or not."[2]

Radical Evil

If it is reduced to an anthropological dictum, the sentence "everything acts in secret" becomes less elusive: it turns into the statement, often expressed as a lament, that everyone acts in secret. The Heraclitean fragment *physis kryptesthai philei* thus translates into the proposition that *human* nature loves to hide itself; the nature of human beings consists in a passion for self-concealment; and this passion itself is so hidden that it cannot be properly brought to light. Not only are all the vices of anthropological reduction contained in these theses, but so, too, is what Heidegger, for one, saw as the common root of such reductions: Christian humanism.[3] If, however, the Heraclitean saying undergoes a more thorough anthropological transformation, and if secrecy is understood in such a manner that it would define terms like *physis*, *theos*, and *anthropos* rather than allowing these terms to direct the interpretation of the idea of secrecy, then the transformed Heraclitean saying can as little be understood under the generic terms "anthropology," "theology," and "physiology," as the sentence "everything acts in secret" can be understood as a sentence of a specifiable type—and it becomes, in turn, ever more difficult to distinguish a secrecy for which there is no corresponding revelation from a mendacity to which one could not confess in all honesty. Heraclitus's saying then approximates Kant's thesis of radical evil: a thesis that is doubtless determined by anthropological, psychological, and especially Christian-Protestant tendencies, but one that cannot be conceived simply as a result of these vectors once it has been thought in all its radicality—if it *can* be thought in all its radicality, which means, at the very least, thought as something other than simply Kant's own thesis, a thesis he posits with complete recognition of its meaning, its point, and its position in a philosophical discourse. Not even the "honest Kant" can say in all honesty that all the members of the species to which he belongs have an "innate" propensity to conceal themselves—not only from one another but from themselves.

Yet, according to Kant, everyone does act in secret. The great attempt to come to terms with the idea of religion that Kant undertakes in *Religion innerhalb der Grenzen der bloßen Vernunft* (*Religion Within the Limits of Reason Alone*, 1793) can be understood as an attempt to explore the dimensions of the secret source from which all action, properly speaking, springs forth. The arena of Kant's self-professed "experiment"[4] in reconciling theological dogma with pure principles of practice is the place where reason is stripped (*entblößt*) of its protective clothing and left bare (*bloß*). As Kant writes to a friend soon after the publication of his work, he too, in making this daring experiment, is exposed: "I have proceeded conscientiously and with genuine respect for the Christian religion but also with appropriate candor, concealing nothing but rather presenting openly the way in which I believe that a possible union of Christianity with the purest practical reason is possible" (Ak., 11: 429). And religion as well, once led into the arena of naked reason under the guidance of a philosopher who "conceals nothing," is also stripped of its clothing: it cannot make use of the "parerga" (Ak., 6: 53–54)—the miracles and mysteries—in which it traditionally wraps itself.[5] Unable to conceal itself in secrecy, religion must rely on the only two modes of revelation that, according to Kant, naked reason can authenticate: on the one hand empirical revelation, which depends on sensuous and thus temporally conditioned intuition, and on the other, purely rational revelation, which does not.[6] What reveals itself in purely rational revelation, according to the famous phrase Kant first proposes in the *Critique of Practical Reason* (1788), is the *Factum der Vernunft*: the fact of moral consciousness, which is to say, the fact that human beings are commanded to act according to a law that reason legislates for itself without help from any source, human or divine, without condition, without promise, and without threat.[7] Under no condition, however, can this *Factum*—as "something made"—disclose the secret of its manufacture and thus make its source, namely freedom, comprehensible: the possibility of freedom always remains impossible to disclose. And this secret source of the moral legislation through which agents become agents in the eminent sense—ones who begin a new series of events—can legitimately be called a secret in absence of all possible revelation: it is, to use the phrase Derrida discovered in Montaigne, the "mystical foundation of the law,"[8] inasmuch as it constitutes the sole basis for the transformation of a pure law of action into a law that a finite being *can*—and therefore must—obey. Since the source of the "fact of reason" cannot be revealed, a door is opened to interpretation. Something like "religion" can then enter into this door, or stand at the threshold, by presenting unconditional imperatives *as* divine commands, which, however, reveal nothing about their source.

Every action for which one can be held accountable presupposes a secret source of which no one can give an account. From the moment he works out his groundbreaking conception of the relation between a law whose facticity is founded on freedom and a freedom that is known only from the fact that the law itself suffices as a motive for action, Kant immerses himself in the ways of radical nonknowledge: no one can know if an action is freely undertaken; no one can know if an action is performed out of duty or in view of certain consequences; and no one can therefore know if the actions one takes are one's own—or merely the result of everything one is given.

The course of Kant's thought after his completion of the three *Critiques* consists in ever-more-refined attempts to come to terms with the secret source from which action draws its power. His first postcritical work, "On the Failure of All Philosophical Attempts at Theodicy," concludes with a melancholic and almost misanthropic reflection on "the impurity that lies deep in what is hidden, where human beings know how to distort even inner declarations before their own conscience" (Ak., 8: 270). Such a deeply hidden impurity—or self-obscurity—points toward the possibility that the secret source of action may be so thoroughly muddied that not only do all attempts at theodicy fail, but all judgments about the justice of things, whether human or divine, become suspect. As if reacting to the radicality of this suspicion—and self-suspicion—into which the closing remarks of "On the Failure of All Philosophical Attempts at Theodicy" issue, Kant steps back and makes a new attempt at working out a conception of religion freed from its dependence on the self-deceptive modes of reasoning that animate philosophical theodicies.

In order to do so, he must disclose the root of every action for which human beings can be held responsible, and thus he must respond—in part and with a certain irresponsibility of his own—to the last and most comprehensive of the four questions he had sought to address in his three *Critiques*: "what is the human being?"[9] *Radical evil* is the expression through which Kant guides his search for an answer.

The route Kant takes in proposing the thesis of radical evil—"The human being is evil by nature" (Ak., 6: 32)—is circuitous and not without a series of impasses, but at least this much is clear: "by nature" means "according to recognizable laws." The only law of practice that pure reason recognizes is the one that commands purely, which is to say, commands without regard to appearances; and this law is, by definition, the moral law.[10] Human beings are evil by nature insofar as the basis of all their subsequent actions is a prior "subordination" of an unconditional command—the command to carry out the moral law—to hypothetical recommendations made by reason in its capacity as calculator of pathological gains and losses. The "nature" of human beings does not then simply consist in freedom; it subsists in a prior or "innate" act (*Aktus*) in which the absolute law of freedom is subordinated to the search for the greatest gain, namely happiness. Such subordination takes place in an act of radical *in*subordination, for—but this is simply to state a tautology—the law alone has a right to order action. This act of insubordination then defines the human species as a species—defines it, however, not in the sense that this species is destined to subordinate the law to a calculus of prudential rules, but in the sense that this act freely determines the "form" in which the three "elements of the vocation [*Bestimmung*] of the human being" (Ak., 6: 26)—those that function as the constituent moments of every human action—are henceforth to be "combined" (Ak., 6: 28): the first "element" in this new *Elementarslehre* is the disposition to "animality"; the second, the disposition to "humanity"; the third, the disposition to "personality." Subordinating the third to either of the first two amounts to insubordination, and insubordination constitutes the fundamental structure of human action. Each individual act is a model of this structure, and the structure "exists" nowhere but there—in its models, which is to say, in every action a human being undertakes. Once these elements of action have been isolated and have been shown to be "combined" in a determinate "form," Kant's impressive version of practical structuralism can then find the resolution to the problem of insubordination in a model of perfect subordination, which, for its part, helps to strengthen the third element and thus to reverse the perverse structure of action.

This model (*Vorbild*) of perfect subordination is derived from an archetype (*Urbild*) of "moral disposition in its purity" (Ak., 6: 61), and the latter, in turn, is rooted in the capacity of reason to form an Idea of moral perfection without any contribution from the power of imagination (*Einbildungskraft*). In place of the power of imagination, which plays a fundamental and indispensable role in the formation of experience as a whole, Kant proposes something like a parallel process of "personification" for the construction of a counterforce to radical insubordination. When the Idea of goodness is "personified," an *Urbild* turns into a *Vorbild* that need not—and here the accent is on *need*—correspond to any empirical example: "There is no need . . . of any example from experience to make the Idea of a human being morally pleasing to God a model for us; the Idea is present as a model already in our reason" (Ak., 6: 63). "The personified idea of the good principle" (Ak., 6: 60) does not have to appear in the same manner as sensible objects, and yet it does not have to remain outside of appearances altogether, as do unpersonified Ideas, ideals, and archetypes. The "person" who results from the process of personification *can* appear; but such an appearance is superfluous, for it remains a *Vorbild* and is recognizable as exemplary only insofar as it wholly conforms to the Idea of moral perfection that reason makes for itself. With the help of the "person," however, Kant can work out the parameters of an "invisible church," the sole function of which is to strengthen each member's resolve to avoid seeking help from anything or anyone that would promise future happiness or threaten future punishments, including any apparatus of the "visible church."

But before Kant can resolve the problem of changing the "form" in which the three "elements" of the "disposition to the good" are "combined" and an invisible church is constructed on the basis of a personified Idea, he must first demonstrate that insubordination does *in fact* describe the form in which the dispositions to the good are combined. Otherwise, not only would there be no need for a *model* of perfect subordination, but the Idea and archetype of moral perfection would suffice. No fact is adequate to this demonstration—not even the "fact of reason," since the latter is just another name for the "element" under which the other two dispositions ought to be subordinated. In a lengthy footnote to the section of the chapter on radical evil entitled "The Human Being Is Evil by Nature," Kant asserts, "The proper proof [*der eigentliche Beweis*] of this condemning judgment [*Verdammungsurteil*] of reason as it passes moral sentences is to be found in the preceding section rather than in this one, which contains only the confirmation of it by experience" (Ak., 6: 39).[11] Yet, if one looks to the preceding section, one will search in vain for anything that proclaims itself "the proper proof" of the thesis of radical evil. And this is hardly surprising, since, as the same footnote proceeds to explain, nothing in experience can ever "uncover" (*aufdecken*) the "intelligible act" that precedes all experience. The radical act of insubordination to the order of the law takes place in secret, without proof, even without the "proof of spirit and power" (1 Cor. 2:4) of which G. E. Lessing, for one, speaks.[12] In the section to which this footnote refers, Kant distinguishes three modes of evil toward which "human nature" is prone, each of which corresponds to one of the dispositions; but nowhere in this analytic exercise does he demonstrate the penchant itself: to borrow a striking image that Kant deploys in his *Laying the Ground for the Metaphysics of Morals* (*Grundlegung zur Metaphysik der Sitten*), this *Hang*, as an "innate" penchant—or as an addiction in advance of all acts of consumption[13]—has no discernible means of support.[14] And neither, therefore, does the thesis of radical evil: it appears to be as much a sheer thesis, a naked positing, as the altogether anterior *Aktus* on which all subsequent ones depend. Kant may define the *Hang* by means of certain critical distinctions, but he cannot justify the application of this term to anything in nature—or in human nature:

The propensity to evil is an act in the first sense (*peccatum originarium*), and at the same time the formal ground of all unlawful conduct in the second sense, which latter considered materially, violates the law and is termed vice (*peccatum deriviatum*); and the first indebtedness remains, even though the second (from incentives that do not subsist in the law itself) may be repeatedly avoided. The former is an intelligible action, cognizable merely through reason, without any temporal condition [*bloß durch Vernunft ohne alle Zeitbedingung erkennbar*]; the latter is sensible action, empirical, given in time (*factum phaenomenon*). (Ak., 6: 31)

Each of these sentences—and in particular the Latin phrases that punctuate them—deserves special attention; but it is immediately apparent that Kant does not demonstrate anything, least of all the thesis of radical evil, for in this passage he grants to the faculty of reason precisely that function from which, according to the *Critique of Pure Reason*, it is positively excluded, namely cognition. And according to the same *Critique*—but this amounts to the same contention—cognition cannot take place "without temporal conditions." The phrase *bloß durch Vernunft* ("merely through reason") echoes the modest words of the title, *Religion innerhalb der Grenzen der bloßen Vernunft*, but it gestures in the opposite direction: toward an elevated *Vernunft* that cognizes intelligible acts in the same manner that it recognizes the "things"—or noumena—of the intelligible world. Such a rational capacity would be in all senses *bloß*: it would be "mere" reason because it would not need the categorial accouterment of the understanding, and it would be an infinite rational capacity before which every finite being would stand naked. Kant would transcend the limits of mere reason were he to claim the capacity to know something *bloß durch Vernunft*—and he *must* do so: he *must* overstep these limits if he intends to make good on his promise and deliver a "proper proof" of the thesis of radical evil on the basis of which a purely rational religion is to be established. Without so much as saying so—and this silence, or this secrecy, is at the heart of his undertaking—Kant improperly "proves" the thesis of radical evil. Kant does not merely refer to an absent proof that he nowhere provides; nor can it simply be said that he reveals the secret by concealing it. Nor can it simply be said that he is mendacious, although many readers of the *Religion* have not refrained from this "sentence of condemnation by reason as it sits in moral judgment."[15] By declaring that the "proof proper" has been demonstrated in the previous section without having conducted anything but "improper" methods of proofs, Kant reveals the secret in secret, and in this way he does not properly reveal it, but does not properly conceal it either.

The thesis of radical evil proves *itself* by the absence of "proper proof." Impropriety is another name for insubordination: human reason does not adopt the proper maxim for its actions, the one maxim that can be maximized to such an extent that it constitutes a universal law of action; yet only a maxim of this kind allows one to be properly oneself in practice. It is of course inappropriate to associate impropriety of proof with impropriety in practice, since the former is an entirely theoretical matter, whereas the latter concerns the principles of practical reason; but if the impropriety in proof concerns the foundation of practical reason and touches on honesty in scholarly matters, this objection is of little consequence. Only improper proofs of the thesis of primordial insubordination present themselves in the *Religion*, and these proofs traverse the distinction between theory and practice—so much so that the *Religion* justifies the universalization of a maxim according to which the evil of the other is presupposed. That human beings are evil by nature, Kant writes, "means . . . that from what one knows of the human being through experience he cannot judge otherwise of him, or, that one can presuppose evil to be subjectively necessary in every human being, even in the best" (Ak., 6: 32).

This "or" is far from being an innocent expansion: if one can presuppose evil in every human being, then one is justified in mistrusting everyone—even the best, even Immanuel Kant, who "spares" himself the trouble of a "formal proof" (Ak., 6: 33) of the thesis, as he expends himself on a series of merely informal or material proofs. The first of these improper proofs concerns the "state of nature." Kant disposes of those "hoping" to find natural goodness in this supposedly pristine state by referring them to various accounts of the "cruelties" that distant, non-European peoples perpetuate upon one another. It is surprising, however, that Kant would trust such accounts, for mistrust is first among the "litany of complaints" altering the mood of those disposed (*gestimmt*) to grant some degree of firmly rooted goodness to others—to such as Kant himself, or to the travel writers he reads, who claim to inhabit an "ethical state" (*gesitteter Zustand*). From the moment that one reflects on "secret falsity even in the most intimate friendships, so that a moderation of trust in mutual disclosure even among the best friends is reckoned a universal maxim of prudence in intercourse [*Umgang*]" (Ak., 6: 33), sanguine trust gives way to melancholic mistrust. Everyone in an "ethical state" must presuppose so much bad will on the part of everyone else, even one's closest friend, that universal mistrust is the only reasonable maxim for social intercourse, even if this maxim cannot be universalized without contradicting itself, and thereby becoming not only irrational but—and for the same reason—evil as well. No wonder Kant loves to repeat the famous saying attributed to Aristotle: "My dear friends, there is no such thing as a friend!"[16] The contradictory character of this "speech act" accords with the self-contradiction into which the maxim of mistrust issues upon its universalization. If it were only "subjectively necessary" to presuppose the thesis of radical evil in practice, and if there were no objective basis in the structure of the dispositions to the good, then the thesis expressing it would be nothing but the uncontested reign of the principle of prudence, and would in this way confirm *itself*: the thesis itself would provide unimpeachable evidence of the evil of which it speaks. And it would be evil in a quite precise sense, for the supposed "principle" of mistrust could not be universalized without undermining the very intercourse, discourse, or *Umgang* in which it was expressed: it could not be communicated—or even articulated to oneself—without at the same time destroying the very medium of communication.

So long as Kant does not properly *prove* that "human beings are evil by nature" (Ak., 6: 32), he can be *trusted* only when he proposes this dismal thesis. Yet the very thesis he entrusts to his readers is reason for universal mistrust, including—or especially—mistrust of anyone who makes universal mistrust appear reasonable. And when Kant then proceeds to clarify the conditions under which he writes the *Religion*, he makes it apparent that there are good "empirical" reasons to mistrust him, even if the precise motives for his "secret falsity" toward his readership, including readers from whom he has sworn to be "concealing nothing" (Ak., 11: 429), remain hidden. In the preface to the second edition of the *Religion*, dated January 26, 1794, Kant asserts:

> To understand this book according to its essential content, only common morality is needed, without entering into the *Critique of Practical Reason*, still less into the theoretical Critique. When, for example, virtue as skill in *actions* conforming to duties (according to their legality) is called *virtus phaenomenon*, and the same virtue as enduring *disposition* toward such actions *from duty* (because of their morality) is called *virtus noumenon*, such expressions are used only because of the schools; the matter itself [*die Sache selbst*] is contained, though worded otherwise, in the most popular children's instruction and sermons, and is easily understood. (Ak., 6: 14)

Kant responds in a quite different manner to an order issued by Friedrich Wilhelm II. After the king's death—and ambiguously breaking his promise not to publish anything on religious matters—Kant publishes this letter in the preface to his *Conflict of the Faculties* (*Streit der Fakultäten*, 1798): "I have," he reassures the king, "done no harm to the public *religion of the country*," although Kant makes clear throughout the *Religion* that religion, unlike a sect or a confession, is indivisible and therefore cannot be attributed to any identifiable church, land, or people. To support a contention that contradicts the direction of his book, Kant then proceeds to inform the king, "This is already clear from the fact that the book in question [*Religion Within the Limits of Reason Alone*] is not at all appropriate for the public: to them it is an incomprehensible and closed book" (Ak., 7: 8).[17] The dedication of the *Religion* could therefore read: "A book for everyone and no one." And if it cannot quite accommodate such a dedication, if it does not quite reach the aporia of address that thwarts every straightforward or merely ironical reading of Nietzsche's *Thus Spake Zarathustra*, its insufficiency cannot be explained away as a consequence of Kant's desire to assure certain members of his readership—the "scholars of the faculty" (Ak., 7: 8)—that the *Religion* was indeed meant for them. Nor can Kant's contradictory statements concerning the intelligibility of his book simply be ascribed to some private failure on his part to measure up to the standards of honesty he so passionately promotes, especially in his last writings. Nor can Kant's contradictory accounts of his intended readership simply be attributed to the systematic dishonesty that prevails, according to Schopenhauer and Nietzsche, whenever philosophers, having turned into "scholars of the faculty," are at the disposal of the state.[18] When Kant writes at one time that the concepts in the *Religion* are "easily understood," and soon thereafter that the book as a whole is "incomprehensible," he may be operating on the basis of a prudential maxim adopted in order to avoid royal displeasure; but this account of his motives—whether psychological or institutional—does not concede the possibility that his book may be "closed" from its inception: impossible to read, even for "scholars of the faculty."

The act of understanding the thesis of radical evil, the act of opening up and comprehending this "incomprehensible and closed" book, demands that the "subjective necessity of evil" (Ak., 6: 32) be recognized in the absence of a proper proof of its objective foundation "in" the human being—and be recognized by every reader in terms of a "secret falsity" traversing all intercourse, including the discourse "before our very eyes [*vor Augen*]" (Ak., 6: 33).

The *Religion* is placed before the eyes of its readership in a much more literal sense than the "cruelties" of the distant peoples that Kant writes about when using this well-worn expression, for these "cruelties" are accessible to the Königsberg-bound "scholar of the faculty" only through the medium of the travel books he enjoys. *Religion Within the Limits of Reason Alone*, in sum, is so subject to mistrust that it could not explicitly proclaim itself "a book for everyone and no one" without ceasing to be such a book. Opening this book means opening oneself to its closedness.

"Opening oneself to its closedness" presupposes, however, that there is some *one* to whom this book would be closed; yet the presupposition of a propensity to "secret falsity" disposes of this, the supposition of subjectivity. For if this propensity is presupposed in all its radicality, then falsity among friends constitutes nothing more than the later "development" of a prior disposition (Ak., 6: 33): the original "secret falsity" lies in the relation of the self to itself. Kant generally calls such falsity "the inner lie"—without investigating the enormous difficulties to which the idea of lying falls prey when it is predicated on an "inner" act.[19] If it makes sense to speak of an "inner lie," then action not only has its source in secrecy but can also take place in a secret secrecy, a secrecy one hides from oneself. Concealing from itself the source of its selfhood in the secret of freedom, the "I" hides from itself the responsibility for the actions it undertakes, and this hiding is itself an action for which it is responsible and from which it hides itself. The possibility that this latter action, too, may be hidden—and so on *ad infinitum*—does not mean that the self consists in the act of hiding from itself, although such a conclusion has given rise to various expositions of "depth." Hiding from oneself the act of hiding from oneself leaves no room for the distinction between the hidden and the revealed, which is to say, no room for anything that can properly appear or properly remain clear of appearances, no room for phenomena or noumena, strictly speaking, or for the critical decision about their difference. Under this condition, reason may be "naked" but can reveal nothing—neither itself nor anything else. As Kant comes to the conclusion of the informal, the material, or in any case the improper proofs of his thesis, he almost inadvertently names the "subjective condition" in which all these distinctions disappear: *Verstimmung*, "out-of-tuneness," "distempered," "misdisposed." Having clearly separated out and shown the "form of combination" of the three "elements of the determination of the human being [*Bestimmung des Menschen*]" (Ak., 6: 26), Kant is nevertheless drawn toward a *Verstimmung* in which *Bestimmung* as "vocation" is revoked, and *Bestimmung* as "determination" rendered thoroughly indeterminate.[20]

Hiding the secret in which every action takes place means concealing from oneself the "fact" that every action is free and ought therefore to find its decisive motivation *there*—in the law of freedom. Hiding the secret thus means concealing from oneself the difference between *virtus phaenomenon* and *virtus noumenon*, legality and morality, positive laws and the law that the rational self posits for itself. The Latin terms may be comprehensible only to "scholars of the faculty," but the concepts to which they refer are nevertheless "easily comprehensible," even among schoolchildren. Or so Kant says, if he is to be trusted. If, however, the distinction between *virtus phaenomenon* and *virtus noumenon* were to disappear in an act of supreme self-concealment, all subsequent actions would cease to be *human* actions and become "devilish." But the term *devilish*, for all of its pathos, is still insufficient to describe the disposition of those who have concealed from themselves the distinction between laws and the law; for the devil, as the "personification" of the evil principle, operates according to an underlying maxim in which opposition to the law—rather than any prospect of happiness—is a sufficient motive for action. By opposing the law for the sake of opposition, the devil, as a great "scholar of the faculty," recognizes the law and thereby reveals, perhaps better than anyone else, the very distinction between *virtus phaenomenon* and *virtus noumenon*. It is quite the contrary for those of "good conscience" or, as Kant prefers to say, those who enjoy *Gewissensruhe* ("peace of conscience"). Not to be troubled by the thesis that one's actions are rooted in evil is an—impassive—act of evil in full bloom:

The *innate* guilt (*reatus*) [is] in the third [stage] . . . deliberate guilt (*dolus*), and is characterized by a certain *perfidy* [*Tücke*] of the human heart (*dolus malus*) in deceiving itself with respect to its own good or evil state of mind [*Gesinnung*] and—provided that its actions do not result in evil, which they could well do because of their maxims—in not troubling itself about its state of mind, but rather considering itself justified before the law [*vor dem Gesetze*]. From this originates the peace of conscience of so many human beings (conscientious in their own opinion) when, in the midst of undertaking actions in which the law was not consulted or at least did not count the most, they escape evil consequences only by luck, and even imagine themselves deserving, feeling themselves guilty of no such offenses as they see attached to others. . . . This dishonesty by which one blows smoke in one's own face [*Diese Unredlichkeit, sich selbst blauen Dunst vorzumachen*] and which thwarts the grounding of an authentic moral state of mind in ourselves, then also extends itself outwardly to falsity and deception of others, which, if this is not to be termed malevolence [*Bosheit*], is at least to be called worthlessness [*Nichtswürdigkeit*], and it lies in the radical evil of human nature, which, inasmuch as it puts out of tune [*verstimmt*] the moral capacity to judge [*moralische Urteilskraft*] how one is to hold a human being [*man einen Menschen halten solle*] and makes accounting entirely uncertain, constitutes both internally and externally [*die Zurechnung innerlich und äußerlich ganz ungewiß*] the foul spot [*den faulen Fleck*] of our species, which, so long as we do not bring it out [*herausbringen*], hinders the germ of good from developing as it otherwise would. (Ak., 6: 38)

Since "peace of conscience" (*Gewissensruhe*) can give rise to the "hallucination of merit" (*Einbildung von Verdienst*) (Ak., 6: 38), it is not entirely at rest; on the contrary, it is enormously productive, and the most proper product of this evil is a strange, unclassifiable, element—perhaps an alchemical offshoot, perhaps a matter of magicians' tricks, or perhaps a side effect of tobacco addiction: namely, "blue vapor" (*blauer Dunst*).[21] Not only does the difference between legality and the law evaporate into this vapor, but so too do the distinctions by which Kant hoped to capture the specificity of human evil. It is not supposed to be sheer malevolence, *Bosheit*, but rather mere wickedness, *Bösartigkeit*: evil of a *kind*; specified, not generalized, evil. Only a few paragraphs earlier, Kant had expressly denied that "malevolent reason (an absolutely evil will) [*boshafte Vernunft (ein schlechthin böser Wille)*]" could be ascribed to human reason, and had therefore exonerated human beings of "devilishness" (Ak., 6: 35). But the uncanny blueness of the vapor, in which the decisive critical distinction between *virtus phaenomenon* and *virtus noumenon* evaporates, sends *Bösartigkeit* in the direction of *Bosheit* and radical evil into the abyss of absolute evil—but only *sends* them: *Bösartigkeit* and radical evil never *reach* these nefarious destinations, because, in order for them to do so, *virtus noumenon* would have to be recognized as such and thereby made into something like a counter-element, to which all elements of the "disposition to the good" would henceforth be subordinated, and in which they would, in combination, be destroyed. The haze in which, as a consequence of clear conscience, all moral judgment—and perhaps the faculty of judgment as a whole—becomes clouded allows for no such recognition: absolute evil is as unreachable as relative goodness.[22] According to one of the doctrines that emerges from the reassessment of subjective powers and principles that Kant undertakes in his *Critique of Judgment*, every judgment presupposes an appropriate *Stimmung* (mood), and the very ability to judge, *Urteilskraft*, consists in a prior "attunement" or "harmonization" of the relevant mental "faculties."[23] Nowhere does Kant, in his discussion concerning the "pure practical power of judgment" (Ak., 5: 68) in the *Critique of Practical Reason*, entertain the possibility of a *Verstimmung* that would, strictly speaking, disable the moral power of judgment altogether. Whereas the power of judgment allows pure practical reason to establish a "typic" of nature in which everything, including the judge, has a dutifully appointed place, the disabling of this power in *Verstimmung* allows judge and judged alike to slip away into some utterly unfixable, fluid, or vaporous landscape: no human being can be "held" long enough to be judged. If, therefore, moral judgment—which consists in the ability to separate out the moral from the nonmoral, the law from mere legality, *virtus noumenon* from *virtus phaenomenon*—does not rest on, and emerge from, a proper *Stimmung*; if it is, from the start, *verstimmt*, then the power of judgment whose very inquiry Kant pursues—"is the human being evil from the outset?"—likewise goes out of tune.

"Peace of conscience" suspends the "court of judgment" in whose image, for Kant, the concept of conscience can enter into consciousness.[24] If there is "peace of conscience," there is neither conscience nor conscientiousness, and if there is neither conscience nor conscientiousness, then evil has free reign. Not only, therefore, does Kant, when supposedly proving that human beings are radically evil and hence untrustworthy, give indications that he is untrustworthy himself, but he confesses as well to a radical untrustworthiness expressed in the strongly negative term *Tücke* ("perfidy," "insidiousness"), mandatory for all who seek to exonerate themselves of the accusation that they are radically untrustworthy. For denying the thesis that Kant supposes he has proved—the proposition, namely, that one must presuppose everyone, oneself included, to be fundamentally insubordinate—amounts to asserting the counterthesis that at least one human being deserves to enjoy a placid conscience. And who better to exempt from the thesis of radical evil than oneself, since the placidity of one's own conscience could serve as incorrigible proof of the counterthesis? All projections of placidity onto others, by contrast, would remain precisely that: mere projections, nondemonstrable conjectures. Any demonstration based on such a projection or conjecture would remain informal, improper, or—in the most precise sense of the term *uneigentlich*—a proof "not-one's-own." And, as Kant vigorously argues in the opening section of the *Religion* in matters of morality, *tertium non datur*: there is no "third" alternative between or beyond the determination that the human being is either good or evil.[25] The very demands of proof, therefore, cast anyone disagreeing with Kant—or, to translate a standard German expression into colloquial English, anyone "not in tune" (*stimmt nicht*) with Kant—into a diffuse atmosphere of "out-of-tuneness" (*Verstimmung*), where there is not only no "third," but no "first" or "second" either. To deny the thesis of radical evil, in short, verges on proving it *e contrario*, according to a mathematical model of which Kant avails himself when describing how the concept of right is constructed.[26] The indirect proof cannot quite work, however, and for the precise reason that the only *proper* evidence that the counterthesis can claim—a calm conscience—distempers "the power of moral judgment," and does so to such an extent that it allows "a human being" to slip away from the sentences pronounced by the court of reason.

As if to indicate this out-of-tuneness *properly*, as if to make the *Verstimmung* reverberate in his *own* vicinity, Kant adds his apparently redundant footnote only a few sentences after he parenthetically mentions the possibility of "the moral power of judgment" being "put out of tune": "The proper proof of this condemning judgment [*Verdammungsurteil*] of reason as it passes moral sentences is to be found in the preceding section rather than in this one." And he thus *lies*. Or lies to himself. Or hides. Or hides from himself the absence of any "formal," "proper," "literal," or "authentic" proof for the judgment that separates out the human species, condemns it, and damns it not to hell but to hope. And in place of proper proof or literal demonstration, Kant does not discover a blind spot, *ein blinder Fleck* that would withdraw from all acts of reflection and could therefore be marked only by reference to something improper or nonliteral; rather, he allows something far more vertiginous to enter into the experimental space cleared by "naked reason": *ein fauler Fleck*,[27] "a foul spot" that besmirches, bespeckles, and thus covers up reason to such a degree that reason ceases to be purely and simply itself, which is to say, "naked." Only this "foul spot," whose devilish provenance is undeniable, remains intact after all the other critical distinctions have evaporated into thin air—or, more exactly, into "blue vapor." *Blauer Dunst* is the unidentifiable element into which all the elements of Kant's "doctrine of elements" disappear. If nature—or only "human nature"—loves to hide itself, it does so in this diaphanous yet all-dissolving vapor.

If the distinction between *virtus noumenon* and *virtus phaenomenon* disappears, so, too, do the distinctions on which an "accounting" (*Zurechnung*) depends for its very operation. Or, in what amounts to the same, the mode of certainty implied in the term through which Kant designates an undisturbed conscience, *Gewissens-ruhe*, makes accounting "entirely uncertain" (*ganz ungewiß*). Whatever else "blue vapor" may do, it thus wipes the slate clean. No wonder it is associated with a clear conscience. But—and this touches on the philosophical-historical problem around which the *Religion* forms, as Kant proceeds from his demonstration of the "failure of all philosophical attempts at theodicy" to an exposition of the consequences for philosophy of this defeat—the atmosphere in which the "blue vapor" ambiguously appears is precisely the opposite of the one in which all "accounting" has been rendered uncertain. On the contrary, the act of accounting has risen to such an unprecedented degree of prominence that the prospect of unlimited "self-selling" presents itself as something like a biblical prooftext for naked reason. The "unworthiness" (*Unwürdigkeit*) that Kant attributes to anyone who enjoys a placid conscience derives from the self-concealing act in which the distinction Kant uses to define "the human being" and to single it out from all other visible things—the distinction between "worth" (*Würde*) and "price"

(*Preis*)[28]—disappears along with all the others. A citation within a citation brings this process of disappearance to an almost eschatological culmination. Without mentioning Paul's reference to his own "proof" of a thesis like that of radical evil—"For we have just proved that all, Jews as well as Greeks, are under sin" (Rom. 3:9)[29]—Kant rescues the apostle's words for critical reflection and completes his account of the vanishing of distinctions with a gesture toward the disappearance of all distinctions among human beings:

> A member of the English Parliament exclaimed in the heat of debate: "Everyone has his price, for which he sells himself." If this is true (which everyone can decide by himself), if nowhere is there virtue for which a level of temptation can be found that is capable of undermining it, if whether the good or evil spirit wins us over depends only on which offers the most and affords the promptest payoff, then what the apostle says may well [*möchte wohl*] be universally true of the human being: "There is no distinction here, they are all under sin—there is none who does good (according to the spirit of the law), not even one." (Ak., 6: 38–39)

"*May well* be universally true": with this startling declaration of uncertainty, Kant renders his thesis radically uncertain at the precise moment when the specter of "blue vapor" arises to make distinctions disappear, rendering all accounts "entirely uncertain." This note of hesitation—"may well"—in matters of morality is among the most unexpected passages in Kant's writings. Such surprising hesitation corresponds to the ambiguity of the term by which Kant proposes to treat the moral-medical problem posed by the "foul spot" on human nature. Like Lady Macbeth, "we" must, as Kant writes, *herausbringen*—"bring out," "eradicate"—this spot; if we do not do so, the "germ of goodness" will not develop "as it otherwise would." If it were not for the "foul spot," in other words, the continuous development of the "dispositions [*Anlagen*] to the good in human nature" would be secure, and it would be possible to interpret (*auslegen*) human history in its entirety, from beginning to end, as the laying out of these *Anlagen*—with no irrevocable interruptions, no breaks, and no breakdowns. Absent the "foul spot," the project, carried out under the title "theodicy," of justifying the creator by showing the justice of the created world would still be subject to irresolvable objections, but talk of a certain providence might still be salvaged.[30] And religion—even religion within the limits of naked reason, interpreting the moral law in terms of divine commands that help strengthen the element of "personality"—might still be possible, although hardly necessary. If the dispositions toward the good would lay themselves out without the threat of interruption, not only would there be no actual historical instance of perfect subordination, no Son of God, but not even its uninstantiated model would be of any value to human action; for the value of this model is a direct function of the devaluation of "dignity," taking place in a prior act of insubordination that finally expresses itself in the universal willingness to sell one's vote—or one's voice (*Stimme*)—to the highest bidder.

Bringing out, and thus confessing, the presence of the "foul spot" would be a demonstration of the perpetual necessity of religion; eradicating this spot, by contrast, would create conditions for the uninterrupted development of dispositions to the good, which, in turn, would make religion unnecessary—or at least would render the model of goodness redundant. The value of religion as a whole—and not simply that of the model of perfect subordination to the divine will—is thus a matter either of bringing out a tainted spot in confession or of wringing it out of naked reason. But this "or" does not represent an alternative: bringing it out is done in order to wring it out, and wringing it out can only be done by bringing it out. All the equivocations of Kant's thesis of radical evil that resolve themselves into the ambiguity *herausbringen* are expressions of the ineluctable duplicity of the supplementary element whose trace is supposed to be brought out and wrung out. This element, which comes into Kant's discourse as "blue vapor," makes all accounts "entirely uncertain." Uncertain accounts are at the origin of unaccountability: those with placid conscience acknowledge only their generally recognizable "public" debts, and they hide—from others as well as from themselves—their "private" indebtedness. From this perspective, the supplementary element displays a devilish, if not a satanic, dimension. But if this element does indeed have the power to decertify all accounts, it can also do away with the prudential calculus by which one fixes a price for oneself. From another perspective—or from a paradoxical perspective that keeps its distance from the calculus of competing values implicit in the very idea of perspective—the same element displays not a devilish dimension but, for want of a better word, a redemptive one: not the redemption from this or that debt but the interruption of the prudential calculation and erasure, if only for a moment, of all accounts and indeed of accounting in general. Such an erasure cannot escape the accusation of unaccountability; but only this erasure is radical enough to dispose of the calculus of prices *for good*—without leaving room for its return under the rubric of "dignity," the exalted name for a price not yet fixed. In his *Religion*, Kant reserves no place for any redemption not undertaken according to the model of "vicarious substitution" (Ak., 6: 73).[31] The place where all accounts and accounting are erased is itself subject to a movement of radical erasure where it appears in the antinomian—or paranomian—guise of devilish blemishes or "foul spots." And therefore this erasure from public as well as from private view *must* appear, provided its appearance, like all appearances, is predicated on the general recognizability of a consistent process of irreversible development—in this case, the flowering of evil. If, however, some appearances are not so conditioned, if an appearance can be uprooted for even a moment, then the decertification of all accounts could appear otherwise: the blueness of the "blue vapor" would not only mark a devilish penchant or ghastly addiction but also testify to an "act" of generalized erasure—a vanishing act that remains unexpected, incalculable, and comprehensible, even according to the law of freedom, and thus an act that always, if ever, disappears only by coming out of the blue.

Crypt of Faith

All of Derrida's work could be dedicated to whatever or whoever—this "or" makes every dedication hesitant[32]—comes out of the blue. Nothing, or no one, can come out of the blue without being in some way remarkable, yet this very remarkability—the ability to be marked, called upon, responded to, named, or merely designated—makes it impossible for anything or anyone purely and simply to come out of the blue. If the only action worthy of its name is without precedent, yet precedence alone makes it recognizable as an action in the first place; if, in other words, every action comes out of the blue without its blueness—or newness—being able to appear as such, then it is impossible to make sure anyone ever acts purely and simply. Or, alternatively, everyone and everything can be said—with a certain bad conscience—to act in secret. Or, as another alternative, as another interpretation of the same impossibility, every action can be said to forfeit its action character in favor of certain omissions or passions—which is to say that everyone not only acts in secret but hides this secrecy from the self it reveals whenever it acts. Clearing up the conditions in which actions and passions take place is one of the more consequential tasks that *Aufklärung* assigns itself. Derrida does not so much challenge the values inscribed into the term *Aufklärung*—clarity, distinctions—as mark out the limits of any clearing-up operation that, assured of its own clear conscience, misses the element out of which clarity comes: a supplementary, out-of-the-blue element to which Derrida, who writes often on tones but rarely on colors, calls.

Thinking through the conditions and consequences of an enlightenment that cannot take the clarity of its conscience for granted—even with respect to its right to the title, lineage, and heritage of "the enlightenment"—has been among the earliest and broadest lines of inquiry Derrida has undertaken, and never with so much insistence as in his altercations with Kant, who, for his part, generally keeps the term *Aufklärung* clear of any association with clarity or light.[33] And Derrida emphasizes as no other philosopher has done the degree to which Kant's critical project, despite—or perhaps because of—its insistence on the values of openness, publicity, and communicability, constantly touches on secrets, especially the secret source of action about which it not only has nothing to say but even commands reverential silence. Three texts of Derrida's serve as guides to this secret source—not because they, going "beyond Kant," reveal anything, but because they disclose the impossibility of a properly philosophical revelation of secrecy, and thus of a properly philosophical revelation in general. These altercations with Kant over the nature of secrecy issue into—or out of—an interrogation of the radicality of evil.[34]

1. Derrida's address "On a Newly Arisen Apocalyptic Tone in Philosophy" does not oppose anything Kant proposes in his essay "On a Newly Arisen Superior Tone in Philosophy," least of all his call for openness, publicity, and communicability. Rather, Derrida adopts a procedure that Kant invented to shore up the doctrine of transcendental idealism. Just as Kant demonstrates that two equally erroneous opponents—generally called "dogmatism" and "skepticism"—share a fallacy of which

they both remain unaware, Derrida shows that Kant and the mystagogues whom he denounces partake of something in common: an appeal to a secret that philosophical labor, no matter how strenuous, is unable to reveal. As Derrida emphasizes, even when Kant denounces "recent" mystagogues, he cannot do without an appeal of his own to a secret, to a mystery, and therefore—inevitably—to a veiled goddess. He may want to distinguish himself as sharply as possible from an inept dogmatist who declares himself on the verge of discovering ineffable secrets, but he cannot oppose himself *completely* to this false, mendacious, and self-deceptive "superior philosopher"; for he, too, acknowledges a secret source at whose threshold philosophical inquiry must come to a close. According to Kant's adversary, the secret appears in the form of a goddess, and so, too, according to Kant:

> The veiled goddess to whom we of both parties bend our knee is the moral law in us, in its inviolable majesty. We do indeed perceive her voice and also understand very well her command. But when we are listening, we are in doubt whether it comes from the human being, from the perfected power of his own reason, or whether it comes from an another, whose nature is unknown to us and speaks through this, his own reason.[35]

The mysterious goddess to whom Kant appeals is a vanishing apparition of this doubt. As Derrida indicates, Kant can distinguish his doctrine from that of the mystagogues on this point alone: the mysterious goddess appears only in order to disappear—and this disappearance or disfiguration is as mysterious and secretive as is she "herself." Once the mystagogues concede that the goddess appears only in this way, critical philosophy can make peace with its last adversaries—although not necessarily with the goddess—and herald the onset of its very own apocalypse: eternal peace in philosophy. Thus Derrida writes:

> No longer, he [Kant] says to the mystagogues, should we personify the law that speaks in us, above all not in the "esthetic," sensible, and beautiful form of this veiled Isis. Such is the condition for understanding/hearing the moral law itself, the unconditioned, and for understanding/hearing ourselves getting along [*pour nous entendre*]. In other words—and this is a trenchant motif for the thought of the law or of the ethical today—Kant calls for placing the law above and beyond, not the person, but personification and the body, above and beyond, as it were,

the sensible voice that speaks in us, the singular voice that speaks to us in private, the voice that could be said in his language to be "pathological" in opposition to the voice of reason.[36]

Derrida does not delve into this "trenchant motif for the thought of the law or of the ethical today" in "On the Newly Arisen Apocalyptic Tone in Philosophy," and he refrains from exploring further the relation between the condition for hearing and understanding the moral law and the undoing of this condition in radical evil. But he nevertheless points—obliquely—in this direction, for the ultimate, if not the final, destination of Derrida's address is *The Apocalypse of John*: not only its announcement of the end of the world in evil, and its corresponding announcement of the end of the evil into which the world has fallen, but also, and especially, its pronouncement—"above and beyond the sensible voice"—of a summons to "come." Such a summons can come only out of the blue; but since nothing that comes out of the blue can be recognized as such, the summons to come cannot properly arrive but must, instead, forever multiply—tragically, comically—into more than a single summons, coming from more than one voice, constituting more than one "to-come," and therefore opening onto more than one future.

2. In "Passions: 'An Oblique Offering,'" Derrida takes up the challenge of thinking a "pathological" language that would not be simply opposed to the voice of reason. He directs his attention to a hyperbolic hypothesis, perhaps even the hyperbolic hypothetical imperative to which all categorical ones secretly appeal as they demand on the one hand that the impossible—moral perfection—be a possibility and thus a necessity that human beings impose on themselves, and on the other hand that the impossible remain what it is: an unrealizable ideal. The hypothesis reads: *Il y a là du secret* ("There is secrecy there").[37] The "there" (*là*) of secrecy does not function as a regular demonstrative, and the secret it "demonstrates" is neither a proper disclosure nor a corresponding revelation. This hyperbolic hypothesis draws Derrida once again into a confrontation with Kant's attempt to secure the moral law against every conceivable challenge to its validity, legitimacy, and univocity. To Kant's Idea of a purely rational voice—one whose source remains hidden but which nevertheless, beyond any doubt, delivers unconditional imperatives that

force human beings to distinguish their "personality" from their "humanity"—Derrida responds with the thought of a nonresponsiveness that not only is *not* irresponsible but also discloses, hypothetically or even apothetically, the ability to respond to the other *as* other.

Throughout "Passions," and especially in two long, dense footnotes, Derrida interrogates morality as opposed to "pathology" and "legality," and he indicates how the very possibility of these distinctions depends upon the secrecy that resides "there"—in the crypt of "motives that act in secret (*insgeheim*)" (*P*, 87). Unless these "motives" are pure, no action is moral; but no one can ever ascertain whether or not they are indeed pure for the precise reason that they themselves "act in secret." Here is the "trenchant motif for the thought of the law or of the ethical today." The "existence" of the distinction between morality, on the one hand, and pathology and legality, on the other—and therefore the very existence of something like "personality" beyond "humanity," which, for its part, transcends "animality"—can no longer be measured with scientific objectivity, or according to the self-consciousness of the agent, the ideal of divine omniscience, or even the court of conscience. For Derrida, this constitutes the most radical dimension of Kant's thought. Derrida, quoting Kant—" 'But it must not be overlooked that it cannot be shown by any example [*durch kein Beispiel*] [i.e., it cannot be empirically shown, J. Derrida] whether or not there is [*ob es gebe*] such an imperative' "—remarks, "This is a most radical claim: no experience can assure us of the 'there is' at this point. God himself cannot therefore serve as an example" (*P*, 87).

The radicality of Kant's claim concerning the uncertainty of the "there is" does not, however, lead Derrida into a direct response to Kant's thesis of radical evil. Rather, the response to this thesis remains "oblique": by rethinking the relation between passion, responsibility, and secrecy, Derrida shows that the least radical moments of Kantian critique are untenable: as long as philosophy *directly* opposes moral responsibility to passion and understands the latter *simply* in terms of pathological—nonspontaneous, heteronomous—phenomena that seek refuge in secrecy and express themselves in irresponsible mendacity, it is not responsible *enough* to the idea of responsibility that it seeks to exemplify. Philosophy—or thought, or practice—must allow for a certain nonresponsiveness and therefore concede, for the sake of an unprecedented politeness and an unprogrammable politics, a secret for which there is no corresponding revelation: a secret that, like the distinction between morality and legality, is so "radical" that it withdraws from the irreducible roots of representation.[38] The hyperbolic hypothesis Derrida addresses in "Passions"—*il y a là du secret*—thus converges at certain points with the thesis of radical evil. If evil is defined as the breaking of the "social bond"—and there is more than one school of contemporary "moral philosophy" that comes down to this thesis—then the secret of which Derrida speaks, the secret that "impassions us" (*P*, 68), cannot fail to appear evil: "the secret never allows itself to be captured or covered over by the relation to the other, by being-with or by any form of 'social bond'" (*P*, 70). But, as Derrida immediately adds, only a radical secret makes the relation to the other—being-with, or the "social bond"—possible in the first place. For without an absolute and therefore unresponsive secret, no one could enter into a relation with someone as someone *else*, as "the other" whose difference from the self—regardless of its closeness—always remains the matter of a secret encrypted into its very existence as other. The hyperbolic hypothesis of radical secrecy "there" undoes all assurances about a univocal account of evil and is, for this reason, also an oblique response to the still-unnamed thesis of radical evil.

3. The term "radical evil" figures prominently in Derrida's recently published "Faith and Knowledge: The Two Sources of 'Religion' at the Limit of Reason Alone."[39] None of the paragraphs that make up this tightly connected collection of aphorisms remains untouched by this term. So far from being merely an allusion or an oblique reference, "radical evil" suddenly appears in bold typeface, as if to disengage itself from the discussion and present itself as an independent force—or as a bold yet figureless face. By the end of "Faith and Knowledge," however, another term vies with "radical evil" for the privilege of being set off in bold typeface: "crypt." These two terms give direction to the title: "faith" (an encryption) and "knowledge" (of radical evil). If the term "crypt" marks a recession from the sphere of knowledge, the phrase "radical evil" does not, for, as Derrida writes, this is what *we now know*—that it is *not* one: "The 'radical perversion of the human heart' of which Kant speaks, we

now know [*nous savons maintenant*] is not *one*, nor given once and for all, as though it were capable only of inaugurating figures or tropes of itself" (FK, 9 / FS, 18). If radical evil is not one, it could be none or many: we could now know that there is no *radical* evil—although there could very well be evils, since the idea of radicality serves to unify evils under a single, basic, and generative "perversion of the human heart"—or that there is more than one. We know, therefore, that if there is evil—and Derrida leaves no doubt on this question, since he asks in one of the opening paragraphs, "Where is evil? Evil *today*, at present" (FK, 2 / FS, 10)—there is more than one radical evil, which means that the radicality of evil must be rethought from its roots. At the root of our knowledge, then, there is uncertainty, for we do not have a mode of calculation that would allow us to enumerate the multiplicity of radical evils. All we now know is that there is more than one. In the course of Derrida's treatment of faith and knowledge, this "more than one" will also turn into the encrypted formula for faith.

Derrida leaves an uncertainty at the root of our knowledge of radical evil for another reason: nowhere does he undertake a reading of Kant's presentation of radical evil, although the *Religion* is, as one might expect, one of the constant points of reference for Derrida's inquiry into the "two sources of 'religion' at the limit of reason alone." Instead of working out the specific ways in which the term "radical evil" takes charge of Kant's text, Derrida confines himself to a single remark about its paradoxical character: "Kant struggles to account for the rational origin of an evil that remains inconceivable to reason" (FK, 9 / FS, 18). Derrida makes this remark not as a prelude to extensive investigations of Kant's attempt to show that the thesis of radical evil affirms a rational faith that, in its turn, converges with the dogma of certain Christian sects, but rather as a gesture toward the immense difficulties that Kant encounters when attempting to demonstrate the thesis of radical evil. Derrida does so in order to pose a question about the consequences of Kant's attempt to make the Christian confession converge with what he calls "religion" pure and simple: "Are we ready to measure without flinching the implications and consequences of the Kantian thesis? The latter seems strong, simple and dizzying: the Christian religion would be the only truly 'moral' religion" (FK, 10 / FS, 21). And there is thus one more reason for uncertainty at the root of our knowledge: by the closing paragraphs of "Faith and Knowledge," Derrida no longer speaks of the *existence* of radical evil, even if it is the ambiguous existence of a thing that is "not one"; rather, he concerns himself with the "possibility of radical evil" (FK, 47, 65 / FS, 62, 86). For Derrida, it is the knowledge of the possibility of radical evil, and not its facticity, that allows us to know how to "act well": "the *possibility* of that radical evil without which nothing good could be done [*sans lequel on ne saurait bien faire*]" (FK, 47, trans. modified / FS, 62). And as Derrida writes in the penultimate aphorism, it is not the facticity of radical evil but its possibility that institutes the religious: "The possibility of radical evil both destroys and institutes the religious" (FK, 65 / FS, 86).

Nothing in Kant's *Religion Within the Limits of Reason Alone* corresponds with this latter phrase: "destroys the religious." In his capacity as a bourgeois defender of *Aufklärung* against its aristocratic assailants, Kant warns that priestly cults, sectarian dogmas, superstitions, and fetishes bring harm to religion, but none of these can "destroy the religious"—and neither, according to Kant's explicit wording, can radical evil; indeed, the latter serves as its foundation, its *raison d'être.* But the destruction of religion may be inscribed in the section devoted to radical evil, and in this way the trajectories of Kant's and Derrida's divergent lines of thought would converge after all. For radical evil, as Kant makes clear, even if none of his readers want to believe him, undermines trust, even trust in oneself, and it thus undoes faith. Understood in all its radicality and therefore understood to be incomprehensible from the start, the thesis of radical evil means that no one can trust any voice, including an "inner" one, even if the source of that latter voice is interpreted as divine. Kant tried to construct religion in a rational manner on the foundation of radical evil without suspecting—or letting it be known how much he suspected—that this foundation took the ground away from every faith. For radical evil destroys the medium of communication within which speech acts are interpretable according to some code, however secret, private, or "personal." Radical evil even undoes the very ability to speak with oneself in the sanctuary of one's "inner voice": what one *does* when one speaks cannot be known with any certainty, even if every sentence, every "thought," can be verified beyond all doubt. Accepting the thesis of radical evil thus means accepting at the very least the possibility that the context of communication has been so thoroughly compromised that it is corrupted at its root. And rejecting the same thesis—which finds its support in the clarity of a clear conscience—means participating in a decertification of accounts that, for its part, turns unaccountability into the self-concealing secret of all future action.

But Derrida suggests another way for the decertification of all accounts to appear—as a radical faith or, more precisely, as an encrypted faith, a faith for which no code exists to make it knowable as faith, a faith therefore that one can hold only in trust. The formula for this faith is "n + One." For one to trust the other, there must be more than one, even if this other—call it "the voice of reason"—is the one by which the self confirms its selfhood. But "n + One" is also the formula for the possibility of radical evil: "The more than One is this n + One which introduces the order of faith or of trust in the address of the other, but also the mechanical, machinelike division (testimonial affirmation and reactivity, 'yes, yes,' etc., answering machine and the possibility of radical evil: perjury, lies, remote-control murder, ordered at a distance even when it rapes and kills with bare hands)" (FK, 65 / FS, 85–86). Radical evil—known to be more than one—undoes the knowledge of faith, and in the place of knowledge there arises a radical yet deracinating crypt: an empty, secret, and mobile place, a "no place," and hardly a utopia that serves as the radix and matrix of knowledge. Derrida does not quite say this, but in the penultimate aphorism of "Faith and Knowledge" the association of radical evil with "onto-theology" suggests it:

> The possibility of radical evil both destroys and institutes the religious. Onto-theology does the same when it suspends sacrifice and prayer. . . . Onto-theology encrypts faith and destines it to the condition of a sort of Spanish Marrano who would have lost—in truth: dispersed, multiplied—everything up to and including the memory of his unique secret. Emblem of a still life: an opened pomegranate (*granade*), one Passover evening, on a tray. (FK, 66 / FS, 86)

No one can swear to an encrypted faith. It has become a secret even to those who share it, and for this reason its singularity implies a paradoxical universality. Because it is encrypted, this faith is not only a faith for no one but also—and here is the para-messianic promise hidden in the explosive image of the opened pome-granade—a faith for *everyone*: a universal faith that absolutely no one could ever profess in good faith. Derrida does not say that *both* onto-theology *and* radical evil encrypt faith; he only suggests it. Yet even as mere suggestion, if the association of radical evil with onto-theology is supposed to be taken only so far, the thesis that radical evil encrypts faith *gives* radical evil—and not simply the thesis of radical evil—a function after all: namely, to encrypt faith and thereby to grant faith a chance to be paradoxically universal. The Marrano, who is perhaps a silent witness to the radicality of an evil rooted in the idea of rootedness, appears as the self-concealing figure of a possibly universal faith. But by assigning radical evil a function, however cryptic, Derrida's collection of numbered paragraphs likewise gives it a *reason* and thus runs the risk of turning into *Nouveaux essais de théodicée*: "As always, the risk charges itself twice, the same finite risk. Two times rather than one: with a menace and with a chance. In two words, it must take charge of—one could also say: take in trust—the *possibility* of that radical evil without which one would not know how to act well [*sans lequel on ne saurait bien faire*]" (FK, 47, trans. modified / FS, 62).[40]

One of the classical solutions to the problem Leibniz treated under his own neologism of *theodicy* can be described in terms of the speculative thesis that only the possibility of evil makes goodness itself possible; and Kant's thesis of radical evil can be interpreted as a critical response to his disturbing discovery that all attempts to make good on theodicical claims exhibit "the impurity that lies deep in what is hidden, where the human being knows how to distort even inner declarations before his own conscience" (Ak., 8: 270). But Derrida's final formulation in "Faith and Knowledge"—"holding in trust the possibility of radical evil without which one would not know how to act well"—can be understood less as a new attempt at philosophical theodicy (or even as a new demonstration of the failure of all such attempts) than as an oblique attempt to free theodicy from its self-defining intention: justification, showing the justice of things as they *now* stand. Holding in trust the worst makes possible the best; but this holding in trust cannot be ascertained or certified, and for this reason it, too, cannot be properly proved, demonstrated, or even shown, but only held in trust. Such a comportment, perhaps like that of the Marrano to whom Derrida refers, testifies to—without being in a place or position to give proper evidence of—extreme injustice. The condition for acting well is this indemonstrable, hidden, secretive trust: a trust that can under no condition be dissociated from a tireless suspicion in and through which all trust is destroyed. For the trust in which acting well is rooted is a trust in the possibility of radical evil—more exactly, a trust in the possibility that acting well is also an activation of a radical penchant for evil. Holding this possibility in trust is not one secret among others; it is not the secret in which everything or everyone acts, but the entirely open secret—without good conscience, known with certainty by no one—of acting *well.*

Lingua Amissa

THE MESSIANISM OF COMMODITY-LANGUAGE AND DERRIDA'S *Specters of Marx*

Werner Hamacher

Cloth speaks. It is Marx who says that cloth speaks. And in saying that, he speaks the language of cloth, he speaks "from its soul" as surely, in his assertion, as do the bourgeois economists he criticizes. Marx's language is the language of cloth when he says "Cloth speaks." But in the language of Marx, this language of the cloth is at the same time translated into the analytical—and ironic—language of the critique of the very same political economy that defines the categories of cloth-language. Marx then speaks, one must presume, two languages: the language in which the cloth expresses itself, weaves itself and joins with comparable fabrics, and another language that speaks *about* and *beyond* that cloth-language, loosens its weave, analyzes its relation to other loosened weavings, entangling it in another categorial warp. But is it truly a question of two languages, two different linguistic structures, or merely of a doubling of one and the same? Does the critique of political economy speak *another* language, a *new* language, or merely a dialect of the cloth language? Doesn't the doubling of a language perhaps belong to the structure of this language itself—doesn't the critique of political economy remain under the spell of this very economy? If Marx is indeed to speak a second, other language, then this new Marxian or Marxist language must fulfill at least one condition that cannot be filled by the language of cloth: it must disclose at least one category which as of yet has no place in that political economy, a category which might betray itself in that language, might even bear witness to itself, yet which cannot itself belong to the repertoire, to the matrix or patrix of that language. This other, this *allocategory*, could—and even must—have an altogether peculiar form incommensurable with the categories of political economy, perhaps not even a form. It would be not the language "of" the cloth, but instead, for example, a language in which a cloth and "its" language first come into existence. Not, perhaps, a talking thing, perhaps a thing that does not—or does not simply—speak, something that, still unspeaking, *nonetheless* promises itself a language in advance of itself.

I am speaking—if I simply "speak"—of cloth for two or three reasons: because, in the chapter that opens *Capital*, in the first volume, "The Production Process of Capital," under the title "Commodities," in the section "The Form of Value or Exchange Value," Marx speaks of it, claiming that the cloth itself speaks; because Jacques Derrida, in *Specters of Marx*, speaks of something like a cloth, an *écran*, as a projection surface for phantoms;[1] and because both references to the cloth sustain an uneasy relationship to one of the most powerful metaphors of the philosophical tradition: the metaphor of covering, veiling, mystification and fetish. And thus also of the fetish-table (*Fetisch-Tisch*), which in the chapter "The Fetishism of Commodities and the Secret Thereof" not only sets itself on its legs and on its head but also dances, and from whose "whims" Derrida draws far-reaching consequences. These consequences concern the structure of the messianic as a dimension—an immeasurable dimension, to be sure—of the commodity and its language, be it table or cloth, screen or fantasy; they concern the commodity's messianic promise and consequently both the language of the commodity and the messianic of capital announcing itself in its commodities. The messianic that Derrida speaks of, the "messianic without messianism," is for him—though he does with respect to Marx grant the religious a special status among ideological phenomena—not just a religious phenomenon, but one that arises from the structure of phenomenality itself—from its spectrality—and that therefore must betray itself in the dominating archiphenomenon of the economic world: the commodity. Developed commodity-analysis—thus we could delineate one of the guiding ideas of Derrida's reading of Marx—must be an analysis of the commodity's spectrality—

and this means both of the phenomenality of the commodity and of the excess beyond this phenomenality, its paraphenomenal spirituality and spectrality. This means as well—and indeed beyond traditional phenomenologies and Marxisms—that this expanded commodity- and capital-analysis must contain an analysis of its messianic power or (and here I am thinking of Benjamin's famous formulation) of its messianic *weakness*, and in no way as an appendix, not as an "ideological" or "propagandistic" ornament, not as a proclamation or as good tidings to be presented beyond this analysis of the commodity-world, but as an integral and indeed "grounding" element of this analysis itself. The commodity cloth not only speaks but promises (itself) something else, and it *is* its promise of something else: as a phenomenon it is, like every phenomenon and every possible and real world, spectrally and henceforth messianically constituted.

Cloth, then, speaks. This is what Marx writes. "We see, then," the section entitled "The Relative Form of Value" reads,

> everything our analysis of the value of commodities previously told us is repeated to us by the cloth itself, as soon as it enters into association with another commodity, the coat. Only it betrays its thoughts in a language with which alone it is familiar, the commodity-language. In order to tell us that labor creates its own value in its abstract quality of being human labour, it says that the coat, in so far as it is worth as much as the cloth, and therefore is value, consists of the same labour as it does itself.[2]

The commodity-language translated—and cited—by the language of Marx's analysis, this commodity-language "betrays" something and indeed "betrays" what one would not commonly expect of commodities, would not expect, for example, of cloth: "thoughts." The cloth not only speaks, it also thinks. But it speaks and thinks exclusively in the exchange with other commodities, with its own kind, with regard to them and to the possibility of finding in them its echo or its reflex. The cloth is *pragma* or even *zoon logon echon* only insofar as it is also a *zoon politikon*. But its politics, commodity politics, is subordinate to the strict dictate of equality among abstract concepts. Commodity-exchange-language is accordingly restricted to a grammatical-syntactic minimum in which only propositions of equality can be formed. Such propositions regularly purport that a particular quantum of one thing is equal to a particular quantum of another thing, regardless of whether this thing currently exists or not. Hence the statements of commodity-language are not propositions of existence but arithmetical propositions of relation that can claim validity even if the existence of one of their members is not assured. They can thus at any time contain a suggestion that is in fact never made good by a reality or that can never be made good. Yet the claim of universal validity of this arithmetical communication among equals means that commodity-language is structured as a functional suggestion of equality, and that its propositions of equivalence—and it knows no propositions that cannot be reduced to propositions of equivalence—only speak, in principle, by feigning the equivalence of their elements. In speaking with one another, commodities *promise* one another their exchangeability: the sole medium in which they can exchange with and change into one another. In speaking, commodities thus promise one another commodity-language as the language of their universal communication. Their propositions, however arithmetical and reduced they might sound, are thus not constative without being at the same time simulations, projections, announcements, or claims. They seem to have—to take up a popular and suggestive word—a performative character.

If the grammar of propositions in commodity-language is restricted by the horizon of equivalence, if the pragmatics of these propositions is essentially that of a fiction, that is, of the performance of a logical claim or a historical announcement, then their semantics is also circumscribed by an economically narrow horizon: they are all propositions about value. In Marx's example, the cloth comes to an understanding with the coat not about its love life or the weather, but solely about the relation the cloth maintains to it and, by way of it, to itself as exchange-value. In its semantics, as in its grammar and its pragmatics, commodity-language is an abstract and speculative language: it disregards all "natural" determinations and relies exclusively upon those formal determinants pertinent to its abstract relation of symmetry. And for this reason it is not only a language of exchange but also a language of turning, of reversal, of specular inversion. In it, every single commodity is abstracted from its individuality and presents itself as a representative, an expression or equation, as the quid pro quo or metaphor of a general substance, of labor. "In order to tell us," Marx says, that labour creates its own value in its abstract quality of being human labour, it [the cloth] says that the coat, in so far as it is worth as much as the cloth, and therefore is value, consists of the same labour as it does itself. In order to inform us that its sublime objectivity as value differs from its stiff and starchy existence as a body, it says that value has the appearance of a coat, and therefore in so far as the cloth is itself an object of value, it and the coat are as like as two peas. (*C*, 143–44)

In order to state the difference—the very difference of its value from its body—the commodity states its equality with something else. It makes itself, it produces itself as value and transforms itself into a value-thing only by disregarding itself as a thing, positing itself as value through its abstract and speculative equation with another. When a thing—the cloth, for example—socializes with another thing in the form of equality, equivalence, symmetry, and reversibility, it—this cloth—gives itself what it formerly lacked; it gives itself a value and thus appears for the first time in the world of commodity-society, appears for the first time in the world and *appears* for the first time. Its turn into the other of itself is thus the very bringing forth of the cloth, rendering it an object of exchange and, by means of that exchange, also one of use. In turning itself, as the logic of its language commands, in standing itself, as Marx says, "on its head," it sets itself first of all on itself, on its "own" feet: it becomes an object only by disappearing as an object and submitting itself to the abstract, the speculative, the "supersensual," "the sublime objectivity as value." Use-value is hereafter "the material through which its own value is expressed" (*C*, 144); it is indeed a material only by the grace of exchange-value, and this means, as commodity-language decrees, it *is* only *as* value. And this value, as it presents itself in the "simple value-form," in the original figure of commodity-language, for its part never exists otherwise than as such, as its "embodiment" in the material of use-value. The coat, Marx writes, is the "'carrier of value,' although this property never shows through, even when the coat is at its most threadbare. . . . Despite its [the coat's] buttoned-up appearance, the cloth recognizes in it a splendid kindred commodity-soul" (*C*, 143). What in one commodity can be recognized by another in a non-sensuous way only, since it never shows through as a "natural" aspect, such a "commodity-soul" is nevertheless incarnated: even the cloth, which "as value" is the same as the coat and thus "has the appearance of a coat" (*C*, 144) such that they are "as like as two peas" (ibid.).

The actuality of general and abstract value—an actuality conferred upon it by what Marx calls the language and soul of the commodity—is from its very inception reversed, inverted into what Marx calls its natural form: the exchange language of commodities is a language of the inversion (*Vertauschung*) of language and the reality of commodities—an inversion that seems all the more unavoidable in that no other language and no other reality than that of commodities appears to exist.

The cloth, the commodity, speaks in man as well. According to the logic of commodity-language, "As he neither enters into the world in possession of a mirror, nor as a Fichtean philosopher who can say 'I am I,'" Peter must "see and recognize himself" as a human being in Paul and win his "form of appearance" as Peter only by identifying himself as the incarnation of his generalizing reflection.[3] Only in the speculative medium of commodity-language, only in commodity-language as a mirror-language, do Peter and Paul come to themselves, come to be selves as specimens of the "genus homo" and come to this genus at all. Commodity-language is thus the pattern of humanization that raises everyone who avails himself of it to the apostles Peter and Paul of general humanity and equality. Hence "man," though Marx explicitly disputes it, does come into the world with a mirror, for before there is a specular other and the I appears as its incarnation or reincarnation, he does not exist as "man." The mirror-I creates the I just as the value-mirror creates the commodity. The speculative dialectic of self-constitution thus follows the speculative pattern of commodity and capital production. And similarly, self-constitution is possible only as the turn (*Verkehrung*) of the prehuman shape of the "I" into the representative of its nonhuman, absolutely formal abstraction. I, man, thing, and commodity appear only by appearing as elements of value-form and as formed by value-form. Their language is solely a form-positing, value-positing, equalizing one—a commodity-language in which they are constituted and conserved as commodities.

Their language forms them—the "humans" as well as the "things"—into commodities. Commodity-language, then, does not mean that there are commodities that, in addition, are endowed with a particular language; it means that they are commodities only by virtue of this language and that this language alone qualifies them as commodities, identifies and forms them. Commodity-language appoints them commodities, syntagmatizing them as commodities and performing them as commodities. Both in *Capital* and in his earlier writings, Marx constantly stresses that the universal commodification prevalent with the development of capitalism result in a complex history of technological, economic, and political developments and indicates an irreversible progress in the freeing up of the forces of production as well as in the liberation from slavery, servitude, inequality, and poverty. Commodity language is not only a historical—that is, finite—language but also, as his footnote on the speculative genesis of the "genus homo" shows, a language of equalization, socialization, and autonomization and hence of the promise of further liberations from the burdens of isolation on the one hand and of hierarchical organization on the other—the promise even of the liberation from concepts of freedom determined by commodity-language. This involves above all the messianic promise of liberation made by Judeo-Christianity. Religion does this, Marx insists in all of his writings, within the boundaries of the speculative proposition of commodity-language. The *Wertsein*, the "being worth," of the cloth, he writes (in the same section about relative form of value), "is manifested in its equality with the coat, just as the sheep-like nature of the Christian is shown in his resemblance to the Lamb of God" (*C*, 143). Christianity celebrates the "cult of abstract man" (*C*, 172), just as commodity-language celebrates the cult of abstract human labor. The sheep's nature and the abstraction of God are reconciled in the lamb as the incarnation of formal equivalence; they appear as equal because equality itself appears in them. Commodity-language is thus not only a language of the bourgeois economy; it is not merely the language of the constitution of the bourgeois abstract subject and hence the language of the ontology of subjectivity; it is also, at the same time, the language of theology and of ontotheology, especially, Marx adds, "in its bourgeois development, in Protestantism, Deism, etc." (*C*, 172). The messianism of Christianity is, in a word, the messianism of commodity-language; its promise of redemption is the promise of commodities; they embody a general, constant, and transhistorical value. It is in this sense that the following comment from Marx is to be understood:

> Let us remark, incidentally, that the language of commodities also has, apart from Hebrew, plenty of other more or less correct dialects. The German "Wertstein," "to be worth," "to be valuable," for instance, brings out less strikingly than the Romance verbs "valere," "valer," "valoir," that the equating of com-

modity B with commodity A is the expression of value proper to commodity A. Paris vaut bien une messe! (*C*, 144)

Marx sees languages, including Hebrew, the holy language and language of the tradesman, as dialects of the universal commodity-language. The Romance verb *valere* articulates its political and theo-economic message most precisely in Henri IV's utterance uniting the conversion to Catholicism with the convertibility of value that is to reside in French capital and its political functions. *Paris vaut bien une messe.* This is the formula of theo-economic transubstantiation, the formula of the messianism of the commodity-language.

The cloth, then, the commodity, speaks. It speaks a historical language that claims to be universal and transhistorical. It speaks an abstract language limited to a single statement, value, and a single grammatical structure, equation, yet claims nonetheless to be valid for an unrestricted variety of singularities. It is a language of exchange (*Verkehr*), but only as a process of turning (*Verkehrung*). Marx brings the three most massive turns into the following sentences: "Use-value becomes the form of appearance of its opposite, value" (*C*, 148). "Concrete labor becomes the form of appearance of its opposite, abstract human labor." And, thirdly: "Private labor takes the form of its opposite, namely its directly social form" (*C*, 150–51). These exchanges and turns can nonetheless be effected only in the medium of commodity-language because its individual elements all refer to a common substratum, to a commodity that belongs to the series of all other commodities but that is simultaneously—in order to guarantee the consistency of this series—the only one that must remain excluded from it, its general equivalent: the money-commodity. Money is the transcendental of commodity-language, the form that vouchsafes all other forms their commensurability, appearing as a copula in all the statements and postulates of commodity-language. This copula, which only apparently has a completely formal character, does indeed refer to a historical referent and is itself both historic and historicizing: it refers, namely, to the "common substance" (*C*, 151) at work in all elements of commodity-language, refers to what is common and—by virtue of its formalization—equal to all: it refers to human labor. Commodity-language is thus—and this would be its more complete if still insufficient characterization—a transcendental schematizing language of the social substance "labor" in a particular historical epoch; it is the transcendental ergologic and ergo-onto-theo-logic of capitalism.[4]

This characterization of commodity-language is not yet complete; among the missing determinants, I name at this point only the most important and apparently most perverse: that it is a language at all. When confronted by the curious double term "commodity-language," every rhetorician or semiotician worth his salt would be immediately tempted to speak of a metaphor or a personfication or, more precisely, of a prosopopoeia. That would not be wrong, but still less would it be right. It would not be wrong because commodities "normally" and "naturally" do not speak. Yet commodities are not natural; rather, as Marx correctly says, they are things with a "supernatural quality," their value, "something purely social" (*C*, 149). Only—and this follows from the analysis of the simple value-form—this "supernatural quality," this being a value-thing (*Wertding*), is of such a kind that it does not remain supernatural but becomes an objective quality, quickly dons a "natural skin" (*C*, 148), becomes "sensuously supra-sensuous" (*C*, 165), that is, supra-sensuous in a sensuous way, and begins to speak as a relatively independent thing. Marx thus does not use a metaphor or a prosopopoeia, but the commodity of which he speaks is itself structured as a prosopopoeia. The cloth does not speak figuratively, but, because it is a commodity and hence a figure, it actually speaks. A language devolves to it—and indeed the only language dominant in the commodity-world—because language is both abstract and material, that is, the incarnated form of man's expression and the form of organization of his labor. That commodities—and moreover everything affected by them—speak a language, and perhaps *the* language, is what Marx calls their fetish character. Commodity fetish—that means commodity-language. What is the secret thereof?

What is it that the cloth veils when it veils itself and speaks? What can't the cloth say? What alone can it *not* say? What, when the cloth speaks, does it keep secret? "Whence," Marx asks in the chapter "The Fetishism of Commodities and the Secret Thereof," "whence, then, arises the enigmatic character of the product of labor, as soon as it assumes the form of a commodity?" And his answer is: "Clearly, it arises from this form itself" (*C*, 164). It is this value-form, he explains—that is, commodity-language as *objective* form—which imprints human labor with the objective character of products, imprints the time of that labor with the character of value, and imprints the relations among producers with the character of relations among products. Production becomes a product, time an object, man a thing. The "enigmatic character," the "phantasmagoric form," the "mystical character" of the commodity as a "twisted thing, abounding in metaphysical subtleties and theological whims," this "deranged form," its fetish character, is not something that can be detached from the product in order to unveil its real, authentic, true character and, as an object, to thereby clear up the self-misunderstanding of worker, labor, and time. Derangement, twistedness, and enigma belong for Marx to the irreducible, constitutive "categories" of bourgeois—that is, to date the most advanced—economy: "They are thought-forms which are socially valid, and therefore objective, for the relations of production belonging to this historically determined mode of social production, i.e. commodity production" (*C*, 169). And he continues: "The belated scientific discovery" (of this fetish character of commodity-form as an objective thought-form) "by no means banishes the semblance of objectivity possessed by the social character of labor" (*C*, 167). If Marx thus notes that "people are not aware of this, nevertheless they do it" (*C*, 166–67), he adds just as quickly that they also must do it *when* they are aware of it. Forms of knowledge, insofar as they are forms and insofar as they are those of knowledge, can for their part be none other than those of commodity-language and thus must be *a priori* "deranged," "phantasmagoric," "mystical," and "fetishistic." Commodity-language itself "objectively veils" social relations "instead of revealing them plainly" (*C*, 169). "Objectively veil" means: objects themselves are the veil that commodity-language spreads over their substance, the social conditions of production; the objectivity of objects is the fetish; the objectivity of materials, of representations and forms, is the covering that presents itself in commodity-language as irreducible. Cloth veils the cloth. The object "cloth" must be the veil over the actual *cloth* that is woven by historical social life. But precisely this weaving of social life results—in deed as in knowledge, in commodity-exchange as in the forms of its recognition in an object—in the object "cloth," and thus is a process of a self-veiling, a self-mystification, self-fetishization. The object named by commodity-language is the fetish by which the conditions of production are not so much veiled as transformed. When the cloth speaks, the cloth, alas, speaks no more. Cloth now speaks exclusively in this way: the cloth "itself" no longer speaks, for it already speaks in the categories, the words, and the grammar, of commodity-language. Only the deranged cloth "abounding in metaphysical subtleties and theological niceties" can speak. Commodity-language itself speaks only as the commodity "language," exchanging itself for equivalent commodities or languages and serving the profiteering of capital. And that is its capital secret: that it can conceal none. It does not veil something behind or underneath it; it does not conceal some *thing* at all; as mere categorial form it veils this very form itself, and with it its formation: the generative structure preceding its transcendental fetishistic frame. What it says, it is, here and now, in objective, material form.

Although he calls it a "derangement," Marx makes no secret of the fact that commodity-language dictates what is to be considered as fact. It does not speak a language other than historical reality; it *is* this reality in the forms of language—in "objective thought-forms," in categories." He writes, once again in the chapter on the fetish character of the commodity:

> If I say the coat, the boots, etc., relate to the cloth as the general embodiment of abstract human labor, the derangement of this expression is obvious. But if the producers of the coat, the boots, etc., relate these commodities to the cloth—or to gold or silver, it makes no difference—as a general equivalent, the relation of their private labor to social collective labor appears to them precisely in this deranged form. (*C*, 169)

The derangement of commodity-language-form lies, then, in the transcendental function appended to the general equivalent—to the cloth, to gold, or to social collective labor—for as a transcendental, it has the structure of a universal measure that simultaneously and *despite* its universality is to be incarnated in a particular form, either material or abstract. The cloth as a *general* equivalent veils or inverts the cloth, a historically determined *single* product. As transcendental form, the cloth must efface the singularity of everything it encompasses and paralyze that history into objects: commodity-language is therefore mystifying and fetishistic, a ghost because it can express not the producedness of products but only their stable form, not the historicity of products but only their perpetual objectivity, not the singularity of labors but only their abstract function. Commodity-language is the language of static categories denying past and future. The task falls to historical analysis to prove them historical and historicizing categories and to disclose for them another future. Marx writes:

> The categories of bourgeois economics consist precisely of forms of this kind [the deranged forms of the general equivalent, of gold, of cloth]. They are thought-forms which are socially valid, and therefore objective [thought-forms which have sedimented in objects], for the relations of production belonging to this historically determined mode of social production, i.e. commodity production. The whole mystery of commodities, all the magic and necromancy that surrounds the products of labor on the basis of commodity production, vanishes therefore as soon as we escape to other forms of production. (*C*, 169)

The escape into other forms of production is an escape from a prison of immobile "objective thought-forms" of the categories of commodity and capital, the escape to a freedom that only historicizing, singularizing, attranscendentalizing language can achieve. (And achieve, perhaps, only at the cost of being persecuted on this flight by the ghost of commodity-language.)

The cloth—and through it capital—thus not only speaks in the transcendental forms of ergontology, not only speaks in the pure forms of measure and equivalence or of controlled surplus and regulated asymmetry, but also exhibits these forms in an objective form, as objective reality, as material cloth. It is a language not only of abstract formalism but also of the deranged material incarnation of this formalism, that is, a deranged transcendental-historical concretism, a *formaterialism.* Abstract value, labor, and time have woven themselves into the warp of cloth and now speak—how else might they speak?—only through it and as it.

—The cloth, the web, speaks; that is: the specter speaks. It speaks—it haunts. Commodity-language, the fetish, is a specter: the material incorporation of universal abstractions, neither flesh nor blood, but materially appearing form, a morphantom.

The "critique of political economy" is understood as the critique of this spectral incarnationism. It bids the table—which, "in relation to all other commodities, stands on its head" and has thereby become a fetish (*C*, 163)[5]—to stand again on its four legs, just as it tries to invert the

Hegelian dialectic in order to discover "the rational kernel in the mystical shell." For, as Marx says in the afterword to the second edition of *Capital*, "With him it is standing on its head" (*C*, 103). Marx here presupposes that those legs exist without a head, that there is a rational kernel without a covering, and that there could be a social form of production unaffected by value-form. Marx does believe in a language other than the transcendental one of formaterialism. He believes in a true language (*eine wahre Sprache*), which remains undisguised by commodity-language (*Warensprache*), but at the same time he offers numerous arguments for the view that this other language, too, is caught in the net of commodity and value categories. He insists that historical-individual labor, with its specific time, is the true, actual substance and the secret of social appearance; but at the same time he leaves no doubt that this substance has until now never appeared other than in the mystifying and theologizing veil of the value-form. He propagates an ontology of production but objects that it has heretofore been possible only as an ontology of products and hence only as a pseudology or spectrology: "The belated scientific discovery that the products of labor, in so far as they are values, are merely the material expressions of the human labor expended in them, marks an epoch in the history of mankind's development, but by no means banishes the semblance of objectivity possessed by the social character of labor" (*C*, 167).

In chapter 48 of the third volume of *Capital*, "The Trinitarian Formula," an often-cited passage opens the prospect of a form of production that is no longer capitalistic. The end of labor, more precisely, of forced and commodity-producing labor, is pledged. "In fact the realm of freedom," Marx writes,

> actually begins only where labor which is determined by necessity and mundane considerations ceases; thus, in the very nature of things, it lies beyond the sphere of actual material production. . . . Beyond it [the realm of necessity] begins that development of human energy which is an end in itself, the true realm of freedom, which, however, can blossom forth only with the realm of necessity as its basis. The shortening of the work day is its basic prerequisite.[6]

What Marx promises here—and he *promises* it even if he states it in the form of a scientifically grounded announcement—and what he hears as the promise of capitalism's production and circulation processes is not so much the liberation *from* labor as the liberation *to* it. That is, to labor itself, to labor as "an end in itself," to labor as the true self of man realized solely in itself and no longer in objective forms, thus no longer incarnating itself, no longer hiding a secret—not even the secret that it has no secret—and no longer cultivating theological whims. Only performance, autoperformance (the promise says) speaks in the substantial labor-language of a future society and defines the "realm of freedom" as a realm of completed ergocracy. But doesn't this promise necessarily remain the promise of capital, of self-capitalizing and abstract labor, the promise that labor itself is capital, a self-producing and self-reproducing substance? The "realm of freedom," Marx states expressly, can "blossom forth only with the realm of necessity as its basis." The future would then be only a prolonged present of capital; there would be, as in every substantialism, no future at all, but only, once again, a present, only an eternal return of the specter that already claims to be the so-called present now. Communism, then, would be only the ideology of capitalism declaring that its further development would culminate in the true unveiling of its theo-economic secrets—of the sacrament of labor. I leave it at this question, for labor or the development of human power as its own end could in its innermost structure, even if Marx takes care not to speak of it in programmatic concepts, also indicate something else: a severing of labor from production, from the generation of the means of subsistence, finally from itself as a substance that shows itself in objects and embodies itself in man; this structure could, in short, indicate an internal disjunction of labor and its autoteleology and thereby its liberation not only from need but from itself as unquestioned necessity. In this sense *The German Ideology* explains that "in all revolutions up till now the mode of activity always remained unscathed and it was only a question of . . . a new distribution of labor to other persons, whereas the communist revolution is directed against the preceding *mode* of activity, does away with *labor*."[7] The "automatic system" of "big industry," he writes in the same connection, "makes for the worker not only the relation to the capitalist, but labor itself, unbearable."[8] With respect to ideology and the practical terror of labor, which reigns in all totalitarian regimes (including those that have called on the legacy of Marx) and also under the "liberal" capital-socialism of western democracies, it is not the last question that one should direct to Marx. It is the first. The liberation from labor is the object of the Marxist promise, the aim of the world-historical development of the capitalistic form of production, the vanishing point of the communist revolution.

There will be no more labor: this is the promise of commodity-language. And this promise no longer simply belongs to the "categories" or "objective thought-forms" of a transcendental commodity-language and the ergontology articulated therein; it no longer simply belongs to its syntax of equivalents and quid pro quos; it does not belong to the dehistoricizing rhetoric of statements of what is and what is not incarnated in commodity relations; this promise says that a language other than commodity-language is possible, and insofar as it is possible it is necessary; it says that categories other than those of commodity-language, and something other than a categorial language, will be invented. This promise is itself already no longer a category; it indicates something structurally different; it is, one could say, an allocategory that speaks beyond—but also in—all "objective thought-forms" of commodity-language, opening up its syntactic arrangement and its meaning to something else beyond any conceivable form.

It is, once again, a question of the language of the commodity-world and what it promises. A question of commodity-language and its promise. It is this promise, deciphered by Marx in the framing of the commodity-world, that Jacques Derrida makes one of the centers of his book on Marx. I have developed the question of commodity-language, which plays no role there, in some detail in order to gain easier access to the questions that this book has prompted for me. They concern the formalism of the messianic promise, the structure of the performative, the status of labor, and the conjunction that Derrida's book establishes between these and the appearance of the spectral. My remarks—even if it is not "written on their face"—have the character of questions in progress; they are not entirely tied to the hope of passing into effective questions or determinations; they do not mean to be immediately productive, nor aim at achieving predetermined theoretical or practical aims. All of these terms are rather implicitly or explicitly simply up for discussion and, if at times in another way, are already under discussion in the texts by Derrida and Marx I refer to here.

Cloth speaks. Derrida translates: the specter—or perhaps the spirit—speaks. And he immediately begins to differentiate, to specify, to classify: there is not just one specter but several, always more than one, and this "more than one" or "no more one" already makes out the constitutive structure, the destitutive structure, of the spectral. The specters are irreducibly plural—for Marx in the texts he cites by way of exorcism or conjuration, for Marxists and for anti-Marxists, the persecutors and doomsdayers of Marxism, and also for those who never believed that Marxist-inspired states existed—Derrida enumerates them, analyzes them, and writes their spectrology. And this spectrology, in turn, is haunted by the specters of Marx, Freud, Husserl, Valéry, Benjamin, Heidegger, Blanchot, and Nicolas Abraham. One might enumerate a few more, but their number is in principle not to be fixed; they are transnumeral. Specters, parting from the departed and on the brink of becoming independent, consist of splits, live in fissures and joints, in intermundia, as Marx, a familiar of the systems of Democritus and Epicurus, says of Epicurus's gods (*C*, 172): they are monsters of difference. The spectral exists, despite this irreducible disparity, if only in the disquieting or self-complacent question of whether it *actually* exists. In the spectral, something past, itself provoked by something to come, something outstanding and as of yet still in arrears, demands its rights here and now. The spectral is, one might therefore say, what is most present among the things that can be experienced because it appears precisely in the open joint between future and past—or more exactly, where its apparently tight connection is out of joint. What appears as spectral is always the future and the future of the past as well, that which is not yet and will never be present. If one can speak of a temporalization of time, as Heidegger and after him Derrida do, then time is temporalized by the future. "The truly temporal in time is the future," claimed Schelling in his "Aphorisms on Natural Philosophy," adding, by way of explanation: "It is the clear product of sheer imagination."[9] But productive imagination, from which time and its various dimensions arise, is neither for Heidegger nor for Derrida the decisive originating instance, the *exstance* of temporalization. It is not the productive *Einbildung* and unifying imagination (*In-Eins-Bildungskraft*); it is much more the *de*imagination or image-*weakness*, the abstinence from images and their retreat, which releases time from itself and temporalizes. Marx, who was never far from placing a ban on images of the future and preferred—but surely any preference can be nothing but paradoxical—reading the future only in the strains and asynchronicities of the "present," speaks of the future only in the mode of proclamations, conjurations, and announcements. Why, then, is the representation of a specter tied to the future?

For Derrida, the specter answers the question of the future. "What of the future?" he asks, and his answer is: "The future can only be for the ghosts."[10] The phantom is also the answer to the question of the "messianic extremity," which Derrida—in one of the most important terminological decisions of his book—gives the name "eschaton." "Is there not a messianic extremity, an *eskhaton*, whose ultimate event (immediate rupture, unheard-of interruption, untimeliness of the infinite surprise, heterogeneity without accomplishment) can exceed, *at each moment*, the final term of a *phusis*, such as work, the production, and the *telos* of any history?" (SE, 37 / SF, 68). This messianic extremity, which goes beyond every telos and every labor; this extremity without which no future can be thought because thinking itself is indebted only to it; this extremity unthinkable in advance, which can be an object neither of knowledge nor of perception, and only precisely because it evades the controls of both perception and knowledge, keeps the possibility of the future open—this *openness* of the future could only attest to itself in the sheerest abstraction beyond form or, if related to forms, only in their irreparable disintegration. Derrida's repeated challenge to distinguish between eschatology and teleology (SE, 37 / SF, 68) seems to insist on precisely this difference between a form determined by telos as its border and the extremity that, in the border or at it, traverses the border and, being external and *exformal*, can no longer fall under the category of form, of categorial thought-form or perception-form. But if the future is an allocategory of the transformative and exformative, if it "a priori" diverges from the categorial framework of forms of thought, perception, and intuition, then it must be without appearance, aphenomenal, and can only attest to itself in the disappearance of all phenomenal figures, in the continued dissociation of its phantasmagorias. The future "is," if it is at all, what shows itself insofar as it effaces the signs it permits. It presents itself only in the retraction of its signs. It is aphanisis antecedent and subsequent to every possible phenomenon. How, then, can it belong to phantoms? What can this sentence mean: "At bottom, the specter is the future, it is always to come, it presents itself only as that which could come or come back" (*Au fond, le spectre, c'est l'avenir, il est toujours à venir, il ne se présente que comme ce qui pourrait venir ou re-venir*) (SE, 39 / SF, 71).

The questions traced out on the background of Derrida's Marx book—at least *some* of its questions—can presumably be paraphrased as follows. How can the future bear witness to itself? And how, *as* the future, can it attest to its futurity? How is it possible that the sheer possibility (under whose aspect alone actuality exists at all) appears not as a void of the actual but rather as the way of its arrival—as a path of actualization remaining open to other arrivals? The figure that comes closest to answering these questions, the figure of figuration, is the specter in all its disparity—as phantom, spirit, ghost, appearance, and spectrum. It is that "figure" which massively and under the most disparate names haunts Marx's texts—whether as phantasmagoria or enigma, as fetish or ideology, as theological whim or objective veil—and which is the phenomenon, or phenomenon of phenomenality, for which the walls and cloths between fields as various as literature and philosophy, psychoanalysis, economics, theology, and politics are permeable. The most disparate types of discourse are haunted by the specter because the specter is what differs from all of them—and from itself. In it transpires something between material and spirit, apparition and disparition, foreclosing both from the outset. But as complex as this figure of figuration and defiguration, this archifigure of difference, might be, it still remains a figure. Derrida's concern is not to conjure it but to analyze the visitations and persecutions, to analyze the rites and formulas of exorcism in which it keeps recurring: a large part of his book on Marx is dedicated to the reduction of the dominant spectral figures to what is irreducibly spectral in them. I will name only three or four of those figures of the figure.

There is first of all the specter of the father, whose "*patrimonial* logic" (SE, 107 / SF, 173) unfolds, as between Hamlet and the ghost of his father, between Marx and his father-in-law, Ludwig von Westphalen, and, more massively, in the metaphorical scenarios of *The Eighteenth Brumaire of Louis Bonaparte.* Derrida introduces the relevant remarks with the ambiguous formulation, used here for the first time, of the *per-*

sécution de Marx: the ghost is what *persecutes Marx*—what he was persecuted by and what he himself persecuted. Derrida, who in *Glas* speaks of a *mère sécutrice*,[11] would not have set the word into this scene of confrontation with the father without deliberation. The *persécution de Marx*, wherever it threatens, is experienced as a *pèresécution*. Testifying to this are the myriad sarcastic remarks aimed at the Pope, the "father of the people," God the Father, all religious and political authorities and institutions that Derrida, in a cadenced rhythm, does not fail to call by name. Even today the history of Marxism is inseparable from the history of this *pèresécution*: it is a history of the persecution of Marxism by presumptive paternal authorities and a history of the persecution that Marxism itself as such an authority must meet with. It is a history of the rivalry for paternity and thus of a doubling of the father, of being a double, of the duplicity of origin and future, of the double gait, of the *double pas*, of the *pas-pas*. In his early texts—most elaborately in "Pas" in 1976—Derrida developed this peculiar structure of the unavoidable and simultaneously deconstitutive doubling of originary instances, the structure of deorigination and disorientation, a bi- and de-structure, in all its complexities. For our purposes here it should be recalled that this duplication first of all splits and de-posits—that it exposes this authority to a movement that, prior to authority, is more powerful than every authority and therefore can no longer be measured against the standard of authority. This duplication of the father and of *pèresécution* also entails a bifurcation of succession, of the persecution, sequence and logic of sequentiality; it thus tears apart the logic of both consequence and genealogy, of both temporal linearity and familial homogeneity. And this duplication also opens the logic of performance—if this is understood as the logic of an originary, inaugurative speech act and therefore as paternalistic, as the logic of *pèreformance*—onto that field in which one father turns against another, a *pas* turns against a *pas*—against its "self": in which it becomes a logic of pas-pas-formance, and consequently no longer of an originary positing, but of a disoriginary one, an ex-positing. Derrida does not make explicit this turn from the logic of performance to the allologic of its internal antagonism and hence to the aporia of performance, but it can be read in his text.

There is, secondly, and not at all far removed from the father in

Derrida's text, the mother in the form of the "mother tongue." She is an indispensable prerequisite for the assumption of the paternal inheritance, but it is equally indispensable that she be forgotten. Derrida writes: "This revolutionary inheritance supposes, to be sure, the one that ends up forgetting the specter, that of the primitive or the mother tongue. In order to forget not what one inherits but to forget the pre-inheritance on the basis of which one inherits" (SE, 110 / SF, 180–81). This "forgetting of the maternal" (*l'oubli du maternel*) is necessary "to bring the spirit in itself to life," but it makes life itself into a "life of forgetting" of the maternal specter (SE, 109 / SF, 180). The life of the Marxist spirit—or of its specter—consequently remains as infinitely bound to the specter of the mother as to this forgetting. The figure of the mother survives solely in its limitless disappearance.

Derrida dedicates his most detailed analysis to the third specter in this familial phantom story, to that of the brother: it is the specter of Stirner and his gallery of ghosts. According to Derrida, Stirner for Marx is the "bad brother" because he is the "bad son of Hegel" (SE, 122 / SF, 198). After Derrida has spoken of his own feelings ("*mon* sentiment," SE, 139 / SF, 221–22), he continues, in the only passage that strikes an explicitly autobiographical tone: "My feeling, then, is that Marx scares himself, he himself pursues relentlessly someone who almost resembles him to the point that we could mistake one for the other: a brother, a double, thus a diabolical image. A kind of ghost of himself [*Une sorte de fantôme de lui-même*]," SE, 139 / SF, 222).[12] Marx has no end of this brother, the double and specter of himself, because he recognizes in him his own jealous identification with Hegel, the father, and sees that he is himself not this father, that he is thus not himself, that he is his own, that is, not his *own* reflection. For him as for Stirner, the proposition of the indubitable ascertainment of self and existence must assume the dubious form "Ego = ghost" (SE, 133 / SF, 212)[13] or "I = my bad brother." The I has *a priori* given itself over to another, to its specter. Its haunting, Derrida says, is "an operation without action, without a real subject or real object"—whereby (which he does not say) the indispensable premise of every speech-act theory to date disappears: that performatives are *acts* of real *subjects.* Every political action consequently threatens to become an automatic farce in a spectropolitical theater. Since Marx least of all can tolerate that, he must separate himself from his Stirnerian specter, from his self and his property, in an endless chain of distancing maneuvers—but precisely for this reason he must incessantly conjure it up, let it return and keep it close at hand. He must promise both himself and the subject of political action a future different from Stirner's specter-future—yet must let this very promise be repeatedly haunted by the threat of its merely phantasmatic character. The *pèresécution de Marx* does not cease to be his *frèresécution* and his *mèresécution*, for the very reason that it was, from the very beginning, a *pèresécution*. "For the singular ghost, the ghost that generated this incalculable multiplicity, the arch-specter, is a father or else it is capital" (SE, 139 / SF, 221).

It is not difficult to find in Derrida's remarks the assumption that Marx, precisely because he took up a permanent hunt for father and capital, wanted to attain this capital in order to maintain himself in it. Whether under the sign of a world-historical law or under the sign of self-preservation, whoever ventures on the persecution of another always intends in this other himself, his own prerogative or his claim on a power equal in principle and, just for that reason, under dispute. He must persecute in another the likeness of himself—but since he pursues only an alienated and estranged figure of himself, his persecution occurs from the very beginning under a doubled and doubly contradictory sign: he cannot be himself without having seized the other, but as this other he can no longer be himself, being merely his alienated, unfamiliar, and false figure, a phantom of himself. From this aporia of self-persecution it perforce follows that a self is possible only as a persecuted and phantasmatic self; that the chance for self-preservation now lies in keeping itself apart from itself; and that the structure of the subject—of the egological, world-historic subject in class struggle—is ultimately determined as an irrecoverable but permanently persecuted head-start: as project and projection, as a persecuted project and as the project of the persecution of projection. The I, as the formula of the Marxist, agonistic, class subject goes, is rendered by Derrida; the I is not only an other but the irrecoverable other that the I persecutes, the phantom of a future I and an I still virtualizing its past figures out of its futurity, of a phantasmal father and of virtual capital. I can only be a future I, and must therefore be an unattainable I—I must be a phantom I. The I *is* only as a promise, and this promise, in which the I speaks beyond every given language in advance of itself and can, from this "advance," first speak to itself at all—this promise must always also be an announcement and a threat, always the threat and what is threatened, the virtual subject and *sujet*, the project of the persecution in the temporal cleft between an irrecoverable "in advance" and an unrepeatable "beforehand."

—The I does not speak; it is always the cloth that speaks: the projection onto the cloth and the cloth as projection. What speaks is the project that the I holds and withholds, veils and presents for the I. What speaks—and promises and threatens—is the fetish: of the I, of the father, of capital. Language exists only as the language of the capital fetish, labor fetish, substance fetish—not, however, as this substance, essence, labor, not as language it*self*: unless its *self* be its absolute advance, its prelanguage, its promise.

—Cloth speaks. But cloth speaks only in order to *attain* the cloth—in order to obtain it, to appropriate it to itself, to pull it to itself and don it, hold it fast and dissolve into its ideal. That the cloth speaks means that a promise alone speaks. And it means that a double threat also always speaks in this promise: it might fulfill its promise—and thereby make an end of language—and it might never fulfill its promise—and thereby degenerate into the infinite simulation of simulations.

—The cloth—promise, project, ideal, capital, and fetish of the I—is always also a religious linen, Veronica's veil, with the impression of abstract man announcing his return, his resurrection and reincarnation; the linen in which capital speaks and this capital, *Monsieur le Capital* as Marx called it, promises only itself, promises only a specter, promises only, once again, the cloth. Capital is an infinite project—a project of its advent, its return, its revenues, and its revolution.

Derrida reconstructs the individual shapes and dramas of this family history of specters, and conjectures "that the figure of the ghost is not just one figure among others. It is perhaps," he offers for consideration, "the hidden figure of all figures." I quote: "And the fantastic panoply, while it furnishes the rhetoric or the polemic with images or phantasms, perhaps gives one to think that the figure of the ghost is not just one figure among others. It is perhaps the hidden figure of all figures. For this reason, it would perhaps no longer figure as one tropological weapon among others. There would be no metarhetoric of the ghost" (SE, 119–20 / SF, 194). But the original figure, the archispecter—as the preceding commentary has shown and as the following will—is the specter of the father and thus the promise that he will be the father, that he will rise again as the son and lead abstract man to real man and to salvation. *La figure cachée de toutes les figures* is certainly not a figure among others, but it is always and above all a figure. It is the figure of figuration itself, the transcendental or quasi-transcendental figure of generation—that which is also figured as a transcendental in the Marxist value-formula and in the commodity-language he deciphers, that which is figured as historical and historicizing, quasi-transcendental, that is: as money (or, in the function of the general equivalent, as cloth) and further as capital. However invisible and hidden among other figures it might be, this figure is not anonymous, nor particularly uncanny or unfamiliar; it bears a name and a familial one; it is called for Marx, as Derrida reads him, the phantom of the father. The archifigure of this ghost bears the name of one of the figures that conceals it. In it, in the name of the father, the metafigure—one is, strangely enough, to assume it is maternal, a mater-figure—becomes a phenomenal figure of generative, paternal phenomenality. The transcendental becomes empirical; phenomenality becomes phenomenal and nominal. The promise of the specter in its paternity, in its spectrality, dictates the drama of the *pèresécution de Marx*, because the promise of the father, the promise that the father makes to himself, precedes his reality and remains after his disappearance, and thus there remains as well the promise of universal capitalization, of the presence of the father, of *pèresence.* In the promise, he is ahead of himself; he is his own grandfather and his own grandson; is himself, both momentarily and invisibly, his own ghost; the promise of the father is his *own* messianic, promessianic operation and aupèreation.

And at the same time, not his own, never his own. For in the promise of the father, ahead of himself, he must at the same time asynchronically and anachronically fall behind himself; he can only promise, not realize, his own paternity, and hence can never promise himself *as* father. The *promise* of the father—this belongs to its aporetic structure, to its irremovable covering—will have never been the promise of the *father.* The father is only promised—and always by something other than the father. The promise does not promise. Its privileged figure, identifiable with what is *called* father, with what is *promised* under the name of father, is entrusted to something other than the father; it is a liminal figure, hidden among all figures, a figure without figure—and consequently a figure that does not satisfy the determinations of figurality and can only by virtue of this insufficiency permit what is called "figure." One could thus say of the "figure hidden beneath all figures" what Derrida does not say, or does not say this way: a finite figure, a figure without figure, it is the disclosure and opening of all figures; it is what in all figures is irreducible to a single figure and thus the event of an *adfiguration*, an a-figuration, an *affiguration.*

—The cloth speaks, and in it, capital. But the cloth, capital, speaks neither in propositional statements nor in categories or objective thought-forms; rather, the cloth speaks in promising itself capital. Thus they do not speak, neither capital nor the cloth, nor commodity-language; instead they disclose the possibility of speaking, which cannot be reduced to their "real abstractions," that is, to the politico-economic grammar and rhetoric of the categories of commodity-language—whose figures, in turn, exist solely in the mode of the promise. Neither capital nor labor are the agents of its project; both are only the historical protagonists of a structure that does not resolve into any grammatical, rhetorical, or pragmatic figure—and therefore also not into the figure of the performative as it is traditionally determined. The promise is not a figure but the promise of a figure. An infinite and always deficient promise, it is the prefigure (Husserl would perhaps say archifigure) of all possible figures that is never fulfilled and closed off in a figure, the unpromissable affiguration of labor, capital, and cloth. Arising from this infinitely generous and generative promise, which always keeps coming, but precisely therefore keeps not arriving and not coming—arising from this ungenerous and ungenerative promise, capital, labor, and cloth never exist *as such.* Always promised and withheld in the promise, neither language nor the promise speaks. Or: language is nothing but this unfulfillable, unrealizable promise of language. (And since it is unfulfillable and unrealizable, one cannot ascertain whether it will ever have been a *promise* of language or a promise of *language.* "It" can always also have been something other than a "promise," and always something other than "language.")

The promise, once again, cannot be a statement, a description, or an assertion. It must play itself out in a mode of saying that corresponds to nothing given, nothing present, nothing extant, and therefore can be in no way placed under the logic of representation, imitation, or mimesis. It is neither some kind of conventional sign—for the future is no future if it corresponds to conventions and can be indicated by means of a conventional code—nor the promise of a sign at all—for at least a representable or ideal signified would have to correspond to it: but this is, for its part, only a promised correspondence. Every promise, foremost, only *promises* to be a promise and to correspond to its concept and, moreover, to its content. The correspondence is therefore not the horizon of the promise; the promise is the horizon of the correspondence. Since this horizon can only be infinite, all adequation and consensus concepts of truth fail to offer a sufficient determination of the promise and of all other future-oriented and future-disclosing speech forms. But not of these alone. For if language, with the cognition possible in it, is always an imparting, then its statements must without exception have the character of assurances or truth claims whose verification can in principle be expected only from future correspondences. Language is language at all only in view of a future language. Even if they are not solely and explicitly offered in the form of the promise, all statements, including those usually termed thetic or constative, are structurally asseverations or announcements whose conditions of verification remain, in principle, unfulfilled.[14]

In order to account for nonconstative speech forms and furthermore for the prospective structure of language in general, a discourse of action developed in Hobbes's late rationalism, Hume's skeptical empiricism, and Kant's transcendental philosophy, then culminated in Fichte's discourse of an originary act (*Thathandlung*), understood either as a contractual promise, as the leading imperative of all linguistic utterances, or as the autothesis of the transcendental I. Language was thus thought of no longer as the correspondence of a statement to a preexisting object but as the autonomous or autonomizing act of a social or individual subject positing itself. It is this theory of the speech act of an empirical, transcendental, and ultimately absolute subject that, by way of labyrinthine detours and transformations, has since then led to what is known as "speech-act theory." Here the promise is one among the possible, so-called performative speech acts that must be conducted within certain conventions to be "successful." Indeed the very choice of the concept "performative" resonates with the assumption of a preexisting rule, of a law or an agreement: the preestablished formal rule is "realized," "executed," or "fulfilled" by a particular performative. Classical speech-act theory does not inquire after the conditions under which conventions can be linguistically prepared and established—and precisely for this reason, it cannot account for the performativity of its performatives. Since it does not inquire after the constitution of conventions and their subjects, it typically proceeds from self-governed, intentional subjects who merely reproduce themselves in their linguistic conventions, thereby deviating from its only productive methodological principle of not recurring to instances independent of language to explain linguistic events.

Since "Signature Event Context," Derrida has repeatedly, critically, and productively concerned himself with the limits of Austin's and Searle's theories, particularly with their conventionalist and presentistic premises, using—as he does again in *Specters of Marx*—the concept of the performative. In the figure of conjuration and conjurement—that is, the figure of exorcism and sworn assurance, like the conspiratorial association of persecutors, which is itself exposed to persecution—he emphasizes the significance of an "act" "that consists in swearing, taking an oath, therefore promising, deciding, taking a *responsibility*, in short, committing oneself in a performative fashion" (SE, 50 / SF, 89); and Derrida speaks of a "performative interpretation . . . that transforms what it interprets." He continues: "An interpretation that transforms what it interprets is a definition of the performative as unorthodox with regard to speech act theory as it is with regard to the eleventh Thesis on Feuerbach ('The philosophers have only *interpreted* the world in various ways; the point, however, is to *change it*')" (SE, 51 / SF, 89). He writes about the future discussed in *The Communist Manifesto* as "the real presence of the specter" of communism: "This future is not described, it is not foreseen in the constative mode; it is announced, promised, called for in a performative mode" (SE, 103 / SF, 186). In, as he continues, the "performative form of the call" (ibid.), this future tries to establish itself in the Communist Party. In the *Manifesto*, as this "manifesto" itself proclaims, the party manifests itself and thereby the future. Its promise, its performative act, is thus staged in Marx's text as the instantaneous positing of what is not yet—and perhaps never will be—present. Derrida diagnoses: "Parousia of the manifestation of the manifest" (SE, 103 / SF, 169). This "absolute manifestation of self" (SE, 104 / SF, 170) can take place only by asserting the actuality of a real, incontestable institution for its future; it can take place only on the double terrain of the not-yet-real and actualization and must therefore be both: unreal and real, *spectreal.* Derrida therefore speaks of "the singular spectrality of this performative utterance" (SE, 104 / SF, 170). He thus emphasizes in performatives the character of parousia, of manifestation, of absolute self-positing; but he does not do so without binding this self-positing to an autophantomization. Every speech act that inaugurates something new, calling to life a subject, a contract, or the Communist Party, posits something under the conditions of reality that has heretofore not existed: it therefore calls to life a thaumaton—a monster or specter. Performatives, one could translate Derrida's thoughts, spectrealize—and themselves are, if, like *The Communist Manifesto,* they institute a novelty, *spectrealities.*

Events, and principally the event of the promise, perform, and to be sure they spectralize in performing; they are phantom-parousias first and foremost because they move in the medium of language and thus of the appresentation of what is never immediately present. The border between the "immediate present" and the future, between the familiar and unfamiliar, is without exception *a priori* porous because it, along with the terrain separated by it, is defined only by language, by both discursive and nondiscursive language, as their common medium. "And if this important frontier is being displaced," Derrida writes,

> it is because the medium in which it is instituted, namely, the medium of the media themselves (news, the press, tele-communications, techno-tele-discursivity, techno-tele-iconicity, that which in general assures and determines the *spacing* of public space, the very possibility of the *res publica* and the phenomenality of the political), this element itself is neither living nor dead, present nor absent: it spectralizes. (SE, 50–51 / SF, 89)

It spectralizes, in other words, because it speaks. And because it promises. All language, whether explicitly oriented toward the future or not, whether explicitly acting or appearing under the screen of neutral statements, promises to communicate something, promises itself the conditions for the preservation and fulfillment of its promise, and promises itself an addressee in whom its statements can achieve their aim. When speaking and promising occur, indissoluble combinations of actuality and suggestion form, combinations of the living and dead, of the present and absent, because, in this language, this "medium of media," no oppositions, but only coimplications, exist. For this reason whatever appears—and only in this medium can anything appear at all—necessarily escapes the opposition being and nonbeing, life and death, and the ontological categories of presence and absence. "It requires, then, what we call . . . *hauntology*," Derrida writes. "We will take this category to be irreducible, and first of all to everything it makes possible: ontology, theology, positive or negative onto-theology" (SE, 51 / SF, 89).

Every logic of capital and labor, every logic of commodity-language, of the form of equivalence, of exchange, and therefore every logic of controlled planning, technological development, and politico-economic prognosis must accordingly be founded in this hauntology of a (as Derrida has it) fundamentally irreducible spectrality of medial language, of the language of the promise, of the futurial and performative, the futuroformative language of an unsecurable project. Labor is no more a given fact than capital; it is not a transcendental form of value determination or essence of anthropo-technological systems without first being a project, a credit, an advance *on* and a head start *into* a future that can in no way be determined as fact, transcendental, or substance. What follows from the idea of "hauntology" is, first of all, that language does not belong to the system of capital, nor to that of labor; that language does not define itself as commodity-language; that it assumes the character of productive or reproductive labor only when the equivalence form is generalized and has repressed the credit-character of capital as well as the project-character of labor; that language does not have under all conditions (and hence not essentially) the character of a communicative exchange operation, of a propositional adequation, or of a positional act; and that, even if it can still be characterized as "performative," the concept of performativity must submit to drastic transformations—transformations that detach it from the instances of both conventionality and positivity, from communicability and continuity with its tradition.

Derrida does think here of language, the medium of media, as a performative engagement, but as one that first of all, essentially and irreducibly, is an engagement *with* others, *against* other others, and *for* a future, which has never been actualized in this performative engagement but possesses, instead, the amphibious virtuality or spectreality that alone is adequate to the medial character of language. Language is the medium of futurity. Whatever enters into it, or simply comes into contact with it, is already pulled into a space where the characters of reality are founded precisely upon the not-yet of this reality—and are unfounded in that conventions are and remain only in anticipation, positings exist only in process and are hence exposed, continuities are suspended, and communications and their rules are not fulfilled but announced, attempted, and promised. If, as Derrida does here—like Benjamin (who seems to have left an impression on *Specters of Marx* hardly to be overestimated)—one thinks of the mediality of language from its relationship to the future, if one thinks of it from its promise—much like Heidegger (whose traces are equally unmistakable and numerous in *Specters of Marx*)—then the futurity of language, its inherent promising capacity, is the ground—but a ground with no solidity whatever—for all present and past experiences, meanings, and figures that could communicate themselves in it. Language is a medium insofar as it opens the place of arrival, opens the gate to what is to come, the entrance of an unpredictable and topographically indeterminate other: the topos of the U-topic. Neither what is to come "itself" nor the purely present, and yet both "at once," language is, in the form of the promise and the announcement, the field of interference where what is to come transforms the meaning of every present figure, rendering it legible *sub specie futurae.* If language did not open itself to future possibilities, if it did not promise itself as something else whose verification is still pending and can only be awaited from another, then it would have no possible meaning, it would be nothing but the superfluous replica of what is already known and could never, in its singularity, impart itself to another. Communication—and therewith every being-with-another, every being—is a promise. Since the other that is to come, that is announced or promised, can never be the object of a theoretical determination within the categorial frame of assured epistemological means, but can only be the project of a practical execution that itself must be determined by this project—and therewith by what is fundamentally indeterminate—this praxis can be thought of no longer as merely the "act" of a constitutive and self-constitutive subject, no longer as a "performance" within a framework of conventions, but only as an event that with every occurrence discloses other rules, conventions, subject forms, performances, alterformances, alterjects, allopraxes. If language is a promise, it is always the other who speaks. And this other cannot be an alter ego, but can be only the alteration—and *alter-alteration*—of every possible ego. What imparts itself in the promise must therefore go beyond all forms of transcendental subjectivity and their politico-economic institutions; it must go beyond capital and the labor which it determines; and from this *exceedence* it must transform all its figures in advance, transform them by promising them and shifting them into the "trans" of every form. From its very inception, it must be beyond everything posited in any way, a monster at the limit of appearance, of visibility and representability. It must be, however so gently, an ex-positing.

If I understand it correctly—and since understanding is also always a "performative" enterprise and therefore an alteration, here too the "correct" understanding does not move along without displacements, transformations, and perhaps distortions—this is nothing other than what Derrida means by the expression "the singular spectrality of this performative utterance" (of *The Communist Manifesto*). It is the spectrality, and more precisely the spectreality, of a project that, prepared from far off, announced for the first time in the history of European societies, in philosophical and scientific form, universal unlimited freedom. "The form of this promise or of this project," Derrida emphasizes, "remains absolutely unique. Its event is at once singular, total, and ineffaceable—ineffaceable differently than by a denegation and in the course of a work of mourning that can only displace, without effacing, the effect of a trauma." And Derrida continues:

> There is no precedent whatsoever for such an event. In the whole history of humanity, in the whole history of the world and of the earth, in all that to which one can give the name history in general, such an event (let us repeat, the event of a discourse in the philosophico-scientific form claiming to break with myth, religion, and the nationalist "mystique") has been bound, for the first time and

inseparably, to worldwide forms of social organization (a party with a universal vocation, a labor movement, a confederation of states, and so forth). All of this while proposing a new concept of the human, of society, economy, nation, several concepts of the State and of its disappearance. (SE, 91 / SF, 149–50)

The event of the Marxist promise—whose singularity, once again, lies in its boundless yet organized universality—precisely because it is an absolute novelty in this determined, universal, organizational form and cannot be reduced to any social, religious, or philosophical conventions that might have anticipated it, is therefore a *trauma*: a traumatizing injury of the politico-economic and social-psychological corpus, of the religious, linguistic, technical, and scientific corpus of all traditions, a traumatic promise that tears apart a techno- and eco-onto-logical topology and its mechanisms of displacement and that cannot be healed by any traditional form of social, psychic, or scientific labor, by any "labor of mourning." The Marxist promise, which pledges the abolition of labor, cannot be recovered by any labor. It marks an absolute limit of ergontology.[15]

—Cloth speaks—but with Marx it speaks for the first time in the form of a universal and infinite promise. No longer as a promise already indicated in the cloth's "indigenous" woven structure and finally, in the mid–nineteenth century, grasped in clear words with teleological resolution, but instead as a promise that unprogrammatically tears its previous weave and its tendencies and, in this traumatization, promises for the first time the cloth in its absolute, universal actuality: beyond every labor, beyond every handiwork and every fabrication, pure mesh. A peculiar mesh, one that is a tear; universal because singular; singular because redeemable in repetitions; in need of repetition because unrepeatable, infinite, and therefore irrecoverably and unrealizably finite.—

The promise in question here must consequently be thought of first of all as the "medium of all media," secondly as the projection into a future that is not the teleologically predetermined goal of a past history, and thirdly—and therefore—as a traumatic experience in which the form of experience itself suffers a tear and is brought to a halt. The medium of all possible media is a tear and an opening, a *rendering possible* of all media, opening the empty place that alone gives room to a spectral actuality, to an actuality only as a specter, and that itself can appear only as a space of spectrality. The promise, the traumatic opening of another time—or, indeed, of something other than time—of another future, or something other than the future perhaps; the promise, which does not continue conventions and does not fulfill the rules of its performance but breaks through conventions and inaugurates other rules—and perhaps something other than rules—the promise does not perpetuate history; it starts and makes history possible. This unique promise of something itself unique and new will, according to Derrida, as "a messianic promise . . . have imprinted an inaugural and unique mark on history" (SE, 91 / SF, 150). This marking of history, which in actuality is its opening and nothing less than the *historizing* of history, is regularly and explicitly characterized by Derrida as its spectralization. He writes of the democratic and the communist promise, of those "infinite promises" that do not govern their own conditions of fulfillment: "*just* opening . . . messianic opening to what is coming, that is, to the event that cannot be awaited *as such*, or recognized in advance therefore, to the event as the foreigner itself, to her or to him for whom one must leave an empty place [*laisser une place vide*]—and this is the very place of spectrality" (SE, 65 / SF, 111). And: "At bottom, the specter is the future, it is always to come, it presents itself only as that which could come or come again" (SE, 39 / SF, 71). And:

> In this regard (that is, with regard to its untimeliness and the untimeliness of the future), communism has always been and will remain spectral: it is always still to come and is distinguished, like democracy itself, from every living present understood as plenitude of a presence-to-itself, as totality of presence effectively identical to itself. Capitalist societies can always heave a sigh of relief and say to themselves: communism is finished since the collapse of the totalitarianisms of the twentieth century and not only is it finished, but it did not take place, it was only a ghost. They do no more than disavow the undeniable itself: a ghost never dies, it remains always to come and to come-back [*il reste toujours à venir et à revenir*]. (SE, 99 / SF, 163)

The specter haunting Europe and beyond is a promise of democracy and communism that traumatically opens up a new world history, a history for the first time neither mythical nor limited, a world history of liberation, justice, and equality. It must announce the most general and most formal form of a future society and at the same time must promise the unpromissable: its absolute singularity and incommensurability with every generalization. The democratic and furthermore communist promise thus announces, in absolute formality and absolute singularity, performatively—*biformatively*—two futures irreducible and irreconcilable to each other: an unlimited universal rule and a singularity free of every imaginable rule. It is the promise of a coming democracy only by being this double and aporetic promise; a performative only by being this *biformative.* But this singular universal promise is aporetic in yet another respect. As the promise of a future that is universal, it must be the promise of a just future of all pasts; but it cannot be the promise of the future of *all* pasts without also being a restrictive promise from a particular generation of *limited* pasts and hence without being itself merely a past promise, a wraith and an echo, the *revenant* of promise, broken over and over or betrayed or fatal. Pluriformative and reformative, the revolutionary performative of the absolute messianic promise is also a *perverformative* that turns against itself and in each of its traits tends to erase itself—and not for any empirical or contingent reason that might have been avoided or eliminated, but from a structural necessity that no single promise can escape, in particular not the promise of singularity.[16]

—The language of the cloth is always also an echolalia. Things said resound in it once more; every shred and tatter of word and phrase pursue the speaker into a future of semblance and echo, into an echo chamber, a tomb: a specter monologue in diverse voices. But this necrophilic language of the nymph Echo is still a language of *philía*, keeping the dead alive and preserving it for other times—or something other than time.—

Specters of Marx is not about this multiplication in the performative structure of the promise, but indeed about the multiplication, the dissociations, and the antagonisms of specters, spirits, phantoms, ghosts, and fetishes—and since it is the promise and the future disclosed in it that Derrida characterizes as the phantom par excellence, his text is, in a mediated way, also about the dissociation and original perversion of the performative. It is about the difference *within* the performative and how this difference can haunt in no other "figure" than that of the monstrous figure of a specter. I cite here three passages that address precisely this problem. (1) "There are several times of the specter. It is a proper characteristic of the specter, if there is any, that no one can be sure if by returning it testifies to a living past or to a living future, for the *revenant* may already mark the promised return of the specter of living being. Once again, untimeliness and disadjustment of the contemporary" (SE, 99 / SF, 162). The specter can come from the past as well as from the future; its spectral quality is its double allegiance, which can in no way be decided upon by theoretical cognition, since every cognition of that kind must already be related to the spectral and, in turn, can do nothing but "performatively" send out its own specters. There is a time fissure through the spectral distributing it across two times that are heterogeneous to each other, distributing it into a double chronicity and an asynchronicity, an achrony that lets the past appear in what is to come and what is to come in what is past. But no matter how even the distribution of times may be, Derrida's formulation suggests with sufficient precision that there is no symmetry between what is past and what is to come: specters of the past can appear only when conjured by the promise of another future. In the final footnote of the book, this theme of an asymmetrical, future-inclined asynchronicity is taken up once again: "Given that a revenant is always called upon to come and to come back, the thinking of the specter, contrary to what good sense leads us to believe, signals toward the future. It is a thinking of the past, a legacy that can come only from that which has not yet arrived-from the arrivant itself" (SE, 196 n. 39 / SF, 276 n. 1). The future delivers specters, and even in the specters of the past, however lethal they might be, it launches the promise of another future for this same past. The promise of an absolutely other future testifies for hope even in the bloodiest pasts. To make other futures possible, they must undergo the risk of their pairing with dangerous futures and confront their own effacement. The performative of the promise, directed toward other possibilities of the past and future, is thus unavoidably linked to a threat to this promise itself and thereby to the effacement of this performative. There is no rendering possible of possibilities that might not also make this rendering itself impossible. No promise in which the possibility of its breach was not also voiced, no act into which its annulment does not intervene.

—No cloth that could not be taken apart thread by thread; no weave that would not end in an open seam, that would not consist of such seams, that was not woven from its unraveling, from its runs. The cloth, a Penelope of itself.—

In principle every performative is an aporetic, agonistic biformative—or, to write the word for French ears and eyes, a *bifformative*: what it inaugurates includes the possibility of its erasure (its *biffure*), and only with the inclusion of this possibility does it have the chance to begin. The performative does not perform—unless it still "performs" the possibility of the "not" of its performing and is in-formed by this "not"; it is, in French once again, a *pas-formative*. It is the start of a speech act in which an egologically structured subject should constitute itself, a start that is close to being this act itself, hence an *adformative*. But since it can be nothing but the start and *opening* of this practical and therein self-sufficient act, an opening in which its possibility is knitted into the possibility of the impossibility of succeeding, it can itself never assume the definitive form of the performative, will never finally be accomplished, and remains, as the event of the threshold before every act, parapractical, an act without act before every possible act, *aformative*. The structure of language is *afformative*—both adformative and aformative—and it is only its onto-ego-logical speech-activist interpretation that is recorded in the concept of performatives, therein maintaining the suggestion that logos has incarnated itself, that it is "accomplished."[17]

The promise, and in particular the Marxist promise, the first and only to announce and prepare the universal actualization of freedom and individuality, opens possibilities; but it opens them with all the dangers and threats linked to this disclosure. These dangers include the repetition of the familial, national, and religious myths that it claims to rid itself of. Here belongs as well the danger—of activating the performative of the promise according to the schema of the jealous persecution of the father. Performatives of *pèresécution* must always be able to be *pèreformatives* as well and thus formatives of the father—and of the kind in which, in the first and last instance, the father and his son and his holy spirit promise and form themselves. And if not a father, then nearby to him a mother in a *mèreformative* of the mother tongue or, perhaps even closer to the father, a rivalrous brother in a *frèreformative*. What else could promise, manifest, and form itself here but the least uncanny and the most familiar specter: the Holy Family beneath its head, capital? Or, as the past 80 years have demonstrated—it amounts to the same thing—the Communist Party, this other Holy Family beneath its head, the capital of labor?

What, once again, would be the difference between specter and spirit, between the phantom of all failed or missed pasts and that spirit of the future in which they would be redeemed from their silence, their distortion and falseness? Derrida expressly poses this question in connection with a passage from *The German Ideology* in which Marx, as Stirner's ventriloquist, sneeringly states, "you yourself are a ghost which 'awaits salvation, that is, a spirit'" (SE, 136 / SF, 217). The difference between specter and spirit, in Derrida's commentary on Marx's citation of Stirner, is *différance.*

The specter is not only the carnal apparition of the spirit, its phenomenal body, its fallen and guilty body, it is also the impatient and nostalgic waiting for a redemption, namely, once again, for a spirit. The ghost would be the deferred spirit [*l' esprit différé*], the promise or calculation of an expiation. What is the différance? All or nothing. One must reckon with it but it upsets all calculations, interests, and capital. (SE, 136 / SF, 217)

If the specter is the holding back and avoidance (*Hinhaltung und Hintanhaltung*) of the spirit, it is the unending longing for the spirit as well. The messianic promise haunts as a specter among the shattered and criminal forms of social and linguistic life and links even its most mythical forms, its terroristic performatives, its familial obsessions, to the expectation of their redemption. A life ruined retains the longing for the just one—and thus, and *only* thus, in a kind of minimal-ontodicy, is itself "justified." For what would redemption be if all pasts were not redeemed along with all their disappointments, tortures, and disgraces? What would freedom be if the dead were not also liberated, at least those who live on in us—and are there others? Even the conditions of capital and labor are subjected to *other* conditions: those of their change, those of their possible other future. Nor would the ontologization of the afformative to the performative, and furthermore into the *pèreformative,* be possible without the afformative, the future-oriented structure of the promise, which vows the transformation of that structure into a prognostically and programmatically untamable other language—and perhaps something other than language—into another form of action—perhaps even something other than form and than action. And, perhaps, something other than the future.

For what would the future be if it could not be something other than the future?

The point is not to conjecture it, design plans, formulate intentions, or suggest precautions for it. Nor is it to speculate about the future or speculate with it. It is a matter of unfolding all the implications of futurity and the only way of access to it, speculation, and thereby of making more audible the language of this futurity and its spectreality, the language of the promise. For the sake of futurity, it must first of all concern its formal structure alone and therefore practice a suspension of all contents that might combine with it. What is offered and what Derrida repeatedly shows in *Specters of Marx* is an ultratranscendental *epokhē*, almost without comparison in political theory up to now, of the objects and contents of a future politics and their rigorous reduction to the sheer form of futurity. Accordingly he distinguishes between the "Marxist ontology grounding the project of Marxist science or critique" and a "messianic eschatology," which, as the unrealized promise of justice and democracy, goes beyond every critical ontology of what is present at hand and of what is prognostically or programmatically graspable. The contentual determinations of the future aside, the *essential* difference between the Marxist critique and the religions, ideologies, and theologemes it criticizes (and that criticize it) dissolves. Their solidarity, notoriously dismissed by both, consists in what neither can think as the content of its doctrines or object of its concepts, but what both are caught up in as the implication of those concepts and doctrines. Derrida writes:

> While it is common to both of them, with the exception of the content (but none of them can accept, of course, this *epokhē* of the content, whereas we hold it here to be essential to the messianic in general, as thinking of the other and of the event to come), it is also the case that its formal structure of promise exceeds them or precedes them. Well, what remains irreducible to any deconstruction, what remains as indeconstructible as the possibility itself of deconstruction is, perhaps, a certain experience of the emancipatory promise; it is perhaps even the formality of a structural messianism, a messianism without religion, even a messianic without messianism, an idea of justice. (SE, 59 / SF, 102)

This suspension of contents with which the messianic structure of the promise—one could say: the structure of the *promessianic*—is exposed must not be misunderstood as indifference toward future or present institutions: it is the only form under which such institutions first become possible. "This indifference to the content here is not an indifference,"

Derrida emphasizes; "it is not an *attitude* of indifference, on the contrary. Marking any opening to the event and to the future as such, it therefore conditions the interest in and not the indifference to anything whatsoever, to all content in general. Without it, there would be neither intention, nor need, nor desire, and so on" (SE, 73 / SF, 123–24). What Derrida calls "the messianic without messianism" is thus what in every promise, every imperative, and every wish—and in language altogether—reveals "the necessarily pure and purely necessary form of the future as such" (ibid.). It is, one could say, the necessary possibility that precedes everything actual, everything necessarily actual, and everything possible. It is the historicity of history itself: a futurity always open and thus open to something else. Marxism—and, since there are several competing Marxisms, among them nationalistic, totalitarian, and terrorist, one must specify: the Marxism that pursues a politics of emancipatory universalism—is the instance of the articulation of this messianic promise. It is the instance of this articulation even when, and perhaps only when, the messianic does not assume the organizational form of one party but of several; even when, and perhaps only when, it is not bound to the sufferings and hopes of a single class and thus not to the traditional conception of the proletariat; and only when the messianic and its Marxism are not corrupted by a program, when they are corrupted neither by their alliance with labor nor by a temporal and historical schema of succession, a development or linear sequence.

The spirit of Marxism—or the one inheritable specter haunting for 150 years—is thus first and foremost the absolutely abstract formality of the promise: the opening of a future that would not be the continuation of pasts but for the first time exposes the claim of these pasts, the opening of another time—a time other than the time of labor and capital—the opening of a history that in fact gives all previous history its room for maneuver (*Spielraum*). The spirit of Marxism is, in short, the promise, the absolute "in advance" of speaking; it is the prestructure, the structure of possibility of every experience—and it is thus essentially temporalization and historization. But as such, it commands an eschatological movement that cannot be halted by any representational content or foreseeable purposes. The messianic eschatology underlying every fundamentally critical thought, every longing, and every one of the simplest statements—and underlying in particular the Marxist project urging justice beyond internationalism, democracy, and all positive legal forms—must, for the sake of the historicity and futurity of these absolutely formal and universal imperatives, be distinguished from classical teleology. Derrida insists upon "distinguishing . . . any teleology from any messianic eschatology" (SE, 90 / SF, 147).[18] There is no preestablished *telos* for "the messianic without messianism" which could be recognizable now, programmatically striven for, and ultimately achieved in some particular organization of social life. As the universal structure of experience, it cannot be presided over by any guiding figures whose design were not already obligated to that structure and therefore were not already surpassed, in every one of their positions, by it. Messianic hope is thus divested of all determined and all determinable religious, metaphysical, or technical figures of expectation; this continued divestment itself opens every past history to a new future one, and can therefore be nothing other than an "expectation without a horizon of expectation" (SE, 65, 192 / SF, 111, 267). From this decisive determination of the messianic, which is repeatedly marked in Derrida's text—that it must remain indeterminate, that it is messianic without a horizon—it follows for the promise, and the structure of its performativity when the messianic tendency first arises, that this promise, too, must *stricto sensu* be open and that it must be a performative without a horizon. Only with this characterization is the ground cleared for the messianic movement, for the Marxist project and a politics of emancipation: it is *performing without a performative horizon*, the *perforation* of every horizon, transcendental—and, more exactly, atranscendental—*kenosis* of all linguistic and nondiscursive forms of action. But what does that mean?

Derrida does not pursue the structure of a horizonless performativity further in *Specters of Marx*. For him, this structure is marked by its mediality—as the "medium of all media"—by its openness, and hence by its illimitable futurity. The way in which these three traits, which join together in the spectrality or spectreality of the Marxist project and affect the structure of the performative, is given no closer investigation. A hint, however, is repeated several times and commented upon in two of Derrida's more recent texts, "Faith and Knowledge" ("Foi et Savoir") and "Avances." In his Marx book, Derrida concedes—and it is important that his statement takes the form of a concession—that the unconditional hospitality that the horizonless promise accords to the other, the future, justice, and freedom could be "the impossible itself"; and he adds: "Nothing and no one would arrive otherwise, a hypothesis that one can never exclude, of course" (SE, 65 / SF, 111–12). One can thus not exclude, but rather must concede and admit, that the promise of an arrival *also* promises *no* arrival, that it promises something not arriving and thus promises precisely what can in no way be promised. But it is clear that this non-advent does not overtake the promise—any promise—like an accident from the outside (perhaps from that other who was promised but who, owing to his volition, power, or impotence, does not come); rather, this nonarriving belongs to the very structure of the elementary promise: insofar as it is a promise, it must be open to something that denies itself knowledge, evidence, consciousness, and the calculability of a program, and thus always and in every single case cannot arrive. The promise would not be a promise if it were a statement of fact or the prognosis for a causal chain of development. It lacks the egologically anchored certainty that should belong to epistemic calculability. Regardless of what is promised, the promise as such already concedes that it may not be kept, that it may be broken and can only be given in consideration of its possible breach. A promise is given only under the premises of the possible retraction of its offering. Since the promise is the initiating act of language altogether (and hence is language "itself")—the opening of both selfhood and relation to the other, of sociability, history, and politics—its structural unrealizability cannot help but suspend them all and, in them, their constitutive relation to the future. Insofar as the future exists, the promise offers it only under the proviso of the future's possible non-advent. And this reserve, this absolute discretion of a possibly impossible future, is inscribed into the promise and inscribed with the promise into the opening of the future; it is inscribed into the very futurity of the future.

The performativity of attestation (*performativité testimoniale*) and the techno-scientific performance discussed in "Faith and Knowledge" are linked by a "performative of the promise," which Derrida emphasizes is at work even in lies and perjuries, and without which an address, a turn to the other, would be impossible. He writes: "Without the performative experience [*expérience performative*] of this elementary act of faith, there would be neither a 'social relation' nor an address to the other, nor any kind of performativity of productive performance joining, from the very beginning, the knowledge of the scientific community to practice, science to technology."[19] Since this elementary promise—and that also means: the promise as the medium of all discursive and nondiscursive institutions—is for its part bound to the iterability of markings, it follows that there can be

> no future without inheritance and without the possibility of *repeating*. No future without *iterability*, at least in the form of a relation to itself and of the *confirmation* of an originary Yes. No future without messianic memory and the messianic promise, without a messianicity older than all religions, more original than all messianisms. No speech, no address to the other without the possibility of an elementary promise. Perjury and a broken promise lay claim to the *same* possibility.[20]

Everything, in short, begins with the possibility—with the possibility of projecting possibilities in the promise and of confirming these possibilities, repeating and transferring them. The possibility of the promise is already the possibility of its repetition. But were this repetition merely to result from the automatism of the perpetually selfsame, the promise would become program and evidence, prophecy and providence. If the opening of the future were ushered in by the iterability of the promise—one could say: if *futuration* were the act of a knowing consciousness—then the future itself would be something entirely knowable and technically executable and would thus be, instead of the future, its annulment. The iterability coextensive with the promise thus has two sides: it opens the future as a field of possible confirmations and even fulfillments, and it discloses it as a future that can block every future. The possibilities of the future always include the possibility that there is no future. The possibilities of iteration always include the possibility that it is not a transformation but rigid fixation; the possibilities of the promise always include the possibility that it is not only unfulfillable but also unperformable: every promise, in principle, necessarily can be interrupted by accident or coincidence. These two possibilities, irreducible because equally original, turn every futuration into *affuturation*: into the opening of a future that, because it must always be able to be a future without future, an annulment of the future, can irrevocably disavow this very opening. Not *the* future is opened, but instead—iteration is immediate pluralization—multiple futures are opened; but to these futures always belongs at least one that no longer permits talk *of* a future or *in* one. At least this one, this annulled and null-future, necessitates the experience of future possibilities always at the foundation of their possible impossibility, futures at the foundation of their future non-advent. There is no relation to the future not undone by the irrelation to its inherently possible absence at every point—thus a relation to irrelation—an irrelation itself—and hence not a relation to the future at all. *Affuturizing*, we speak and act at the future, on its *threshold*, not *in* it, not in the open but in the opening—and in an opening that (otherwise it were none) can always be the opening to an end, to a conclusion or obstruction.

The possibilities disclosed in the messianic opening of the promise do not relate to this promise as external addenda following a logic other than that of the promise. They are possibilities only insofar as they are possibilities disclosed by the promise. If for Derrida the promise is messianic, this does not mean that it is the promise of a messianic lying outside it; still less the promise of a messiah; rather simply this: it means that the grounding structure of the promise itself is the announcement and expectation of another, a just life and another, a true language. Consequently—and therefore alone—the irreducible possibilities imparted in the structure of every promise also necessarily include the possibility that it is the promise of a god or a messiah. The messiah of a promise is nothing but this promise that the promise is real and in truth a promise; he is nothing but the promise to say the truth about the promise and to keep this promise as it was made. God himself would be the promise that the promise *is* a promise: the one who testifies to its truth as its highest guarantor. To be able to promise something, the promise itself must first of all secure its own status and to this end project an absolute—and therefore ungeneratable—instance of its attestation. To be a promise at all, every promise, even the most profane, must produce a god. "Without god, no absolute witness. No absolute witness who could bear witness to the attestation itself."[21] What the promise takes as the witness to its truth must be absolute, must be a god, *one* god—but must also *not* be god, not an absolute, and not a witness, for if the promise were certified by an absolute witness then it would be no longer a promise, no longer directed toward the future, and no longer the precarious opening of a possibility; it would be the statement of an absolutely certain actuality. The one absolute witness must be able to be none—no god. He can be a god only in that he can also not be one; he must remain able to let his potency go, beyond all capacities—and he can attest to the promise only as this one and none. "Without god, no absolute witness [*point de témoin absolu*]. No absolute witness who could bear witness to the attestation itself." The necessary possibility, posited by the structure of the promise itself, of a god is, by the same necessity, ex-posited to the necessary impossibility of god. If the messiah is heralded, summoned, and called into life by the messianic structure of finite language, then he must be held back by the same structure, withheld, always overdue and longed for. No god, no messiah, who would not be missing. None who was not still absent in his presence. None who was not promised and promised away by language: spoken away and removed, removed and re-moved. None who would speak. The messiah cannot be promised—but can *only* be promised, and thus only promised as an unpromissable that breaks every promise.

What makes the messianic structure of language and experience into not a theological but an anatheological and atheological structure is precisely what the titles "messianic" and "the messianic" still mask. Just as the messianic, like the title "god" for a theology (whether positive or negative), is valid only as the name for an absolute entity if an element from the structure of the promise is isolated, semanticized, and ontologized, so the carefully chosen, purely formal title "the messianic without messianism" could still arouse the misunderstanding that it indicates a stable transcendental structure of projective actions directly aimed at an open future, disclosing the future. Not only would that lead to a messianization and theologization of the future (Derrida cites Lévinas's "Dieu est l'avenir"),[22] not only would it mean the ontologization of an isolated element from the structure of the promise, but it would also be contrary to precisely those aspects that Derrida stresses in his analyses of the promise and to his question of what could be a more consistent inheritance than an "atheological inheritance of the messianic" (SE, 191 / SF, 266). The messianic is always what longs for, discloses, and promises an unanticipatable, unprefigurable other. But exactly because it is not prefigurable, because it is an other, the messianic must of necessity refuse to promise it, must thwart its promise to retain its promissability; and instead of pledging a future, the messianic appresents, in its ex-position, futurity. Only the *ammessianic* is messianic: that which opens the messianic tendency and concedes at the "same" time the possibility of its discontinuance, *hic et nunc.* Just as there must be a possibility of no future for there to be a future, so must the messianic always be open to its lapse, if it is to be messianic at all. It—every it—must also possibly not exist so that it might exist: the law of that law issued by the promise, the law of the exposing of the law "itself," an atranscendental movement that precedes every transcendentality of hope, belief, wish, and ontologization or semantization. This movement precedes every being as something in which every "pre" is given up. "Messianic promise"—that means the anasemiosis even of the "pre" of every *pro*mise in a possibility potent to the extent that it is impotent; a possibility that can mean only by preceding nonmeaningfully every meaning and every bidding. "The messianic," like "the future," is a misnomer; its gap cannot be filled by the misnomer "ammessianic" but can only be made more precise and commented upon.

"Avances," Derrida's preface to *Le tombeau du dieu artisan* (The tomb of the artisan god), by Serge Margel, is a study on the aporetic structure of every promise. It argues the connection between doing (*Machen*) and lack (*Mangel*), performance and finitude. Promises are possible only under the conditions of their possible breach. They are the most exposed forms of linguistic and consequently existential fragility. "In order to be a promise," Derrida writes, "a promise *must be capable* of being broken and therefore capable of *not* being a promise (for a breakable promise is no promise)."[23] Though Derrida does not pursue it in this way, the consequence for the structure of performativity is clear: since this structure cannot grant the certainty that it is really the structure of *performativity*, since it *must not* grant this certainty if the structure is to have a chance to correspond to it, the *form* of the performative in its performance must itself be suspended. The performative is what exposes its form, the horizon of its determination, *ex-poses* itself as an act—a doing not lacking something else but lacking this doing "itself"—a completion from which both the plenitude and the carrying through "itself" immediately slips away—and whose "self" can lie in nothing other than permitting this exposing and slipping away. An *actus ex-actus.* A performative that must be structured, distructured as *afformative* to be able to operate, open, or posit: as open *toward* the form of an act, but for this reason *divested* of the form of this act; an amorphic or anamorphic event over which no figure rules and from which no final figure results because it is essentially *affigurative*; moreover it is, each time, a singular, noniterable—and therefore *errable*—occurrence because the conditions of its repetition must also always be the conditions of its unrepeatability. Therefore Derrida's reference to the "perversion" of the promise into a threat[24] can only be misleading: every promissive, every promessianic performance, without changing its character, is of necessity itself already the threat not only of not being kept but of *not being one* at all.

If, once again, a future can be, then it can be only as one that can also *not* be. This possibility is not an alternative articulable in the disjunction "either a future or none," for only insofar as there is a future is there none; only insofar as there are open possibilities is there also the possibility that none will be preserved *as a possibility.* But if what is called presence or actuality is always determined by the opening toward the future and *as* this opening, then presence *appresentating* (in a sense other than a Husserlian one) is always that in which every future is pending. This opening that is the present must, *hic et nunc,* be something other than future, more than *a* future: it must be pluralities of futures, but also more than futures, a pluperfect-future; not only another time and other times, but what would no longer be time. The promise would be the place where this other time and this other-than-time occur. It is the place—the atopic place—where possibilities are indeed opened, but only those constitutively lacking the conditions of their verification and actualization. Whatever might *become* a promise without ever indeed being so belongs to at least two "times": a time of a future that can come and a time of a future that cannot come; a time that renders possible and one that renders impossible this very rendering. The promise is thus the place of the aporia of temporalization; hence the place of an *attemporalization* that must precede every possible time, every possible future, every possible possibility, and with which, here and now—for this too is a promise—not only other times occur but also an other-than-time.

—A cloth before time and before temporally determined speech—a cloth of promises, a prediscursive material that promises "itself": the cloth is originally twofold, the cloth of the promise, and another (which is not there) of the confirmation that it is a promise. They do not exchange with each other, do not communicate with each other under a common discursive ideal, yet, in their absolute disjunction, they are a community—a possible-impossible community before every equivalence, before capital and before the labor and its time measured by capital. And because it is before labor, it is also beyond it: atranscendental material. Now.—

As a promise exposed to the uncertain possibilities of the future, every act risks not being one. Each act, however closely determined it might otherwise be, must *a priori leave open* at least one extreme possibility—and leaving open means risking and risking failure—the possibility of no longer falling under the regime of an intentional subject and thereby no longer qualifying as an act. The open place of this extreme possibility that (in)determines the field of any and every action is a place no longer of doing but of *letting*. Every performative must contain the structural concession that its horizon is not its own, that it is not altogether the horizon of performativity—of positing, of productive imagination, of labor—that it is instead open to other horizons and, at the limit, ahorizontal, open to possibilities not given *by* it but given *to* it, ceded, imparted, or left. Performatives, speech acts positing facts or opening possibilities, exist only when they are conceded room for maneuver and when they give themselves over to this maneuvering: when, even before they can be performatives, they are admitted into a field that one can provisionally call a field of *admissives* or *amissives*. These admissives or amissives cannot be thought of as fundamental speech acts, for they involve neither acting nor executing; they are, rather, admitted and conceded, granted and left, and in such a manner, a manner unregulatable and unique each time, that an admission or cession can at the same time be a letting go and discarding, an abandonment and a loss.[25] To say "I promise" I must also say "I admit my promise" and "I admit it in view of its admission by the other to whom it is addressed." But to *admit* a promise means unavoidably to concede its potential failure, its potential breach and even its potential inadmissibility, hence to treat its admission not as an assured fact but as a rendering possible that does not exclude its rendering impossible as well—the possibility of the impossibility of this rendering possible. "I promise" therefore always also means: "This promise is admitted on the condition of its unreliability and its possible inadmissibility." All performatives are therefore (even if, in programming, semanticizing, ontologizing the field of their projects, they deny it) structured as admissives, and all admissives are structured as amissives: they admit, concede, and leave themselves to a field over whose determination they have so little defining power that they cannot even grant it being, not even an unlimited, secure, solid possible being, an actual or necessary being. They admit and leave themselves to what is not projected with them: they are amissives insofar as they risk their own loss, their impossibility. Admissive, amissive: the Marxist promise is the opening of a world, of a society, of a language, which—*lingua missa, lingua amissa*—aims at a just life in every trait, and for this very reason, in every trait, must be open to another and still another—and also to none. But if the opening onto another life and another language still follows the temporality of a rendering possible, then this never excludable—and, for the sake of the opening itself, indispensable—opening onto another life that would be none and onto a language that would be no language, this opening onto the occlusion of the opening follows at the same time the temporality of the rendering impossible; and the promise of language knits itself—for the sake of this promise—into the promise of the prohibition not only of a particular language but of every language. A promise, above all the most relinquished, the most admitted of promises, exists not in a language but in the cleft of language.

The promise, the messianic, ammessianic promise, opens itself as a time cleft. And indeed as the time cleft of a world, as a world cleft. Marxism is historically the first promise that made a claim of unlimited universality in freedom and justice, the first and only not biased by racisms, nationalisms, cultisms, or class ideologies, but promising instead a world common to all and to each his own.[26] This world must be promised, demanded, desired, and made possible before it can exist. But if it is ever to exist, it will be a world under the conditions of this promise, of this longing and this rendering possible; it will therefore be an aporetic world whose idea lies in infinite conflict with its every singular actualization and in conflict with its always possible annulment. This conflict is as unavoidable as the promise from which it arises. What can never be conclusively avoided but, to be sure, can be opposed—what *must* be opposed—is the possibility contained within the promise's tendency not to be a promise but instead to be a totalitarian program, an immutable prescription, or a plan, or instead, quite simply, not to be at all. What must be opposed is the organization of the future; and what fights against it is the longing that the future might be otherwise, other than other, not merely *a* future and not merely *future.* This is the rift in the world that the world has opened up with the Marxist promise of a *world.* It has become no longer necessarily a cleft between different classes—but it is still this class antagonism as well. It is first of all a rift between a future that opens other futures and not merely futures, and a future that would be the end of all futures, the end of history in the automatized terror of private interests, in the tortures of exploitation and self-exploitation, in the vacuous self-sufficiency and ritualized mutilation of others and of the other possibilities of history. What must be opposed is the mutilation of past history—but how past?—and future history—but future beyond every arrival—and thus the destruction of the present that opens itself to the entrance of history. What *must* be opposed is the death of the promise in theoretical certainty and practical complacency—of the promise that precedes both, declaring that neither is sufficient, that both must let themselves be opposed, and that this "must" and this "let" must be able to exist beyond certainty and complacency, beyond this death.

The promise, *afformatively*, Derrida makes clear, is a desert, formal, *afformal,* in its infinite abstraction and limitless expanse, an insurrection against the suggestions of fulfillment and of successful culturation, a landscape of fury and longing for all that is absent. This insurrection and this fury and this longing of the promise could be the beginning, the perhaps unconscious and unpractical, surely inconsolate beginning both of language—of another language—and of politics—of another politics and of something other than politics. They speak, askew and "deranged," spectreal and compromised, in commodity-language as well. The point is to articulate it more clearly, and not merely to articulate it.

—Cloth of sand. "Language, too, is desert, this voice that the desert needs," Blanchot writes.[27]

> The desert, not yet time and not yet space, but space without site and time without generation. . . . When everything is impossible, when the future, given over to fire, burns . . . then the prophetic word announcing the impossible future still says the "nevertheless" which breaks the impossible and restores time. "Truly, I will give this city and this land into the hands of the Chaldeans; they will invade it, burn and raze it, and *nevertheless* I will lead back the inhabitants of this city and this land from every region whither I have cast them away. They will be my people, and I will be their god. Nevertheless! *Laken!*"[28]

Translated by Kelly Barry

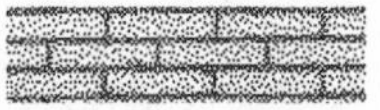

The "Mujic of the Footure"

FUTURE, ANCIENT, FUGITIVE

Jean-Michel Rabaté

In *Of Grammatology* Derrida announced early and forcibly "the end of the Book and the beginning of Writing."[1] For a thinking that opens itself to the possibility of a radical alteration of the basic concepts of logocentrism, the future can only loom ahead under the figure of absolute danger. The future as *l'avenir* appears thus as a monstrosity for which an epigraph is still lacking (*il n'est pas encore d'exergue*). In a more paradoxical if similar way, Derrida comments in the recent "Archive Fever" ("Mal d'archive," 1995) on Yerushalmi's "Monologue with Freud," linking the function of the archive with the experience of an unthinkable yet absolutely affirmative future:

> But it is the future which is at issue here, and the archive as an irreducible experience of the future.
>
> And if there is a single trait about which Yerushalmi remains intractable, if there is shielded from all discussion (psychoanalytic or talmudic), an unconditional affirmation, it is the affirmation of the future *to come* [*l'à-venir*] (in French, I prefer saying this with the to-come of the *avenir* rather than the *futur* so as to point toward the coming of an event rather than toward some future present).
>
> The affirmation of the future *to come*: this is not a positive thesis. It is nothing other than the affirmation itself, the "yes," insofar as it is the condition of all promises or of all hope, of all awaiting, of all performativity, of all opening

toward the future, whatever it may be, for science or for religion. I am prepared to subscribe without reserve to this reaffirmation made by Yerushalmi.[2]

Just as Benjamin, in a famous remark of the last thesis in his "Theses on the Philosophy of History," notes that while the Torah prohibits any investigation of the future, the future has nevertheless to keep all its messianic potentialities,[3] so too Yerushalmi stresses the foundational function of a Messianic posture. His "Judaism Terminable and Interminable" implies hope, not just a vague "hope for the future" but "the anticipation of a specific hope for the future." Jewishness, which is not exactly the same as Judaism, appears indissociable from a valorization of the "to come" as a French term (*l'avenir*), not to be reduced to the futurity of *le futur*. The assertion of *l'avenir* is assertion itself, a pure *yes* insofar as it conditions all promises and hopes.

Can the specifically French opposition between *avenir* and *futur* be translated into English, or must it remain trapped in the singularity of an idiom? One observes a bifurcation between, on the one hand, Latin languages such as French, Spanish, and Italian, three languages possessing two terms for the future, and, on the other hand, Germanic languages such as English and German, containing one term only (future; *Zukunft*).

In French, an etymological investigation yields a first opposition between *l'avenir*, indicating the *coming* of a future event (or the coming of the future as an event), and *le futur*, indicating the *being* of the future. For *futurus* derives from *esse*, the supine of the Latin verb "to be," a component of the future participle *futurus*, which, as a plural neuter, *futura*, in classical Latin means "things that are to come or to happen." *Futur* was current in the thirteenth century, whereas *avenir* was a later creation, appearing in the fourteenth century as a modification of the verb *advenir*, signifying "success in the future." A century later (around 1427), *avenir* would mean a "future time"—a time *à venir*, a time yet to come. And Littré's famous nineteenth-century dictionary opposes Pascal, who systematizes the finality of *l'avenir* by playing on means, ends, and endings—as when he writes: "The present is never our end. The past and the present are our means, the future alone our end [*le seul avenir est notre fin*]"[4]—to Gide, who insists on the potentiality inherent in *futur*, as when he asserts: *Je confonds possible et futur* ("For me, possibility and futurity are identical"). However, as Littré concludes etymologically, but also a little enigmatically: *Le futur est ce qui sera, l'avenir est ce qui adviendra.* "The future is what will be, and the 'to come' is what will come"—to which one could add: *Comprenne qui pourra!*

To progress a little beyond mere etymological quibbles, let us remember that Pascal's mathematical (and metaphysical) calculations of the future introduced the new science of probability—even as Pascal himself derided the Jesuits for relying, in their casuistics, on theological "probability" (he did so after having invented his "calculating machine," the earliest prototype of the computer). Pascal's overall strategy here relies on the distinction between *avenir* and *futur. Avenir* supposes a distinction between stretches of time (time can be *proche*, "near," or *lointain*, "remote"), which itself presupposes the possibility of programming a shift from one time to another: *prospective* is often implied. The French *futur* is at once more ancient (with the overtones of *fut-fût* linking the preterite to the subjunctive) and more distant, opening up onto science fiction (and—why not?—onto futility, as we shall see with Mallarmé). Hence that influential science-fiction series published by Denoël bears the apt title *Présence du futur* (The presence of the future). Hence, too, that colloquial English phrase expressing despair about a hopeless situation—"no future"—can be translated into French only as *pas d'avenir* or *aucun avenir*. Translating it as *pas de futur* would indeed sound like an anglicism, because in French, one is usually understood to have a *futur*, or several *futurs* (in the sense, for example, of having "future brides"), even if *l'avenir* may appear to be bleak. Similarly, one would not really say *je travaille pour le futur* (*je travaille pour l'avenir* is correct) since one is generally expected to toil not for some hypothetical *futur* but for a directly foreseeable *avenir* yielding concrete results. *Futur*, moreover, through its grammar of shifting tenses, rather than calling up another time introduces a modalization of being.

With all this in mind, I shall first try to bet that the term *futur* can provide us a vantage point from which to assess the *avenir*'s posterity. Next, I will advert to chance, casting the dice to question the calculation of "generations," since it seems that "posterity" is contained more often in *l'avenir* than in *le futur*. Along the way, we need to pay attention as well to the commercial overtones of "futures" as a term designating uncertain commercial "shares." The word "wager," for its part, implies a calculation combining the plural and the future: it yields a plural "futures" that has to do with debt and risk, all thrown in a balance whose equilibrium depends upon a measurement capable of calculating "times to come."

We shall turn to Pascal's famous wager, but before doing so, let us review a Christian apologue, the story of the "Steward of Iniquity," which sketches some aspects of a fundamental structure linking futurity to writing.

The Steward of Iniquity and the Master of Prudential Grammatologies

My attention was first attracted to the famous parable when I saw how Joyce used it as the culmination of his satire on a perverted Catholicism in *Dubliners.* At the end of the story titled "Grace," Father Purdon's sermon in the Jesuit church on Gardiner Street epitomizes a moral complacency and a spiritual simony that Joyce associates with degraded petty-bourgeois values. Dublin is presented as the capital of simony: all values have been bought and sold, reduced to commodities, while commercial interests still require a religious sponsor to disguise their cynicism. The preacher (whose name calls up a then-famous street in the red-light district of Dublin, also evoking a Jesuitical "pardon" all too easily granted to sinners) concludes his sermon with these words:

> "*For the children of this world are wiser in their generation than the children of light. Wherefore make unto yourselves friends out of the mammon of iniquity so that when you die they may receive you into everlasting dwellings.*"
>
> Father Purdon developed the text with resonant assurance. It was one of the most difficult texts in all the Scriptures, he said, to interpret properly. It was a text which might seem to the casual observer at variance with the lofty morality elsewhere preached by Jesus Christ.[5]

The modernized text of Luke 16 used by Father Purdon is at variance with both the King James Version and the Catholic Bible, where one finds not "when you die" but "when you fail" (this may be a deliberate distortion, by means of which Joyce points out the Jesuitic "veil" thrown over a purely commercial meaning). The basic story is well known: a master, a lord, an *adon*, who is also a "rich man," upon hearing rumors that his *oikonomos* (or *villicus*, in the Vulgate) has "wasted his goods," tells the *oikonomos* two things that are slightly contradictory: first, that he has to "give an account of [his] stewardship," and second, that he will soon be dismissed ("for now thou canst be steward no longer"). The steward, aware that he has little time before being dismissed, does not attempt to "give an account" or defend himself. Instead, the steward approaches his lord's debtors, devising a trick "so that they may receive (him) into their houses": with one debtor, he reduces the debt from 100 barrels to 50 barrels; with another debtor, he reduces the debt from 100 quarters of wheat to 80 quarters. This curious scene is also a scene of writing and dictation: "And he said to him: Take thy bill [*gramma*] and sit down quickly and write [*grapson*] fifty. . . . He said to him: Take thy bill and write eighty" (Luke 16:6–7).

The story of the Steward of Iniquity (*Villicum iniquitatis*) is a parable linking debt and writing: the steward (whose cleverness in practical matters and lack of natural wisdom in religious matters establish his exemplarity by default) shows how to steal from a debt, which exhibits, after all, a rather wise and exhilarating perspective on the future. Because the *oikonomos* has been asked to give an account of his stewardship, he suddenly—all too quickly—launches into a systematic anti-economy. The steward, who has always mediated between a capitalist lord and a crowd of debtors, begins perverting this relationship. There is indeed a degree of anarchy in the large reductions he authorizes, which may be ascribed to a lack of preparation, to pure and ingenious improvisation. The steward steals from the debt (takes away even more of his master's money) or gives from the debt (to the debtors, who will profit marginally): this is an instance in which stealing is exactly synonymous with giving. But he does not erase the debt, even though he might have been tempted to do so: could he not simply cancel the debt, and destroy these incriminating tablets altogether? No, this would go beyond his power—and would undo the force of the parable: its meaning is connected to a particular writing, a writing that keeps a trace of another trace that has nevertheless to be read through partial cancellation or obliteration.

One of the ironies of the parable's outcome is that the master, instead of being furious, praises him ("And the lord commended the unjust steward, forasmuch as he had done wisely," Luke 16:8). In fact, whether the steward knew it or not, this was the best way to be rehired by the lord. However, his original strategy aimed at being invited into the homes of all or some of the debtors, who no doubt would then have shown some measure of gratitude. He expects to be without money or job, and is above begging or working with his hands ("To dig I am not able; to beg I am ashamed"), and he will therefore have to depend upon others. The context of the lord's potentially scandalous commendation of an "unjust" man is revealing: Luke, writing in the name of Jesus, means to attack the Pharisees, who, as we know, were, with the Scribes, the staunchest defenders of the old dispensation, and the guardians of the Mosaic faith after the destruction of the Temple by the Romans. Luke's story questions the Pharisees' aristocratic self-righteousness, their denial of debt, and ultimately their blindness in the face of impending catastrophe. The steward who, in the hope of a future charity, "gives" by reducing debts that are not his own is aware that somehow his accounts, like everyone else's, will not tally. One cannot pay back fully: it is far wiser to gain new accomplices than to bet on one's purity in the face of the Law. The righteous Pharisees are said to be "covetous": above all, they are indeed misers because they feel secure. They labor under the delusion that they are the elect, the *ariston*: their economic and spiritual wealth, which should prove their moral distinction, is in fact spurious—precisely because they believe mistakenly that they have no debt to pay.

The steward's predicament can be universalized to all humanity: we are all going to account for our lives, and we are going to be found wanting. The catastrophe of death and judgment is impending. The only way we may postpone its terrible effects seems to be through a cunning calculation: if we cannot make our accounts look right, we can at least deflect a prior prevarication in the direction of others. Thus we partly atone for the misdemeanor. In one sense, we add to our wrongdoing (instead of justifying the past—there is no time for this; it would be a waste of one's time), by risking the speedier dissipation of the master's fortune. But we gain the friendship of the people whose complicity we try to buy in advance. Luke's wager is a human one, since it bets not on a divine pardon but on a sense of a human reciprocity. It moves toward the community, not toward a transcendent relationship.

This parable about economy supposes an economy of debt, in debt, hinging on a sense of futurity but also supported by a reciprocal sociability. Real economy is based upon the accountants, debtors, IOU's, and account books where the names and the quantities one owes are inscribed. God is indeed the arch-capitalist in this story: the *adon* as master is pleased to have discovered that even if his steward steals a little, at least he is very clever. He will not find a better one (if he loses some money, it will be only a fraction of his sound investments and astute transactions). The steward functions precisely as Jesus is supposed to act according to Christian doctrine. He takes away from our sins, which appear as a sort of eternal debt, a debt that can be diminished, and he also takes away from the old Jewish Law. The steward facing his master is in the same position as Jesus the Son facing his divine Father, or as Moses facing God. Both steal from the debt of sin, lessening it in order to reduce the burden of humanity. Jesus' conclusion—"for the children of this world are wiser in their generation than the children of light"—initiates a paradoxical economy: in order to be as wise on the spiritual level as on the practical, one must learn to play on sharing and shares, on proportions and fractions; one must see the point of calculating a reduction of 50 percent or only 20 percent in a debt of Sin.

Money is indeed seen less as a "general equivalent" measuring future exchange than as a measure of inequity, and this is essential to the parable, since it explains how it can be read as a sort of negative "wager" argument: it is better to bet on some future outcome of one's actions than to attempt to justify past deeds. Money cannot be mistaken for a sign of election. A rapid evaluation of chances with the others has to prepare a new start in life, since a half-clean slate looks more secure than the uncertain outcome of a real trial. It is not necessary to try to justify oneself before the Law. In a time of haste, a prudential judgment, implying one's interest, is to be preferred to an evidential judgment, implying proofs, evidence, testimonies. There is simply no time for the endless deferral of a Kafkaesque or Simpsonesque trial. . . . This prudential grammatology (in which a stroke of the pen reduces a debt) culminates in the translation of death as a "failure": the parable points to the function of Christ as a Redeemer, who buys humanity out of original sin. Thus we learn that failure can be positive, and that we can live with an interminable debt, provided we have been wise enough to bet on the Future. This Future, however, is also a past event (the coming of Christ), which will be duplicated in a messianic moment (the Second Coming). All of which leads us to the Pascalian argument.

Pascal's Wager

Pascal's famous argument entails a double series of calculations. The first level is deliberately simplistic: the decision that "either God exists, or He does not" should be solved by a simple decision favoring infinity over a finite stake ("if you win, you win everything; if you lose, you lose nothing," *P*, 151). But this too-easy solution does not take into account the price to be paid, which soon appears as exorbitant if one has to "give everything" ("you must risk all"). There then begins a really complex calculation of chances:

> Though there may be an infinite number of chances [*hasards*], only one of which is in your favor, you would still be right to wager on one in order to win two; and being obliged to play, you would be acting wrongly in refusing to stake a single life against three, in a game where, out of an infinite number of chances [*hasards*], one is in your favor, were there the infinity of an infinitely happy life to win. (*P*, 151)

In fact, as most commentators agree—whether they think that the argument is directed only at the Libertines, or at all men—this wager could never convince or convert anyone. Faith is not a matter of chance-taking, and one cannot bet with belief. What, then, is Pascal's aim? First, he shows very effectively that the "argument" in fact describes an ontological situation in which not to bet is already a bet. Not to choose is already to choose against. The *pari* (wager) is in fact a demonstration of the *parti* / *partie*[6] axiom: a game is being played, and each player should know the stakes. "A bet must be laid. There is no option: You have joined the game [*Vous êtes embarqué*]."[7] The saying "Nothing ventured, nothing gained" cannot obtain here in any simple way: one has both to risk and to venture.

But this ontological situation (which has often been described as leading to modern Christian existentialism, for instance to Kierkegaard) displaces the issue of ontology—and this is why, no doubt, Heidegger quotes Pascal approvingly in the first pages of *Being and Time*: just as God cannot be "proved" rationally, so the concept of Being is indefinable (Pascal had written, "in order to define *being* one must say 'It is . . . ' and hence employ the word to be defined in its definition").[8] If one cannot prove rationally the existence of God (as in Descartes's metaphysics, for instance), then what remains is a personal dilemma, which one might hope to solve through a rational calculation of risk. The wager replaces traditional proofs with a pragmatic assessment stressing decision and choice. Choosing implies a risk, but this risk can be calculated. As Nicholas Rescher writes, "the level of the discussion is shifted from *establishing a fact* to *justifying an action.*"[9] Pascal announces contemporary decision theory; the second level of the argument, taking into account the cost of the wager, has recourse to preponderant expectations. But beyond the relatively complex mathematical structure of double bifurcations, which I shall not reproduce here, what stands out self-evidently is Pascal's conclusion that it is not simply absurd to believe in God, even if this belief entails the *abêtissement* (humiliation) of reason. The calculation aims at establishing the rational rights of the heart's "reasons" over Reason. The "heart" is the locus of the undoing or autodeconstruction of reason. Thus, if one remains unconvinced at the end of the demonstration, Pascal suggests help from a community: "Follow the way by which they began" (*P*, 152) and join a community of believers.

However, there is a second level in Pascal's argumentation, which supposes another type of proof: the Bible. His main strategy has been in fact less to frighten the Libertine than to convince him to start reading the Book in a correct way. Writing offers a different type of proof, which supposes that one can learn to read—the way to man or God—between the two infinities, in the "mean" of meaning between extremes. Paul de Man's epigraph to *Allegories of Reading* ("When we read too fast or too slowly, we understand nothing")[10] could remind us of a good speed or indeed proportion necessary for the right kind of understanding. The principle of the "mean" applies to every domain: "First principles are too obvious for us; too much pleasure causes discomfort; too much harmony in music is displeasing; too much kindness annoys us: we want to pay back the debt with something over" (*P*, 92). Pascal then quotes Tacitus's cynical comment ("Kindness is welcome to the extent that it seems the debt can be paid back. When it goes too far gratitude turns into hatred," *P*, 92), which may help understand why the steward does not want to abolish his lord's debts altogether... The calculation of an exact reading-focus similarly presupposes a good use of time: "We never keep to the present. We recall the past; we anticipate the future as if we found it too slow in coming [*Nous anticipons l'avenir comme trop lent à venir*] and were trying to hurry it up, or we recall the past as if to stay its too rapid flight" (*P*, 43). The ontological vertigo created by the argument of the two infinities and the difficult "mean" also applies to the time (and to the subjective poise or position) that any reading activity presupposes.

The outcome of the "wager" has thus been to transform the hesitant Libertine into a literary critic, whose main assumption it is that nothing has been left to chance in a text.[11] The notion that we are all "embarked" upon a game of decision making plunges us radically into a hermeneutic situation. The text at hand is indeed the Bible, which may seem so obscure at a first sight. Pascal's starting point is that the contradictions and ambiguities in the Bible all make sense: "Every author has a meaning which reconciles all contradictory passages, or else has no meaning at all; the last point cannot be said of the Scriptures and the prophets: they were certainly too sensible [*avaient trop de bon sens*]. We must therefore look for a meaning which reconciles all contradictions."[12] One must find the plane of meaning on which all the surface contrarieties of the text are harmonized. This is why Pascal founds his hermeneutics on Augustine's symbolism, in which the model of meaning is prophetic discourse. It implies four elements:

(a) an enunciator who is supposed to be conscious of the double level of meaning;
(b) a tropologically encoded message working through a mixture of figurative and plain statements;
(c) a key to the rhetorical tropes used, distinguishing between passages that keep a literal meaning and passages in need of a tropological interpretation;
(d) a consideration of the inherent temporality of the text, distinguishing between events that have already taken place and events still to come in the future.

For instance, Adam is not to be understood as a "literal" character. Pascal quotes the Latin phrase (*Adam forma futuri*) from Romans 5:14 ("Adam is the figure of him that was to come," *P*, 228). In typically Augustinian fashion, Pascal regards Adam's sin and fall as necessary for the coming of Christ, and even for the fact that time exists, which immediately entails the coexistence of several different times: "If Adam had not sinned and Christ had not come, there would have been only one covenant and one age of man, and creation would have been represented as accomplished at a single moment" (*P*, 228). Adam is not just the "figure of him that was to come," meaning Jesus, but also the figure of a distinct type of futurity, a futurity that is underpinned by a past and eternally future *felix culpa.*

In a similar way, circumcision is shown to have been merely a sign (*P*, 173). It is from this point of view, for instance, that Pascal can deduce that the true Jews and the true Christians share the same religion (but the stubborn Jews are wrong in taking circumcision literally). The threat of absurdity or contradiction becomes a methodological weapon: "All these sacrifices and ceremonies were therefore either figurative or nonsense. Now some things are too clear and lofty to be considered nonsense" (*P*, 109). In his approach to the ambiguous figures of the Bible, Pascal relies heavily on Raymond Martin's *Pugio Fidei adversus Mauros et Judaeos* (A Dagger against Moors and Jews) the exposition of rabbinical hermeneutics by an obscure thirteenth century Spanish divine, republished in Pascal's time. From Martin's *Pugio*, Pascal learns the use of techniques of interpretation invented by the Rabbis, but, of course, often fights against their conclusions. One of the main ideas Pascal has found there is that the prophets of the Old Testament clearly announce Jesus as the Messiah and God's son (this is based on complex numerological issues). The role of the unbelieving Jews then acquires a crucial function: they are both witnesses to the sacred nature of their religion and misguided readers whose blindness forces one to interpret better. Their relationship to a division of time (*templum*) is thus crucial: "Anathema of the [Greeks] against those who compute the periods of time" (*P*, 130). Michel Le Guern replaces "Greeks" with "Jews" in his edition of *Pensées,* since he supposes that "Greeks" is a slip of the pen for "Jews": Jews, not Greeks, hate those who distinguish "before the Law, during the Law, under Grace."[13] As Pascal keeps repeating, Jewish prophecy stopped after the coming of Christ, sending us back to the need to read the doubleness of the Law. "Double law, double table of the law, double temple; double captivity" (*P*, 133). This confirms the link between hermeneutics and prophecy: the "proof" of religion lies in the already inscribed futurity of the event in Scripture.

The demonstration of existential hazard (throwing us between couples of infinities) should lead one to conversion, a conversion less to religious fervor than to textual rigor. The uncertainty in man's lot as *l'avenir*—which has to be transcended or sublimated into the order of faith or the heart—nevertheless permits the certainty of a knowledge of a *futur*: there is a futurity already inscribed in the text of the Bible, which converges upon the Event of the Incarnation. For Pascal, indeed, the Messiah's futurity has already happened; Christ has come at the right time as the announced Messiah: without this, no reading is possible, no textuality can be defined. The Event alone provides the keystone of textual hermeneutics. The more uncertain our *avenir* looks, the more certain and convincing will the textual proofs of religion appear. This is why, indeed, "to have no time for philosophy is to be a true philosopher" (*P*, 212). A. J. Krailsheimer's translation of the *Pensées* distorts in an interesting and creative fashion the original statement (*Se moquer de la philosophie, c'est vraiment philosopher*). To deride philosophy, to mock philosophers, is also to have "no patience" with a certain type of discourse, as Nietzsche knew too well. Pascal's hermeneutics, just like Luke's parable, never leaves us enough time to think and consider: we are hurried and bullied into realizing that we have always already been "embarked" upon a wager acquiring universal and ontological dimensions.

Wagering the *Wagnis*, from Pascal to Rilke Through Heidegger

Heidegger, another philosopher who was impatient with all other philosophers—including Nietzsche, who believed too soon that he had put an end to metaphysics—alludes often to Pascal's "heart," though with a certain ambivalence. We saw that Pascal figures very early in *Being and Time*, and that he reappears in a significant context—a reading of Rilke's poetry—in Heidegger's essay "Wozu Dichter?" ("What Are Poets For?").

There, Heidegger glosses Rilke's notion of *das Offene* ("the Open") and develops the associated idea of "unshieldedness" into a "sphere of consciousness."[14] Heidegger then opposes, as two complementary versions of the "invisible interior," Descartes's *cogito* and Pascal's heart: "At nearly the same time as Descartes, Pascal discovers the logic of the heart as over against the logic of calculating reason. . . . Only in the invisible innermost of the heart is man inclined toward what there is for him to love: the forefathers, the dead, the children, those who are to come" (WAPF, 127–28). "Those who are to come" (*die Kommenden*) is a phrase that quotes a passage from a letter by Rilke in which Rilke speaks of "the dead" and of "those who are to come" (*die Künftige*) as those in need of a refuge, of an abode. This, for Heidegger, circumscribes a typically metaphysical attempt aiming at converting consciousness into an expanding sphere, until it becomes "the widest orbit" capable of containing the whole world. But the specific feature of the "heart" is that it is free from "the arithmetic of calculation," and becomes the "supernumerary" existence praised by Rilke in the majestic conclusion of his ninth *Duino Elegy*:

> Siehe, ich lebe. Woraus? Weder Kindheit noch Zukunft
> werden weniger. . . . Überzähliges Dasein
> entspringt mir im Herzen.
> Look, I am living. On what? Neither childhood nor future
> are growing less. . . . Supernumerous existence
> wells up in my heart.[15]

From this point, Heidegger then returns to a previous analysis of an "improvised" poem by Rilke, in which Rilke expands the notion of Nature as actively "risking" the creatures that are in it and borne from it whenever they find themselves "in the Open." The key word glossed at length here is *Wagnis*, which calls up both risk *and* balance (since Heidegger links them etymologically: *wiegen* means to weigh, a balance is a *Waag*—in old German a *Wage*). All of this is close to *wägen*, "to open paths in a forest" such as these *Holzwege*, providing a neat title to the collection of essays. This is the improvised poem written by Rilke in a letter:

> As Nature gives the other creatures over
> to the venture [*Wagnis*] of their dim delight . . .
> so too our being's pristine ground [*Urgrund*] settles our plight;

> we are no dearer to it; it ventures us [*er wagt uns*].
> Except that we, more eager than plant or beast,
> *go with* this venture, will it [*es wollen*], adventurous
> more sometimes than Life itself, more daring [*wagender*]
> by a breath (and not in the least
> from selfishness).[16]

Heidegger pounces on the verb "to will" so as to conflate Rilke's position with Nietzsche's will-to-power: according to him, both Rilke and Nietzsche thus complete Western metaphysics. Heidegger concludes, "Being is the venture pure and simple. . . . The Being of beings is the venture" (*Das Sein ist das Wagnis schlechthin. . . . Das Sein des Seienden ist das Wagnis*).[17]

The exercise in poetic close reading, which takes a good twenty pages, brings Heidegger back to questions about the essence of this "venture"—a wager as much as a risk. It seems at first that Rilke follows more in the steps of Pascal than of Nietzsche—until we realize that all three affirm the same thing. Heidegger asks: "What do they dare, those who are more daring?"[18] Since Being cannot transcend itself to reach into something else—for Being is the *transcendens* pure and simple—one has to conclude that the only "venture" more daring than Life itself is a risk that takes poetic language—hence all language—as its stake. Heidegger has already situated the heart's space as the only inwardness that can meet the Open: "The interiority of the world's inner space unbars the Open for us. Only what we thus retain in our heart (*par coeur*), only that do we truly know by heart" (WAPF, 130). After positing Being as both presence and language—"Being, as itself, spans its own province, which is marked off (*temnein, tempus*) by Being's being present in the world. Language is the precinct (*templum*), that is, the house of Being" (WAPF, 132)—Heidegger meditates, in a famous passage, upon the fact that when we go through the woods, we already go through the word "wood" even if we do not speak or think the word, and he describes the object of the "dare," of the *Wagnis*, as language: "We have an intimation of what they dare who are sometimes more daring than the Being of beings. They dare the precinct of Being. They dare language." The "venture with language" (WAPF, 133) confirms the "inner conversion" that turns the world's openness into the unshieldedness of consciousness or vice versa.

The Being that accomplishes such a feat of conversion is called the

"Angel" by Rilke—and the Angel is identical with Zarathustra: "the creature which is Rilke's angel, despite all difference in content, is *metaphysically the same* as the figure of Nietzsche's Zarathustra" (WAPF, 134). Like Zarathustra, the poet, because he is "more willing" than modern men who believe in willing self-assertion, can will nothing (WAPF, 140) and can thereby let the holiness of Being resound in a song. Although, for Heidegger, Hölderlin was, even more than Rilke, the one who could rise up to the lofty expectations of this risky wager with language (*Wagnis mit der Sprache*), it is my contention that Mallarmé was the first to understand the radical implications and the nature of this risk half a century after Hölderlin, and half a century before Rilke.

Mallarmé's Die or Dice; or, Mallarmé Dies

> *Die,* (7) plur. Dies: a block of metal on which the design of a postage stamp is engraved, used in making the repeated impressions that form the printing plate.
>
> —*Webster's* dictionary

To link Mallarmé's and Rilke's wagers, I shall start with a curious historical coincidence: Mallarmé, as his letters show, discovered the aesthetics of Nothingness and the pleasure of the casino at about the same time. In a letter he sent to his wife in April 1866, after a three-days' trip to Nice and Monaco with his friend Lefébure, Mallarmé mentioned that the "Monaco excursion was delicious," and that he won "some money at roulette" with which to buy a surprise gift for Maria.[19] He enthusiastically comments on the experience a little later, explaining that he is "resuscitating": "Lefébure lifted the veil forever hiding Nice, and I was deliriously drunk with the Mediterranean. Ah, my friend, how divine is this sky of earth!" (*C,* 300). The almost Nietzschean overtones, coming from a scene that likewise inspired the German thinker, acquire only retrospectively the dimension of an existential and intellectual crisis. Two years after the fact, in April 1868, Mallarmé commemorates the fecund "stay in Cannes" that allowed him to "dig down into verse" (*creuser le vers*) and reach a major artistic breakthrough after the dismal encounter with utter nothingness.

A letter to Villiers de l'Isle-Adam comments upon the famous crisis:

"For the future [*pour l'avenir*], at least for the near future, my soul is destroyed. My thought has reached the point where it can think itself, and has no available strength to evoke, in a unique Nothingness, the void disseminated in its porosity" (*C*, 366). Mallarmé nevertheless announces the "interior dream" of two parallel books, one on "Beauty," the other on "the sumptuous allegories of Nothingness," books he feels impotent to produce: "Really, I am afraid to *begin* (although, it is true *Eternity* has scintillated in me and devoured any surviving notion of time) where our poor and sacred Baudelaire ended" (*C*, 367). But the same letter concludes on a more optimistic note, begging forgiveness for a silence that is "ancient about *Morgane* . . . and future [*futur*] about the riches the *Journal* will bring me" (*C*, 367). The mention of Villiers's drama *Morgane* suggests, as an echo, a "martingale" with which the poet can hope to win some money, if not at roulette, then at least as a journalist or a *littérateur*. Throughout the correspondence, one observes a systematic bifurcation between *l'avenir*, which describes the time of the future work whose "vague plans" he cannot make more precise and has to postpone (*C*, 369), and *le futur* or *futur* used as an adjective, which he reserves for a potentiality of writing as a gamble still determined by past calculations: "You would save from Nothingness very divine pieces of work that suffer from being half-immersed in the future [*navrées d'être à moitié plongées dans le futur*]" (*C*, 373).

In 1869, we then find an extraordinary series of letters to various addressees, all dictated by Mallarmé to his wife because he was suffering from a strange writer's hysteria and his doctor had forbidden him to touch a pen. In the first of these, Maria's erratic spelling (her native language was German) transforms *futur* into *fûtur*: "the simple fact of writing installs hysteria into my head, which I want to avoid for you, dear friends, to whom I owe a Book and future years [*des années fûtures*]" (*C*, 425). The submerged pun on "fût-il?" suggests a creative futurity quite aware of its risky status, and still in need of specific studies, among which one would find what Mallarmé calls his "egyptology." This is how he describes his situation through his wife's pen: "The first phase of my life is over. Consciousness, overburdened with shadows, wakes up slowly to shape a new man, and has to find back my dream after its creation. This will last a number of years during which I must relive the life of humanity after its childhood as it becomes conscious of itself" (*C*, 425). This second—and last—"crisis" of 1869 relegates to the past of the work everything that preceded it, including the text whose title "The Future Phenomenon" ("Le phénomène futur") points in the direction of Hegel's phenomenology.

The correspondence keeps promising a work to come, even when the metaphysical encounter with absolute Nothingness commemorated by *Igitur* is past, the poet having accepted that he is a simple *littérateur* (not a philosopher or a hero of the mind). In 1871, he again postponed the essential writing: "But to begin immediately, no. First, I must get the needed talent, and my thing has to become ripe, immutable, instinctive; almost anterior, and not of yesterday" (*C*, 509). Mallarmé's future creation is thus based upon a sense of some archaism inherent in a consciousness ready to throw it out again, to disseminate it along the unpredictable lines of chance. In order to document the evolution, one would have to follow all the thematic links between the prose-poem entitled "The Future Phenomenon" and the "last" realization of a project such as *A Throw of the Dice Will Never Abolish Chance* (*Un coup de dés jamais n'abolira le hasard*). But, for want of time and space, I shall limit myself to a few hints gleaned from the poems, which all testify to a similar sense of a paradoxical futurity:

> "A Fan (*Madame Mallarmé's*)"
> With nothing else for speech
> Than a pulsing in the skies
> The future verse is freed [*Le futur vers se dégage*]
> From a precious lodging.[20]

Or again in "Funerary Toast":

> . . . We are [*Nous sommes*]
> The sad opacity of our future ghosts [*La triste opacité de nos spectres futurs*].
> Is there, of this destiny, nothing that remains? . . .
> A solemn agitation of words in the air,
> In honor of a calm catastrophe.[21]

The even more momentous last stanza of "The Tomb of Edgar Poe" states:

Calm block here fallen from obscure disaster,
Let his granite at least mark the boundaries evermore
To the dark flights of Blasphemy scattered in the future [*Aux noirs vols du Blasphème épars dans le futur*].

A lighter sonnet dedicated to Méry Laurent plays on similar tensions:

You know always, since years ago
Your dazzling smile has prolonged for me
The rose that plunges with its fair season
into the past and then into the future too [*Dans autrefois et puis dans le futur aussi*].[22]

I can merely point to deep affinities and convergences between Mallarmé's letters, his rare published poems, and his numerous notes for an unfinished "Book."[23] Blanchot has demonstrated in his *Livre à venir* (The Book to come) that Mallarmé's absolute "Book" was in essence always future in the sense of always yet "to come," against Schérer's shortsighted optimism (Schérer edited the notes as if they constituted an actual book).[24] However, more recently, another thesis on the lost or vanishing "Book" has been proposed, a thesis that would stress the past and "future perfect" realization of the "Book," closer to the sense of *le futur* than to Blanchot's *à venir.* Roger Dragonetti, in *Un fantôme dans le kiosque* (A phantom in the kiosk), starts from the idea that Mallarmé's meditation on the absolute "Book" implies also, as a dialectical counterpart, the contingent inscription of the vanishing author in a futile everyday life, from which at least a few postcards or sonnets are occasionally sent to contemporaries. A rigorous reflection on the interaction between the theory of modernity and its social locus of production can lead to a radical thesis: this is why Dragonetti, in his study of Mallarmé and the ghost of the "quotidian," claims that the perfect (and only possible) realization of Mallarmé's "Book" was his own correspondence.[25] Mallarmé worked more with a view to the social inscription of his writings—especially toward the end of his life, when he busied himself with countless poems for anniversaries, banquets, commemorations, burials, and all the rituals surrounding the busy but empty life of a literary *Maître*—than with a view to the neo-Hegelian agenda presupposed by Blanchot. With the *loisirs de la poste*, Mallarmé invented a new genre in which futility and ingenuity triumph: the address of his correspondent became the pretext for a brief poem, almost always a quatrain, which the mailman must decipher in order to forward the message. His poems were indistinguishable from gifts for friends, since they were written on fans, fruits, and packages of candies, tobacco, or coffee. For lack of the absolute "Book," poetry seemed condemned to fulfilling the function of miniature decorations: ornamentation appeared as the bourgeois rewriting of an ontological futility, a systematic Pascalian *divertissement.*

Dragonetti shows how Mallarmé's ghost was less the real ghost of his dead son Anatole than the impossible, tyrannical, and totalitarian *bouquin.* Even if one harbors some skepticism toward the exegetical feats by which Dragonetti transforms each letter sent by Mallarmé into fragments of an aborted *ars poetica,* one can admire the forceful and easy solution to Mallarmé's apparent contradiction: just as he was describing to his disciples the absolute task of a "Supreme Fiction," his real activity consisted in producing rhyming addresses and a few rare sonnets. The death of the Hero (perhaps his own son Anatole), for which the notes for the "Book" elaborate several scenarios, is surely a demise that Mallarmé reserved for himself in a self-fulfilling prophecy: he would confirm his inability to create a Work to which it seemed that he had devoted his entire life. Is it hardly accidental, then, that he died of a laryngeal spasm while struggling with the fantastic creation of the "Book"? It is less that a physical demise indicates the "elocutionary disappearance" of a poet vanishing with a vengeance into a pure but inaudible language, than that the crisis that seized him is called in French by a name derived from English, *faux croup* (spasmodic croup): a *faux coup* or "false throw of the dice" grabbing you in the throat, leading to death throes that parody the final dice throw of Death as a dishonest croupier. Caught in this fatal spastic throw, Mallarmé seems to have literally died from the discrepancy between his sublime aspirations to the "Book" and an awareness that he would never fulfill them.

Like Rilke's Orpheus, the poet identifies with a pure Trace, his exile becomes writing, in a last metamorphosis that is not devoid of pathos. Mallarmé's lifelong effort to combine Hegel's ghostly phenomenology of negativity with Poe's gothic specters and apparitions needed additional help from the *Geist* of History. He remained trapped between the Ghost of all Ghosts, the absolute but impossible "Book," which might embody his French solution to a radically new poetical language, and the *Angelus Novus* of a pure language, a "new angel" similar to the figure that Walter Benjamin evokes after Klee's painting, an angel who can see the chain of historical events as "one single catastrophe which keeps piling wreckage upon wreckage." And the storm blowing from Paradise "propels him into the future with his back turned, while the pile of debris before him grows skywards."[26] Mallarmé could have concurred with Benjamin that this storm is identical to a doubtful "Progress," and he had to await the last gasp of his fateful "croup" to meet his own ghost—a specter suddenly speaking all languages at once, without him.

Conclusion: Toward a Ghostlier Futurity

When he died, Mallarmé was conscious that he left "no legacy": no son (since the boy had died), no daughter (although she was still alive), no heir could take up the project. The last letter written for his family, between two horrible seizures, stresses the desperate character of this past futurity. Alluding to the "half-centenarian heap of notes" that he alone could have deciphered or used, Mallarmé advocates utter destruction: "Burn, therefore; there is no literary heritage there, my poor children. . . . Believe that it was to be very beautiful" (*C*, 642). Nevertheless, the gesture leaves us with the task of rethinking his poetics of chance: *Un coup de dés jamais n'abolira le hasard, A Throw of the Dice Will Never Abolish Chance.* The grammatical link between "Never" and the future points toward an endless calculation of chance. So much will have always already depended upon the chance echoes in the rhymes provided by a given language, rhymes that are then yoked together in a new type of ideality. Such an ideality supposes that one forgets the time it takes to read or even to write the "Book." This was, after all, Joyce's idea of an "ideal reader" suffering from an "ideal insomnia"—a reader who was expected to devote his or her entire life to the reading of the Book.[27]

Joyce, the modern semiotics of Eco, and Pascal would agree on a crucial point: that there exists not just a "good" reader but an "ideal" reader—to be constructed—and that the concept is intimately bound with the text's specific futurity. Pascal's ideal player or ideal hermeneute confirms the ideality of the reader, a reader functioning as the "faithful steward" of textual economy. However, with Mallarmé and perhaps Derrida, such a perfect adequation of speed with writing has become all but impossible. My belief is that we cannot help reading too fast or too slowly, just like Luke's "unjust steward." This forced speed, playing with strategic delays, should allow us to bypass an all-too-limited economy of textuality, and force us, in a daring wager or "risk," to venture the very future of language. Is this mere illusion, just a *Zukunftsmusik*? Such a conceptual crux seems to be evoked again in a question posed by *Finnegans Wake*: "The mujic of the footure on the barbarihams of the bashed?"[28] Is this once more the anthem of a "music of the future"—a *Zukunftsmusik*: meaning in German empty promises, willful delusions, illusions created by deception or wishful thinking—played with the barbaric instruments (the barrel organs / *orgues de barbarie*) of the past? Or are the "new men" allegedly created by the Soviet revolution a new avatar of the Barbarians of the past? Whatever our doubts may be, Joyce never seems to have questioned the prophetic nature of his book. He sent a letter to E. Jolas early in 1940, at the time of the Russian invasion of Finland: "The most curious comment I have received on the book is a symbolical one from Helsinki, where, as foretold by the prophet, the Finn again wake, and volunteer Buckleys are running from all sides to shoot that Russian general."[29]

In the absence of any real solution—of a Mallarméan martingale magically providing a key to futurity's hazards—to all the aporetic disjunctures between the *to come* and the *future* I have called up, I would like to conclude by quoting from a book by a young French poet, Olivier Cadiot. The title of his recent collection of experimental prose and poetry, *Futur, ancien, fugitif* (Future, ancient, fugitive), should help clarify my use of the *futur*. It could also be said to develop the promise implicit in Rimbaud's cryptic allusions to the "ghosts of the future nocturnal luxury" (*les fantômes du futur luxe nocturne*).[30] This curious poetic narrative that begins with a shipwreck and ends with "Zero-sum" is said to follow a general program. This could be the textual futurity promised to our still uncertain postmodernity:

> This book contains: the complete list of what you need to do when you are in exile. Precise advice about the making of simple objects. A retrospective view of

things that have taken place. A systematic manual of poetic exercises. A memento of table manners and polite usage. A rehabilitation of hidden memory. A description of different everyday lives. An analysis of potential recurrence. Observation techniques applying to people you know. A concentrate of individual sensations and their explanation. A method of one-voice dialogue. A plan to visit nature.[31]

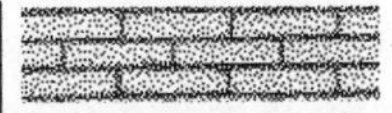

Elijah's Futures

Elisabeth Weber

In the frequently quoted first supplement to his "Theses on the Concept of History" Walter Benjamin writes:

> We know that the Jews were prohibited from investigating the future. The Torah and the prayers instruct them in remembrance, however. This stripped the future of its magic, to which all those succumb who turn to the soothsayers for enlightenment. This does not imply, however, that for the Jews the future turned into homogeneous, empty time. For every second of time was the strait gate through which the Messiah might enter.[1]

The hinge on which this gate moves, as Benjamin writes in his preparatory notes to the "Theses," is *Eingedenken*, "remembrance."[2] It is through remembrance that a fact understood as cause is transformed "posthumously, as it were," into a *historical* fact, "through events that may be separated from it by thousands of years." A historian who keeps this in mind "stops telling the sequence of events like the beads of a rosary. Instead, he grasps the constellation which his own era has formed with a definite earlier one"(*GS*, 263). *Eingedenken* thus happens as the constructive seizure of the constellation between two unique moments of the past and the present, a construction that is destructive insofar as it destroys the illusion of a "homogeneous course of history," of a chronological continuity of events in terms of causes and effects. For Benjamin, this seizure reflects the recognition of "a revolutionary chance in the fight for the oppressed past" (*GS*, 263), and consequently for a different future. The (messianic) interruption of history's so-called "continuum" replaces historicism's "'eternal' image of the past" with "a unique *experience* with the past" (*GS*, 262, my emphasis), which expresses the conviction that "even the dead will not be safe from the enemy if he wins. And this enemy has not ceased to be victorious" (*GS*, 255).

Significantly, Benjamin compares the materialist historian's work "to the method of the splitting of the atom [*Atomzertrümmerung*]," liberating the "enormous [or monstrous: *ungeheure*] forces of history, that lie bound in the 'once upon a time' of classical historicism."[3] However, it is not peaceful nuclear fission that Benjamin has in mind. Through remembrance, he writes, the historian ignites the "explosive" (*Sprengstoff*) that lies in the past.[4] Benjamin's belligerent tone is not softened in the affirmation that the materialist historian's work is an "attempt" or an "experiment in the technique of awakening," namely an "attempt to become aware of the dialectical, the Copernican revolution of remembrance."[5] For "the coming awakening stands like the wooden horse of the Greeks in the Troy of the dream."[6]

Benjamin's reflections on the relation between these two concepts and practices, history and remembrance, have deeply influenced recent discussions on the possible conflicts between the writing of history, on the one hand, and memory and testimony on the other—conflicts that have proven to be particularly acute in the field of "Holocaust Studies."[7] According to Benjamin,

> history is not only a science, it is no less a form of remembrance. What science has "established," remembrance can modify. Remembrance can transform the unfinished (happiness) into something finished, and the finished (suffering) into something unfinished. That is theology; but in remembrance we experience something that forbids us to conceive of history in fundamentally atheological terms, as little as we are allowed to try to write it in immediately theological concepts.[8]

If some of the outstanding figures participating in the debate on history and memory have warned against the use of history as a narrative of redemption,[9] none of them has put into doubt the power of disruption and awakening that memory can carry into history. It is legitimate to bring remembrance and memory close to each other in this context, since it is memory, or, in Saul Friedländer's terms, "deep memory,"[10] that prevents historiography from closure, just as for Benjamin, remembrance transforms "the finished (suffering)"—the suffering of the dead victims and of those who are still alive (a suffering treated by historiography as a thing of the past)—into "something unfinished": something that still awaits, if not "redemption," then testimony.

The following pages intend to trace back a practice of remembrance and awakening in Jacques Derrida's work. This work can indeed be read as a relentless attempt to bring the past and the present into a constellation, very much in Benjamin's sense of that word. I will venture to follow such traces of remembrance in Derrida's texts on meditations of mystics such as Meister Eckhart and Angelus Silesius.[11] The justification of this choice lies in a notion that in recent years has provoked, and not by chance, nothing less than *interpretations at war*,[12] namely the notion of "desire." As will be shown, desire is the unlocalizable heart of Derrida's remembrance of certain mystical texts. Desire could thus be one of the crystallization points for the constellating of past and present, that is, an explosive element whose interpretations would decide on the future, not only on the different shapes the future may take but on its very possibility.

I

In his text on the German mystic Angelus Silesius, "Post-Scriptum: Aporias, Ways and Voices,"[13] Derrida unfolds the notion of desire by starting with two questions: "Isn't it proper to desire to carry with it its own proper suspension, the death or the phantom of desire? To go toward the absolute other, isn't that the extreme tension of a desire that tries thereby to renounce its own proper vigor, its own proper movement, its own movement of appropriation?" (PS, 285 / *SN*, 19–20). According to Derrida, then, the "extreme tension" of desire is tantamount to a renunciation of its movement of mastery or domination. If, however, it can give up its movement of "appropriation," this is because its *raison d'être* does not lie in what it can appropriate, or possess. And if desire's goal is not to appropriate, this is because it does not need to appropriate, for it does not lack anything. As Derrida writes elsewhere: "Desire, of which no modern language on seduction, simulation, originary repetition, etc., will render breathless the untamed affirmation. Older than the beginning. Doesn't lack anything."[14] Just as the mystics' desire cannot be described in terms of lack and appropriation, neither can desire in general.

"Older than the beginning." The next step in "Post-Scriptum" pursues this an-archy: Describing the mystical desire as "the desire *of* God," Derrida notes the "equivocity" of this phrase, an equivocity that is "essential, signifying, decisive in its very undecidability," namely,

> the equivocity that the double genitive marks ("objective" and "subjective," even before the grammatical or ontological upsurge of a subject or an object), in other words, that of the origin and of the end of such a desire: does it come from God in us, from God for us, from us for God? And as we do not determine ourselves *before* this desire, as no relation to self can be sure of preceding it, to wit, of preceding a relation to the other, all reflection is caught in the genealogy of this genitive. (PS, 285 / *SN*, 19–20)

Not only, then, is it impossible to describe desire in terms of appropriation and domination, but it is also impossible to describe it in terms of origin, in terms of end (or goals), and thus in terms of possible objects for a subject: in short, it cannot be reduced to the economy of so-called object relations. Furthermore, if "we do not determine ourselves *before* this desire," and if all reflection is caught, as Derrida affirms, in the genealogy of this strange genitive, then remembrance is caught there too. This entanglement necessarily affects the three dimensions of the relation to the other that define remembrance: the other as radically past and radically other in death (even the dead are not safe); the relation to the other as a still-open past (remembrance may intervene radically and transform what had seemed to be "finished," *abgeschlossen*); and the relation to the other as unpredictable future (remembrance may activate the hinge of the strait gate through which the messiah might arrive to interrupt the course of history).

This desire—before which, according to Derrida, we do not determine ourselves—is, strictly speaking, the desire of nothing. Angelus Silesius's texts, for example, as quoted in "Post-Scriptum," insist: "To become Nothing is to become God" (PS, 289), and "*One must go beyond God. . . .* What should my quest then be? I must beyond God into a desert flee" (PS, 298). In a similar vein, Meister Eckhart affirms: "Who are they who are thus equal? Those who are equal to nothing, they alone are equal to God. The divine being is equal to nothing."[15] And John of the Cross describes the path of the perfect spirit, the "path of Mount Carmel," in seven steps: "Nothing, nothing, nothing, nothing, nothing, nothing, and even on the Mount nothing."[16] Moreover, the desire of nothing does not leave its marks any less powerfully on women's mystical experience. Mechthild von Magdeburg states, "You must love the nothing [*das niht*] and flee the something (flee what is [*das iht*])";[17] and in one of her book's sections, *Von der verbranten minne* (About burned love), she implores: "Oh dear lord, have pity on the one who has burned here in the fire of your love and disappeared in your humility and has become nothing in all things."[18] The admirable Marguerite Porete, whose book was condemned as heretical by the ecclesiastic authorities and was burned a few months before the burning of Marguerite herself, entitled her work *The Mirror of Simple Souls Who Are Annihilated and Who Only Remain in the Will and Desire for Love.*[19] And Hadewijch of Brabant writes, "To be reduced to nothingness in Love is the most desirable thing I know." In one of her visions she sees herself being engulfed as a young eagle, an "eaglet," as she says, in the "abyss" of this desire of nothing, together with an older eagle,[20] who stands for the one whom Derrida himself calls a "compatriot," and in whose "traces" or "tracks" he writes his "Circumfession"—namely, Saint Augustine.[21]

As an articulation of the desire of nothing—the desire to desire nothing, the desire to become nothing, and thus to become nothing's desire—mystical language, especially in the form of "negative theology," "does not cease testing the very limits of language, and exemplarily those of propositional, theoretical, or constative language";[22] it tries to *exceed* "essence and language" (PS, 299), resulting in an "inexhaustible exhaustion" (PS, 295) of its discursive possibilities. At the same time, however, and for the same reason, the mystical text, as Derrida writes, would be "above all the most thinking, the most exacting, the most intractable experience of the 'essence' of language: a discourse on language . . . in which language and tongue speak of themselves and take note of this, that *Die Sprache spricht*" (PS, 299):

> In any case, negative theology would be nothing, very simply nothing, if this excess or this surplus (with regard to language) did not imprint some mark on

some singular events of language and did not leave some remains on the body of a tongue. . . .

—A corpus, in sum.

—Some trace remains right in this corpus, becomes . . . [the] survivance of an internal ontologicosemantic auto-destruction: there will have been absolute rarefaction, the desert will have taken place, nothing will have taken place but this place. . . . "God" "is" the name of this bottomless collapse, of this endless desertification of language. But the trace of this negative operation is inscribed *in* and *on* and *as* the *event.* (PS, 300)

The "divinity of God" is, according to Derrida, interpreted in these texts as nothing else than a "gift or desire of giving" (PS, 300). And although the space of the desert seems at first sight to be diametrically opposed to a place of giving, the two coincide in the notion of the desert, since it stands for the opening as such: of language, of desire, of giving. In sum, the name of God is conjugated "with the experience of place," the desert being a "figure of the pure place." But this "most intractable experience of language" leads Derrida to affirm that "figuration in general depends on this spatiality" of the pure place or the pure space, on this empty "locality of the word (*parole*)."[23] Figuration and, one could say, language in general depend on this pure spatiality. Language exposes this dependence in the most open terms, exposes it as its own desire, and, impatient with the insufficiency or the limits of its own *topoi*, it "orders" one to go where one cannot go, "there where it is impossible to go: over there, towards the name, towards the beyond-the-name *in* the name."[24] Derrida provides a "universalizing translation" (PS, 305) of this command: "To go where it is possible to go would not be a displacement or a decision, it would be the irresponsible unfolding of a program. The sole decision possible passes through the madness of the undecidable and the impossible: to go where (*wo, Ort, Wort*) it is impossible to go" (PS, 302 / *SN*, 63).

If, as Derrida writes a little further on, "the desire of God, God as the other name of desire, deals in the desert with radical atheism," and if "desert" is yet another name, "the other name, if not the proper place, of desire" (PS, 318 / *SN*, 103), then desire as such indicates the place or non-place where it is impossible to go. I will come back to this impossible but unavoidable (un)locality.

But first, what is *our* place in all this? There is no doubt that "we come *after the fact*; and the discursive possibilities of the *via negativa* are doubtless exhausted," but this is precisely, according to Derrida, "what remains for us to think" (PS, 294 / *SN*, 43). Toward the end, "Post-Scriptum" gives a hint of the extent or the scale of what "remains for us to think"; it hints that although we might "come after the fact"—an *après le fait* that is also an *après-coup*, a *Nachträglichkeit*, a deferred fact—the event for which the *via negativa* stands might be calling for us to reconsider it within the conditions of our present world, to rethink it, if not to reread its distant traces within our psychic economy: "Yes, the *via negativa* would perhaps today be the passage of the idiom into the most common desert, as the chance of law [*droit*] and of another treaty of universal peace (beyond what is today called international law, that thing very positive but still so tributary of the European concept of the State and of law, then so easy to arraign for particular States): the chance of a promise and of an announcement in any case" (PS, 319 / *SN*, 105). Thus Derrida acknowledges some link or some however distant affinity between these two deserts that appear at first sight extremely different, describing the second—"our own," as it were—as the dried-out formalism of "the poorest, most arid, in effect the most desertlike technoscientificity" (PS, 318 / *SN*, 103). It is this arid discourse that has become the universal tongue. It is at this point that our own present and that of the mystics might enter into a constellation. And at this point I want to add another thread of reflection.

II

In his *Ethics of Psychoanalysis*,[25] Lacan describes the discourse of modern science, "the kind that was born with Galileo," in terms of the "increasing power of symbolic mastery [that] has not stopped enlarging its field of operation since Galileo, has not stopped consuming around it any reference that would limit its scope to intuited data." By "allowing free rein to the play of the signifiers" (EE, 122), it has given rise to a science for which "the vault of the heavens no longer exists, and all the celestial bodies, which are the best reference point there, appear as if they could just as well not be there." Lacan refers here to Alexandre Koyré's analysis of the unification of terrestrial and heavenly physics accomplished by Copernicus, Galileo, and Newton, which resulted in the "destruction of the cosmos," the complementary "geometrization of space," and, in turn, the mathematization of nature and science.[26] As Koyré puts it: "Modern science broke down the barriers that separated the heavens and the earth. . . . It did this by substituting for our world of quality and sense perception, the world in which we live, and love, and die, another world—the world of quantity, of reified geometry, a world in which, though there is place for everything, there is no place for man."[27] With the destruction of the cosmos, with the unification of the *physica coelestis* and the *physica terrestris*, modern physics has opened the way for a discourse, in which, according to Lacan,

> we see revealed for the first time the power of the signifier as such. That question is our very own. . . . The sudden, prodigious development of the power of the signifier, of the discourse that emerged from the little letters of mathematics and that is distinct from all previously existing discourses, becomes an additional alienation . . . insofar as it is a discourse that by reason of its structure forgets nothing. . . . At a certain moment in time, man learned to emit and place the discourse of mathematics into circulation, in the real as well as in the world, and that discourse cannot function unless nothing is forgotten. It only takes a little signifying chain to begin to function based on this principle, for things to move forward as if they were functioning by themselves. So much so that we even wonder if the discourse of physics, as engendered by the omnipotence of the signifier, will reach the point of the integration of nature or its disintegration. (EE, 236)

This discourse forgets nothing, which also means that it forgets the nothing, the "fundamental omission in which the subject is situated" (EE, 236). This "fundamental omission," however, has everything to do with the "peripeties" out of which modern science itself was born: "science, if one looks at it closely, has no memory. Once constituted, it forgets the circuitous path by which it came into being; otherwise stated, it forgets the dimension of truth that psychoanalysis seriously puts to work."[28]

In this new universe there is "no place for man," as Koyré states in his humanistic terminology, because the decentering effected by science is tantamount to the destruction of the concept of "man." Consequently, for Lacan, the notion of "human sciences" is a misnomer: "There is no such thing as a science of man, because science's man does not exist, only its subject does."[29] It is crucial to keep in mind that Lacan analyzes this situation without nostalgia, since psychoanalysis cannot be thought of outside the parameters introduced by modern science.[30] The subject of science is the subject of psychoanalysis, the subject of the signifier. As such, it is located at the heart of difference, at the "nexus," as Lacan writes, of the specific difference between modern science and all that had been called "science" before: "One thing is certain: if the subject is truly there, at the nexus of that difference [*le noeud de la différence*], all humanist references become superfluous in science, the subject cutting them short."[31] One inherent consequence of a subject located at the node of difference in general and of the specific difference just mentioned is, as Wolf Kittler states, the "shift from determinism to probability."[32] Kittler notes further, "No one had ever dreamed of applying what Pascal called the geometry of chance in order to describe the physical world, because this world was not supposed to be and operate just like a game of chance."[33] When Lacan, in his lecture "Psychoanalysis and Cybernetics," mentions the replacement of a "science of what is found at the same place" by "the science of the combination of places as such,"[34] he explicitly refers to game theory, and continues:

> I've told you how the entire movement of the theory converges on a binary symbol, on the fact that anything can be written in terms of 0 and 1. What else is needed before what we call cybernetics can appear in the world? It has to function in the real, independently of any subjectivity. This science of empty places, of encounters in and of themselves [*cette science des places vides, des rencontres en tant que telles*] has to be combined, has to be totalised and has to start functioning all by itself.[35]

But if modern science culminates in a "science of empty places," what is being forgotten? Before addressing this issue, let me take a step back to mystical experience. In one of his sermons Meister Eckhart voices a question his listeners doubtlessly asked numerous times:

> If a man is in such a state of pure nothingness, is it not better to do something to beguile the gloom and desolation, such as praying or listening to sermons or doing something else that is virtuous, so as to help himself?

> No, be sure of this. Absolute stillness for as long as possible is best of all for you. . . . Do not imagine that God is like a human carpenter, who works or not as he likes, who can do or leave undone as he wishes. It is different with God: as and when God finds you ready, He has to act, to overflow into you, just as when the air is clear and pure the sun has to burst forth and cannot refrain. . . . You should know, God cannot leave anything void or unfilled, God and nature cannot endure that anything should be empty or void. . . . If there were anything empty under heaven, whatever it might be, great or small, the heavens would either draw it up to themselves or else, bending down, would have to fill it with themselves. God, the master of nature, will not tolerate any empty place.[36] Therefore, stand still and do not waver from your emptiness.[37]

Nature does not tolerate anything empty, and neither does God. This, then, is precisely how one can *force* God to enter the soul: through its emptiness. God will hasten, and *cannot but* hasten, toward such an empty soul in order to fill it. He cannot resist the call of the emptiness of a speaking being, an emptiness that originates in his or her inscription into language, into the signifying chain. Referring to Heidegger's description of the vase in his essay "The Thing," Lacan takes the vase as the signifier in epitome: "It creates the void and thereby introduces the possibility of filling it. Emptiness and fullness are introduced into a world that by itself knows not of them."[38] The signifier is what introduces emptiness, a gap or a hole in the real (EE, 121). Against the Aristotelian philosophy that only conceives of things as made of matter—nothing can be made from nothing—Lacan stresses, with Heidegger, that the potter creates the vase around emptiness, out of nothing, *ex nihilo*, starting with nothing.[39] The pursuit of this pure void, the desire of this emptiness or the desire of this desert, the desire to cross the limit of that emptiness and the desert of this desire, would, according to Eckhart, hasten God's entry into the soul. And it is this very emptiness, this no-place, that the discourse of modern science not only has to forget but has to "foreclose," as it does by attempting to "suture" the subject.

Before addressing the issue of the subject's "suture," let me recall a few points concerning the concept of foreclosure, which translates Freud's *Verwerfung*. According to Lacan, "foreclosure" entails the exclusion of something that will return from without, as real[40] (psychotic hallucinations exemplify such a return from without). More precisely, this exclusion from the subject "constitutes the real as the domain that subsists outside of symbolisation."[41] In other words, "*Verwerfung*, foreclosure, cuts off every manifestation of the symbolic order," and most significantly, it cuts off a primordial *Bejahung*, or affirmation, that Freud "poses as a necessary precedent for any possible application of *Verneinung* (negation),"[42] the latter being a preferred "way of taking cognizance of what is repressed [*verdrängt*]."[43] To speak with Franz Rosenzweig, whom Derrida quotes in his "Nombre de oui" (Number of yes), his homage to the scholar of psychoanalysis and mysticism Michel de Certeau, foreclosure would cut off the *Ja*, the *Yes*, as the original word (*Urwort*) that *opens* language and thereby exceeds it.[44] As Samuel Weber puts it, "*Verwerfung* differs from repression in that it leaves no traces from which future symbolization could be structured, but simply a hole, a gap in the symbolical or, more precisely, a rent in the Symbolical."[45] If the primordial affirmation bears, as Lacan asserts, on the signifier, then foreclosure is precisely the "foreclosure of the signifier."[46] It is thus highly significant to note, with Derrida, that if mystical discourse tends to practice the self-abolition of discourse in a "sweet rage against language" (PS, 303 / *SN*, 63), its postulate is nonetheless an "irreducible and essential infinity of affirmation, of 'yes.'"[47] From a Heideggerian perspective, Lacan reads Freud's primordial affirmation as the "primordial condition that something of the real comes to offer itself to the revelation of being" (*la condition primordiale pour que du réel quelque chose vienne à s'offrir à la révélation de l'être*), whereas foreclosure cuts off this possibility, which is one of an "opening towards being" (*ouverture à l'être*).[48]

It is the very emptiness of this "opening towards being" that the discourse of modern physics tends to foreclose. However, at the moment it does so, it also reveals something of this fundamental emptiness. For just when we "wonder" whether, to quote Lacan again, "the discourse of physics, as engendered by the omnipotence of the signifier, will reach the point of the integration of nature or its disintegration" (EE, 236), we find "the revelation of the decisive and original character of the place where human desire is situated in the relationship of man to the signifier." *Our* question, *today*, is: "Should this relationship be destroyed?" (EE, 236). Lacan continues:

> It is because the movement of desire is in the process of crossing the line of a kind of unveiling that the advent of the Freudian notion of the death drive is

meaningful for us. . . . It is a question for the here and now, and not *ad aeternum*. . . . The question is raised at the level of the relationship of the human being to the signifier as such, to the extent that at the level of the signifier every cycle of being may be called into question, including life in its movement of loss and return. (EE, 236)

Earlier, Lacan had commented: "in the end what is expressed for us in the energy/matter equivalence is that one final day we may find that the whole texture of appearance has been rent apart, starting from the gap we have introduced there; the whole thing might just disappear" (EE, 122).

We have known since the first explosion of what Lacan refers to as "the absolute weapon" (EE, 104) that this is not an insane apocalyptic fantasy but the possibility of a destruction so absolute that no trace of that destruction would be left. To put the Lacanian argument in a nutshell, one could say that modern science occupies the very place of desire (EE, 325), which is not a specific place but the pure spatiality mentioned earlier, the emptiness, the nothing introduced by the signifier. It forecloses the fact that desire is in its heart, as it were—desire of nothing, desire of that pure exposition to the other that cannot be reduced to a specific goal, object, or satisfaction. If the signifier introduces a gap into the real, opening thereby the space for the metonymy of desire, the foreclosure of the signifier introduces a rent into the symbolic, a rent that tears the world apart (as, literally, in the individual psychotic experience, in hallucinations). On the level of the discourse of the community, modern science, occupying that empty space of desire but at the same time foreclosing it, threatens to tear the world apart, "the world" understood in ontological, phenomenological, or scientific terms, as well as, to speak with Heidegger, in terms of a "vulgar understanding."

It should, however, be emphasized that Lacan's perspective is not antiscientific.[49] For him, the subject correlates with science, although in an "antinomial" way, since science "turns out to be *defined* by the deadlocked endeavor to suture the subject." The "logical form" of the knowledge communicated by science "*includes* a mode of communication which sutures the subject knowledge implies."[50] In the same text, "Science and Truth," Lacan formulates the same statement from the perspective of his own science, psychoanalysis: "our science's prodigious fecundity" needs to be "examined in relation to the fact, sustaining science, that science doesn't want-to-know-anything about the truth as cause. You may recognize therein my formula for *Verwerfung* or foreclosure."[51] An attempt at "suturing" the subject thus corresponds to a foreclosure of the "truth as cause." As Bruce Fink states: "Science 'sutures' the subject, that is, neglects the subject, excluding the latter from its field" because "the speaking subject is considered irrelevant to the field. . . . What distinguishes psychoanalysis from the sciences is that it takes into account the cause, and the subject in his or her libidinal relation to the cause."[52] This cause is the cause of desire: in science, on the one hand, "the effect [*l'incidence*] of the truth as cause . . . must needs be recognized in its guise as formal cause"; in psychoanalysis, on the other hand, one "emphasizes the guise of material cause, a fact that qualifies its originality in science. This material cause is truly the form of impact [*l'incidence*] of the signifier as I define it" (ST, 22, trans. modified / SV, 875). In Wolf Kittler's words: "Psychoanalysis reveals the reverse of science, which is the material side of mathematical formulas and formalisms. The truth of this matter and, therefore, of any possible signifying effect, however, is sexual difference, which is to say that sexual difference as such cannot be written down, because it is the unsolvable question, on which the very possibility of writing depends."[53] Therefore, desire has no object; "it has a cause," as Fink notes, "a cause that brings it into being."[54]

This cause—which simultaneously determines and decenters the subject, introducing into it an unbridgeable "gap," the space of nothingness—cannot be taken into account by the discourse of the modern sciences. But science is nonetheless deeply—and structurally—haunted by it:

> Throughout this historical period the desire of man, which has been felt, anesthetized, put to sleep by moralists, domesticated by educators, betrayed by the academies, has quite simply taken refuge or been repressed in that most subtle and blindest of passions, as the story of Oedipus shows, the passion for knowledge. That's the passion that is currently going great guns and is far from having said its last word. (EE, 324)

In spite of the clear Heideggerian influence on Lacan's *Ethics*, it would be wrong to say that for Lacan as for Heidegger "science does not think" (*Die Wissenschaft denkt nicht*). It *does* think, and actually thinks more than its subjects, since it carries its secret host, desire—to which it offers refuge—to its very limits. Desire is realized today in the form of modern physics, which, "determined" by the foreclosure of desire's cause, the foreclosure of nothing, approaches this "nothing" literally "going great guns." For "what is foreclosed in the symbolic reappears in the real" (EE, 131).

If the "massive destruction" that our century has witnessed "seems to us to be an inexplicable accident, a resurgence of savagery" (EE, 235), we should remind ourselves with Benjamin that the "astonishment that the things we are experiencing are 'still' possible in the twentieth century is *not* philosophical. This amazement is not the beginning of knowledge—unless it is the knowledge that the view of history which gives rise to it is untenable."[55] The view of history that gives rise to such astonishment is untenable not only because it subscribes to the idea of the imperturbable advance of progress toward a better future but also because it ignores the fact that the "massive destruction" of our century is "necessarily linked to the leading edge of our discourse [*l'avancée de notre discours*]" (EE, 235 / EF, 276), "our discourse" designating here the "discourse of the community, of the general good," carrying in itself the effects of science (EE, 236). This discourse pursues in the real what is foreclosed, not repressed, in the symbolic: the desire of nothing in its ambiguous genitive, monstrous and absolutely terrifying in the deformed reappearance of its foreclosure. Desire would then be our question, a question for here and now, and not *ad aeternum*, insofar as the foreclosure of this question has the potential, and already the reality, of disastrous consequences.

III

But let me take a step back. As Derrida's "Post-Scriptum" states in a passage mentioned earlier, mystical discourse tends to practice the self-abolition of discourse in a "sweet rage against language" (PS, 303 / *SN*, 63); yet its postulate remains an "irreducible and essential infinity of affirmation, of 'yes.'"[56] It is well known that many mystics had to face violent repression from the ecclesiastic authorities, "repression" in the psychoanalytic as well as the political sense. This repression, from the Crusades to the end of the thirteenth century,[57] went hand in hand with the growing appeal of mystical experience—an experience so widespread that the lay movement of the "Beguines," to which Hadewijch, Mechthild, and Marguerite belonged, has been termed the "first European women's movement."[58] But with the advent of the scientific revolution, something else may have happened to the repression of the mystics' experience. An "exigency of the symbolic," voiced in their discourse, could not be integrated into the discourse of a geometrized universe. The desired self-abolition of their discourse may have become readable in a new light with the ontological leveling of the hierarchy between heaven and earth. It may have become readable as a desire inhabited by the most radical finitude, as the relationship "to man to the extent that language demands of him that he realize the following, namely that he is not" (EE, 298). It may have become readable as the reiterated, irreducible, essential, infinite affirmation of finitude, of difference as such, of desire as such. The question may be posed as to whether this new readability itself revealed the limits of the mechanism of repression: with the impossibility of integrating the signifier of the mystics' language into the new scientific order, the "symbolizing compromise" or "symbolic mediation" constituted by repression[59] revealed itself to be impossible, making this signifier's foreclosure imperative.[60]

The self-abolition of discourse, of the signifying chain that is possible today, is, then, of another, although related, kind. The mystical self-abolition of language can be described as desire in the name of the name, desire of nothing in the name of the name. Obversely, the scientific tendency toward the abolition of discourse is a foreclosure of that desire and of its signifier—of the name of the name, the name in epitome. Nevertheless, that tendency is still an expression, however deformed, of a desire for the name. Expelled from the symbolic, this name threatens to return in the real. One of Derrida's "seven missiles, seven missives" in "No Apocalypse, Not Now" states exactly this: "The name of nuclear war is the name of the first war which can be fought in the name of the name alone, that is, of everything and of nothing":[61]

> This war would be waged in the name of something, whose name, in this logic of total destruction, can no longer be borne, transmitted, inherited by anything living, that name in the name of which war would take place would be the name of nothing, it would be the pure name, the "naked name." We think now the nakedness of the name. That war would be the first and the last war in the name

of the name, with only the non-name of "name." It would be a war without a name, a nameless war, for it would no longer share even the name of war with other events of the same type, of the same family, these small, finished wars whose memory and monuments we guard. Beyond all genealogy, a nameless war in the name of the name. That would be the End and the Revelation of the name itself, the Apocalypse of the Name. *Now*: End and Revelation of the Name. *This is* the Apocalypse: Name. *This is*: strange present, now. We are there. In a certain way we have always been, and we think it, even if we don't know it. But we are not there yet, *not now*. (NC, 30–31 / NA, 384–85)

We have always been there, in the pure spatiality, the nothing of the name, but the knowledge of it, the practice and the desire of it, have been repressed. For it is impossible to be in nothing, impossible to be in the purity of desire, given that *pure* desire is nothing other than "the pure and simple desire of death as such."[62] We have always been there without being there. But the foreclosure of that pure space is particularly *our* question. That question has become ours, *now*, as if it had become readable, *for us*. Confronted with the possibility that the "breaking of the mirror would be, finally, through an act of language, the very occurrence of nuclear war," we have to face the question voiced by Derrida: "Who can swear that our unconscious is not expecting this? dreaming of it, desiring it?" (NC, 23 / NA, 370). "The hypothesis of this total destruction watches over deconstruction, it guides its footsteps; it becomes possible to recognize, in the light, so to speak, of that hypothesis, of that fantasy, or phantasm, the characteristic structures and historicity of the discourses, strategies, texts, or institutions to be deconstructed" (NC, 27 / NA, 377). This is why Derrida's work was earlier referred to as a practice of remembrance and awakening. For the realization, in every sense of that word, of what is at the heart of desire will be an awakening—revealing desire as an explosive element whose interpretations decide on the mere possibility of the future.

IV

Language orders us, as we have seen, to go where it is impossible to go; desire indicates the place or nonplace where it is impossible to go. The crossing of a borderline, the crossing of limits, is thus inscribed in both: according to Lacan, "it is always through some beneficial crossing of the limit that man experiences his desire" (EE, 309 / EF, 357), for the subject's desire cannot place itself elsewhere than within the "space" of the "desire of the Other."[63] As Lacan affirmed in his seminar in 1972, one of the limits that mystics such as Hadewijch of Brabant, Teresa of Avila, and John of the Cross explore is the crossing beyond what he calls the "phallic function." It is this crossing that he describes as a "*jouissance* which one experiences and knows nothing of" and "which puts us on the path of ex-istance."[64] This could be called the path of our "being held into nothing" (as Heidegger calls it in "What Is Metaphysics?" before diagnosing the "denegation," *Verneinung*, with which the public sphere responds to this nothing).[65] If for Lacan desire, and even the outline of a theory of desire, is inscribed more than anywhere else in the mystical experience,[66] it is because such experience respects this nothing (EE, 130), its emptiness. Many texts of the mystics can be described in the terms that Derrida uses to describe desire: as the "song of an immortality without proof, prayer without religion, tears."[67] They could also repeat the following affirmation by Benjamin: "My thinking is to theology what the blotting paper is to ink. It is entirely soaked with it. However, if the blotting paper had its own way, nothing of what is written would be left."[68]

In concluding,[69] I want to make a last step back to the very beginning. What would "Elijah's futures" be in this context? In the Jewish tradition, Elijah participates in all kinds of discussions, appears in an unexpected way throughout the Talmud and the centuries. One could say that he stands for the question, for the insistence of the question that will not be brought to a close by any answer—and as such, the question is a figure of desire.[70] Moreover, as Derrida notes in "Circumfession" (the precursor to "Le livre d'Élie," "The Book of Elijah," planned since 1976), Elijah is "the most 'eschatological' and thus the most awaited of the prophets." Since he had "condemned the Israelites for breaking the alliance, God supposedly . . . appointed him to be present at each circumcision as at the renewal of the alliance." In the Bible, the "guardian of circumcision"[71] is mentioned several times as frequenting Mount Carmel. As Derrida notes in quoting Michel de Certeau, the ascent to this "Mount" signifies the pursuit of the "science of circumcision,"[72] which can be called, in the perspective of the mystics as well as from the psychoanalytical standpoint, a science of desire. It is of course not by chance that Elijah is one of the prophets who lived for some time in the desert, and that John of the

Cross gave the title "The Ascent to Mount Carmel" to one of his compositions. "This mountain," writes de Certeau, "is the silent foundation of the languages that crown its summit."[73]

Furthermore, Elijah is the one for whom a place and a glass of wine are reserved in each house during the Passover meal, the meal that commemorates the crossing of a borderline, of a limit. Elijah is thus the guardian of an alliance that requires the crossing of a borderline; he is the guardian of the inscription of a name. As Derrida writes: "This is what God's name always names, before or beyond other names: the trace of the singular event that will have rendered speech possible even before it turns itself back toward—in order to respond to—this first or last reference. . . . Language has started without us, in us and before us. This is what theology calls God, and it is necessary, it will have been necessary, to speak."[74]

Defying unilinear chronology, insisting on the recurrence of the question, Elijah might also be called the guardian of remembrance.

Remembrance transforms "the finished," such as the experience of the medieval mystics, into "something unfinished": something still awaiting to be deciphered together with the history of its foreclosure. In the context of Derrida's work, the writings of the mystics are brought into a constellation with the "present," constituting thereby, in Benjamin's words, an "experiment in the technique of awakening," an "attempt to become aware of the dialectical, the Copernican revolution of remembrance." The mystic's desire for nothing might become decipherable in the blinding light of today's possibility of total destruction, and of this century's catastrophes. To address the questions of these disasters, a revolutionary awakening, indeed, is required. If, as Derrida writes, the "hypothesis" of "total destruction watches over deconstruction" and "guides its footsteps," if, moreover, "it becomes possible to recognize, in the light, so to speak, of that hypothesis, of that fantasy, or phantasm, the characteristic structures and historicity of the discourses, strategies, texts, or institutions to be deconstructed" (NC, 27 / NA, 377), then the constellations that deconstruction performs demand to be read as repeated "experiments[s] in the technique of awakening." Its readers are challenged to awaken.

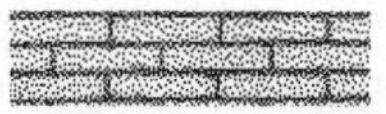

Notes

BENNINGTON, "RIP"

1. Paul de Man, *The Rhetoric of Romanticism* (New York: Columbia University Press, 1984), p. 81.

2. Plato, *Phaedo,* trans. Hugh Tredennick, in *The Collected Dialogues of Plato,* ed. Edith Hamilton and Huntington Cairns (Princeton, N.J.: Princeton University Press, 1961), 64a–b. See also 67d–e: "If a man has trained himself throughout his life to live in a state as close as possible to death, would it not be ridiculous for him to be distressed when death comes to him? . . . Then it is a fact, Simmias, that true philosophers make dying their profession [αποθνηισκειν μελετωσι: practice dying] and that to them of all men death is least alarming."

3. Ibid. 68c. The argument is that goodness is to be had not in an economic system of exchanges of emotions (so the nonphilosophical version of courage exchanges one fear for another, and that of temperance one pleasure for another), but in the absolute measure of wisdom, which is to be approached only through philosophy as the sort of living death we have seen. See also 82b–d. The application of a "logical" criterion to ethical questions might provide a further link to our later discussion of Kant.

4. Plato makes very clear the link between death and transcendence that Derrida insists on in, e.g., "Signature Event Context"; at *Phaedo* 79c–d, for instance, Plato states: "Did we not say some time ago that when the soul uses the instrumentality of the body for any inquiry, whether through sight or hearing or any other sense—because using the body implies using the senses—it is drawn away by the body into the realm of the variable, and loses its way and becomes

confused and dizzy, as though it were fuddled, through contact with things of a similar nature? . . . But when it investigates by itself, it passes into the realm of the pure and everlasting and immortal and changeless, and being of a kindred nature, when it is once independent and free from interference, consorts with it always and strays no longer, but remains, in that realm of the absolute, constant and invariable, through contact with beings of a similar nature. And this condition of the soul we call wisdom."

The earlier section I have been quoting has made it clear that this condition of the soul called wisdom is in fact attained only in death: "If [true philosophers] are thoroughly dissatisfied with the body, and long to have their souls independent of it, when this happens would it not be entirely unreasonable to be frightened and distressed? Would they not naturally be glad to set out for the place where there is a prospect of attaining the object of their lifelong desire—which is wisdom [φρονεσιζ]—and of escaping from an unwelcome association? Surely there are many who have chosen of their own free will to follow dead lovers and wives and sons to the next world, in the hope of seeing and meeting there the persons whom they loved. If this is so, will a true lover of wisdom who has firmly grasped this same conviction—that he will never attain to wisdom worthy of the name elsewhere than in the next world—will he be grieved at dying? Will he not be glad to make that journey? We must suppose so, my dear boy, that is, if he is a real philosopher, because then he will be of the firm belief that he will never find wisdom in all its purity in any other place. If this is so, would it not be quite unreasonable, as I said just now, for such a man to be afraid of death?" Plato, *Phaedo* 67e–68b.

5. G. W. F. Hegel, *Phenomenology of Spirit*, trans. A. V. Miller (Oxford: Oxford University Press, 1977), §32. That Socrates is proposing a general dialectics is clear from the passage, beginning at *Phaedo* 70d, establishing that the soul must have been alive before the body and must survive the body's death: "Let us see whether it is a necessary law that everything which has an opposite is generated from that opposite and from no other source."

6. This is a tempting reading, which would center on Socrates' past enunciation as reported in the "current" discourse by Phaedo to Echecrates, that enunciation stretching through the time of *arrêt de mort* between dawn and dusk of the day of execution. The *execution* itself of course occurs only after the much longer *arrêt de mort* incurred by the coincidence of the date of the pronunciation of Socrates' death sentence, his *arrêt de mort* in the usual sense, and the departure of the ritually garlanded Athenian ship for Delos.

7. This possibility (what I earlier called the "half-life" of philosophy) returns explicitly in Socrates' reconstruction of Cebes's objection to the doctrine of the immortality of the soul: "Indeed the very entrance [of the soul] into the human

body was, like the entrance of a disease, the beginning of its [the soul's] destruction; it lives this life in increasing weariness, and finally perishes in what we call death" (Plato, *Phaedo* 95d). Socrates' long refutation of this view, however it may convince Cebes, leads, precisely via the supposedly established immortality of the soul, to the intractable problem that that very immortality incurs the risk that the soul will carry evil (i.e., bodily contamination) with it into the next world, the existence of which has nonetheless been proven by appeal to the soul's essential *purity* with respect to just such bodily contamination. The subsequent fable about the souls of the dead being led to Hades by a guardian spirit provides us with another link to Kant via its motif of *guiding* that it entails (107e–108a). The fact that according to this fable souls cannot easily find their *own* way into the underworld spawns further aporias I cannot detail here.

8. Derrida is often accused of generating paradoxical formulations, as though the discovery of paradox were the end of deconstruction. But it seems to me he is still a traditional enough philosopher to see in paradox a challenge to thinking that must be taken up as a problem rather than held up for admiration. The "I am dead" deduction in *Speech and Phenomena*, for example, is less concerned merely to be striking and shocking than to show up an insuperable difficulty (or an ineradicable dogmatism) in the concept of the transcendental ego insofar as that concept allows and indeed entails that deduction. See Jacques Derrida, *Speech and Phenomena*, trans. David B. Allison (Evanston, Ill.: Northwestern University Press, 1973), p. 96.

9. " . . . the wandering of a thought faithful and attentive to the world irreducibly to come announcing itself [*qui s'annonce*: English words like 'looming' or 'brewing' might catch this better in some ways, but would lose the allusion to the annunciation] in the present, beyond the closure of knowledge. The future can only be anticipated in the form of absolute danger. It is what breaks absolutely with constituted normality and can therefore announce itself [*s'annoncer* again], *present* itself, only in the form of monstrosity" (Jacques Derrida, *De la Grammatologie* [Paris: Editions de Minuit, 1967], p. 14). Derrida has of course reflected on these formulations and the apocalyptic impression they make, in "On a Newly Arisen Apocalyptic Tone in Philosophy" (in *Raising the Tone in Philosophy: Late Essays by Immanuel Kant, Transformative Critique by Jacques Derrida*, ed. Peter Fenves, trans. J. Leavey, Jr. [Baltimore: The Johns Hopkins University Press, 1993]), in the context of a reading of Kant very germane to what I shall argue shortly, and in "How to Avoid Speaking" (in H. Coward and T. Foshay, eds., *Derrida and Negative Theology* [Albany: SUNY Press, 1992]). At the time I first wrote this paper, I had not read Derrida's "Résistances," where birth and death are explicitly linked to the concept of "analysis": "for what here doubles the *archeological* motif of analysis, is here an *eschatologi-*

cal movement, as if analysis carried extreme death and the last word, just as the archeological motif in view of the originary would be turned towards birth." Jacques Derrida, *Résistances: De la psychanalyse* (Paris: Galilée, 1996), p. 33.

10. Jacques Derrida, "La structure, le signe et le jeu dans le discours des sciences humaines," in his *L'écriture et la différence* (Paris: Seuil, 1967), p. 428.

11. Immanuel Kant, *Prolegomena to Any Future Metaphysics*, trans. Paul Carus (Indianapolis: Hackett, 1977), p. 94.

12. In *Aporias*, Derrida reminds us, in the context of a discussion of death, of Cicero's reflection on the Latin translation of the Greek *telos*, and the suggestion that it might advantageously be translated by the Latin *finis*. The whole of what I will suggest here might be summarized in the phrase "the end is the end." See Jacques Derrida, *Aporias*, trans. Thomas Dutoit (Stanford, Calif.: Stanford University Press, 1993), p. 5.

13. Especially Jacques Derrida, *Spectres de Marx: L'état de la dette, le travail du deuil et la nouvelle Internationale* (Paris: Galilée, 1993).

14. Immanuel Kant, *Critique of Pure Reason*, trans. Norman Kemp Smith (New York: Macmillan, 1929), A68–9 / B93–4.

15. See also Immanuel Kant, *Anthropology from a Pragmatic Point of View*, §42.

16. This attempt has at the very least many affinities with what Peter Fenves exposes about the notion of "tone" in Kant, and especially about how only attention to tone allows philosophy to avoid the twin deaths of peace and *Schwärmerei*. See *Raising the Tone of Philosophy: Late Essays by Immanuel Kant, Transformative Critique by Jacques Derrida*, ed. Peter Fenves, trans. J. Leavey, Jr. (Baltimore: The Johns Hopkins University Press, 1993).

17. Immanuel Kant, *Critique of Judgment*, trans. Werner S. Pluhar (Indianapolis: Hackett, 1987), intro., §2.

18. Ibid.

19. At Dartford, to the east of London, north-bound vehicles cross the Thames through a tunnel, whereas south-bound vehicles cross using a bridge over the same spot. This gives a working image of the relationships in Kant between theory and the practical.

20. Kant, *Critique of Judgment*, intro., §2.

21. "*Being*-law of law" is of course already too ontological a formulation of this situation, but the fact that there is no satisfactory non-ontologizing alternative—"law of law" being perhaps not ontological *enough*—tends to confirm Kant's point about the originality of the practical realm.

22. With the same proviso as in the previous note, we might say that this pre-prescription shows up as a sort of prior "Obey me!" which forms the being-prescription of the prescription.

23. As Peter Fenves has so brilliantly insisted; see his *A Peculiar Fate: Metaphysics and World-History in Kant* (Ithaca, N.Y.: Cornell University Press, 1991).

24. Kant, *Critique of Judgment*, §76. See, too, §64, which argues that the contingency of certain natural objects in terms of any mechanical explanation calls for a teleological explanation, and §67, which extends this logic to the whole of nature considered as a system. This antinomy of judgment between mechanical and teleological explanation is complicated by the fact that its *apparent* resolution (according to which one or the other type of explanation is adopted as appropriate or convenient by a judgment appealing to each only as a subjective maxim) tends to conceal another "resolution" whereby nature as a whole, considered as a totality, cannot be thought of as subject to the mechanical causal laws that are to be preferred for intra-natural explanation. This leaves the curious situation, which I shall explore elsewhere, in which teleological explanations are *necessary for necessity.*

25. In the third *Critique* Kant describes an object as monstrous "if by its magnitude it nullifies the purpose that constitutes its concept" (§26), in the immediate context of the remarks about the colossal. The latter remarks are the focus of the fourth part of the "Parergon" section of Derrida's *La vérité en peinture.*

26. See my very preliminary discussion of this relationship in Geoffrey Bennington, *Dudding: Des noms de Rousseau* (Paris: Galilée, 1991), pp. 143–48.

27. This would be the point at which, sometime in the future, to append an analysis of Heidegger's analysis of Kant's analysis of reading from §35 of the *Kantbuch.*

DAVIES, "THIS CONTRADICTION"

1. Martin Heidegger, *The Principle of Reason*, trans. R. Lillie (Bloomington: Indiana University Press, 1991); abbreviated hereafter as *PR.* The German edition is *Der Satz vom Grund* (Pfullingen: Verlag Günther Neske, 1957); abbreviated hereafter as *SG.* References to these works will be given in my text, with the English page numbers first, followed by a slash and the German pages. English quotations are from the Lillie translation.

2. Note that this subordination is not akin to the Kantian interpretation of Leibniz, where one identifies the types of knowledge defined and governed by the principles: for Kant, of course, the principle of contradiction provides the criterion for analyticity and thus for logic, the principle of (sufficient) reason for the synthetic *a priori* and thus for metaphysics. For Kant it is a matter of determining the particular realm over which each of the principles exerts its authority. In the case of logic and analytic knowledge, this exhausts what needs to be said about the principle of contradiction. For Heidegger, although the principle of reason is released from its equiprimordiality with the principle of contradiction

in order to facilitate a new investigation into the nature of metaphysics, this cannot be the last word on the principle of contradiction. It is a matter of the principle's subordination rather than its proper demarcation.

3. Aristotle, *Metaphysics*, trans. Hugh Tredennick, Loeb Classical Library (London: William Heinemann, 1933), γ 4.1006a. See also the text and translation in Appendix III of R. M. Dancy, *Sense and Contradiction: A Study in Aristotle* (Dordrecht: Reidel, 1975).

4. Although Heidegger wants to prevent the principle of contradiction from dictating how we hear and examine the principle of reason, notice that this is not quite the case when he treats Silesius's lines. As we noted above, they are first introduced as a contradiction of the principle of reason and so, in accordance with at least one reading of the principle of contradiction, as a problem for the principle of reason. If there is a way of bringing Silesius's "because" and the principle's "because" together, must it not also thereby count as a successful way of dealing with a contradiction?

5. Graham Priest, *Beyond the Limits of Thought* (Cambridge, Eng.: Cambridge University Press, 1995), p. 5.

6. Jacques Derrida, *Specters of Marx: The State of Debt, the Work of Mourning, and the New International*, trans. Peggy Kamuf (New York: Routledge, 1994), p. 35.

7. "Le *sans* s'auto-affecte de tout autre (*sans sans sans* . . .)." Jacques Derrida, *Parages* (Paris: Galilée, 1986), p. 92.

8. In this connection, recall the answer Derrida gives to John Llewelyn's question about the principle of identity. Llewelyn asks: "In your writings identity turns out again and again to be infected by difference. Would you say that this holds for the principle of identity itself, if P then P? Does this assert or otherwise present a self-possessed eternal validity or truth?" Derrida replies: "The identity of the principle of identity itself is, I wouldn't say 'contaminated,' but is constituted by difference—and this is not original on my part. Hegel, and Heidegger on Hegel, emphasised this point: the principle of identity implies difference. . . . My answer is yes. Difference is indispensable for the principle of identity itself; and then we have to follow the consequences." Jacques Derrida, "Some Questions and Responses," in *The Linguistics of Writing: Arguments Between Language and Literature*, ed. Nigel Farr, Derek Attridge, Alan Durant, and Colin MacCabe (Manchester: Manchester University Press, 1987), p. 258.

9. Compare this passage from Deleuze: "The force of paradoxes is that they are not contradictory; they rather allow us to be present at the genesis of the contradiction. The principle of contradiction is applicable to the real and the possible, but not to the impossible from which it derives." Gilles Deleuze, *The Logic of Sense*, trans. Mark Lester with Charles Stivale (New York: Columbia University Press, 1990), pp. 74–75.

10. Priest, *Beyond the Limits of Thought*, p. 244.

11. Arkady Plotnitsky, *Complementarity* (Durham, N.C.: Duke University Press, 1994), p. 279 n. 22.

12. Jacques Derrida, *Limited Inc* (Evanston, Ill.: Northwestern University Press, 1988), p. 116.

13. It is interesting, regarding this all-too-quick discussion of Derrida, to note a relatively recent willingness on Derrida's part to use the words "paradox" and "contradiction." *Aporias* opens with a sort of retrospective listing of contradictions, along with antinomy, paradox, etc. ("a plural logic of aporia [which will be] paradoxical enough"; Jacques Derrida, *Aporias*, trans. Thomas Dutoit [Stanford, Calif.: Stanford University Press, 1993], p. 20). Most revealingly, as we have said, in both *Aporias* and *Specters of Marx*, Derrida explicitly reinvokes the disarticulation of contradiction he finds in Blanchot. For many readers of those books, my take on this disarticulation must seem misguided. In *Specters of Marx*, although warning against the comfort of a philosophical paradoxy, the familiarity of the trope, Derrida appeals, if not quite to the paradox of the specter, then to something like the specter of paradox. Might not that "only ostensibly" best be thought of as "spectrally"? Is one of the specters of Marx not the specter of contradiction? The whole drama begins again; but this would be perhaps its most traditional staging—the principle warning against a specter, a specter haunting a principled and only putatively protected philosophy.

14. Martin Heidegger, *What Is Called Thinking?* trans. J. Glenn Gray (New York: Harper and Row, 1968), p. 154; the German edition is *Was Heißt Denken?* (Tübingen: Niemeyer, 1954), pp. 99–100.

15. Martin Heidegger, "What Is Metaphysics," in *Pathmarks*, ed. William McNeill (Cambridge, Eng.: Cambridge University Press, 1998), pp. 85–86; the German edition is *Wegmarken* (Frankfurt am Main: Vittorio Klostermann, 1978), pp. 107–8.

16. Ibid.

17. Heidegger does, however, speak of the principle as being "the most enigmatic [*der rätsellvollste*]" of principles (*PR*, 5 / *SG*, 16). Nor is it quite accurate to say that Heidegger never addresses the issue of self-reference. In the first lecture he admits that inquiries into the "principle-character" of principles are deemed to be best undertaken by logic and grammar, and "especially wherever it is a question of statements and principles in which all that matters is the content of the sentence, and above all wherever the content of the sentence refers to itself [*worauf der Satzinhalt selbst sich bezieht*]" (*PR*, 7 / *SG*, 19). Yet for this type of logical and grammatical observation, Heidegger claims that the self-referential sentence is simply immediately related to the object of its inquiry, as though here were an ideal proximity, self-evident and self-justifying. Our question thus remains: if the enigmatic quality of the principle of reason lies in the uncertainty

as to whether it refers to itself, why not describe this as the enigma of self-reference or as a self-referential paradox?

18. Heidegger, *What Is Called Thinking?*, p. 155.

19. Martin Heidegger, *Nietzsche*, vol. 3, ed. and trans. David Farrell Krell (San Francisco: Harper and Row, 1987), p. 112; the German edition is *Nietzsche*, vol. 1 (Pfullingen: Verlag Günther Neske, 1961), p. 603.

20. Ibid., pp. 111–12; in German, p. 603.

21. Martin Heidegger, *Being and Time*, trans. John Macquarrie and Edward Robinson (Oxford: Blackwell, 1962), p. 23; the German edition is *Sein und Zeit* (Tübingen: Niemeyer, 1979), p. 4.

22. G. W. F. Hegel, *Encyclopaedia Logic*, trans. T. F. Geraets, W. S. Suchting, and H. S. Harris (Indianapolis: Hackett, 1991), p. 190.

23. Ibid.

DERRIDA, "HISTORY OF THE LIE"

1. "The first problem, then, centers upon the question as to what constitutes a lie, for the person who utters a falsehood does not lie if he believes or, at least, is of the opinion that what he says is true [*si credit opinatur verum esse quod dicit*]. There is a distinction between belief and opinion. Sometimes, he who believes realizes that he does not understand that which he believes, although if he believes it very firmly he does not doubt at all about the matter which he realizes he does not understand. On the other hand, he who holds an opinion thinks that he knows what he does not know. Whoever gives expression to that which he holds either through belief or opinion does not lie even though the statement itself be false [*etiamsi falsum sit*]." "On Lying," chap. 3 in Saint Augustine, *Treatises on Various Subjects*, vol. 16 of *The Fathers of the Church*, ed. Roy J. Deferrari (Washington, D.C.: The Catholic University of America Press, 1952), pp. 54–55.

2. Ibid., chap. 5, p. 60.

3. Ibid., chap. 4, p. 57.

4. Hannah Arendt, "Truth and Politics," in her *Between Past and Future: Eight Exercises in Political Thought* (New York: Viking, 1961), pp. 227–28. Henceforth, references to this essay, abbreviated TP, will be included in my text.

5. Hannah Arendt, "Lying in Politics: Reflections on the Pentagon Papers," in her *Crises of the Republic* (New York: Harcourt, Brace, Jovanovich, 1972), pp. 3–4. Henceforth, references to this essay, abbreviated LP, will be included in my text.

6. Reiner Schürmann, *Heidegger on Being and Acting: From Principles to Anarchy*, trans. Christine-Marie Gros (Bloomington: Indiana University Press, 1990), p. 351 n. 194.

7. Immanuel Kant, "On a Supposed Right to Lie Because of Philanthropic Concerns," in *Grounding for the Metaphysics of Morals*, trans. James Ellington (Indianapolis: Hackett, 1993), p. 64, translation modified.

8. Ibid., pp. 64–65.

9. Ibid., p. 65.

10. Prime Minister Tomiichi Murayama, quoted in *New York Times*, Aug. 16, 1995, p. A1.

11. Jean-Pierre Chevènement, "Vichy, laver ou noyer la honte?" *Libération*, Aug. 7, 1995, p. 6.

12. Alexandre Koyré, "La fonction politique du mensonge moderne," *Rue Descartes*, no. 8/9 (Nov. 1993). Koyré's essay has also been reissued under its original title: *Réflexions sur le mensonge* (Paris: Allia, 1996).

13. Alexandre Koyré, "The Political Function of the Modern Lie," *Contemporary Jewish Record*, 8, no. 3 (June 1945): 290–91.

14. Ibid., p. 291.

15. Ibid., p. 291.

16. J. L. Austin, *How to Do Things with Words*, 2d ed. (Cambridge, Mass.: Harvard University Press, 1962), twelfth lecture, p. 150. If it were possible to refine things here a little, one would have to analyze closely Austin's distinctions between, for example, a promise made in bad faith, without the intention to fulfill it, and a lie. A bad-faith promise remains an effective promise, "but it is not a lie or a misstatement" (first lecture, p. 11).

17. Koyré, "Political Function of the Modern Lie," p. 291, Koyré's emphasis, translation modified.

18. Koyré, *Réflexions sur le mensonge*, p. 25.

19. "The story of the conflict between truth and politics is an old and complicated one, and nothing would be gained by simplification and moral denunciation." Arendt, TP, 229.

20. "Image" is the key word or major concept of all the analyses devoted to the political lie in our time ("lying image," "image makers," "propaganda image," "image" versus "event," etc.; Arendt, TP, 255–59). The word and concept of image here invite some confusion. The analysis of this transformation of the icon is merely sketched by Arendt, it seems to me. What is at stake—and she does not say this—is a mutation affecting the substitutive status of a substitute that there is a tendency to represent and accredit (for example, in the allegation of "live" broadcasts) no longer as, precisely, a representative, as a substitute-replacement-representative-referring, but as the "thing-itself" come to replace, in perception itself, the "thing-itself." The "thing-itself," assuming that it ever existed as such, then disappears forever without anyone ever dreaming of "demanding" it or requiring its difference. Not to mention framing, selection,

interpretation, and all the kinds of intervention that are now technically possible in a fraction of a second between recording and its reproduction-broadcast.

21. "To look upon politics from the perspective of truth, as I have done here, means to take one's stand outside the political realm" (Arendt, TP, 259). "The standpoint outside the political realm—outside the community to which we belong and the company of our peers—is clearly characterized as one of the various modes of being alone. Outstanding among the existential modes of truth-telling are the solitude of the philosopher, the isolation of the scientist and the artist, the impartiality of the historian and the judge, and the independence of the fact-finder, the witness, and the reporter. (This impartiality . . . is not acquired inside the political realm but is inherent in the position of the outsider required for such occupations)" (TP, 259–60). "It is quite natural that we become aware of the non-political and, potentially, even anti-political nature of truth—*Fiat veritas, et pereat mundus*—only in the event of conflict, and I have stressed up to now this side of the matter" (TP, 260).

22. This motif is very present from the first pages of "Lying in Politics." For example: "A characteristic of human action is that it always begins something new, and this does not mean that it is ever permitted to start *ab ovo,* to create *ex nihilo.* In order to make room for one's own action, something that was there before must be removed or destroyed, and things as they were before are changed. Such change would be impossible if we could not mentally remove ourselves from where we physically are located and *imagine* that things might as well be different from what they actually are. In other words, the deliberate denial of factual truth—the ability to lie—and the capacity to change facts—the ability to act—are interconnected; they owe their existence to the same source: imagination" (Arendt, LP, 5). One should of course relate this organizing concept of *imagination* to the discourse on the "image" to which we referred above.

23. For example, "the images, on the contrary, can always be explained and made plausible—this gives them their momentary advantage over factual truth—but they can never compete in stability with that which simply is because it happens to be thus and not otherwise" (Arendt, TP, 257–58). Or this even more optimistic statement: "Power, by its very nature, can never produce a substitute for the secure stability of factual reality, which, because it is past, has grown into a dimension beyond our reach. Facts assert themselves by being stubborn, and their fragility is oddly combined with great resiliency—the same irreversibility that is the hallmark of all human action" (TP, 258–59). In "Lying in Politics," Arendt writes with a valiant optimism: "No matter how large the tissue of falsehood that an experienced liar has to offer, it will never be large enough, even if he enlists the help of computers, to cover the immensity of factuality" (LP, 7). But assuming, *concesso non dato,* that one subscribes to these statements when they concern facts of the type "In August 1914, Germany

invaded Belgium"—an example that Arendt is very fond of—how can one still subscribe to them when the "facts" in question are already phenomena of performativo-mediatic discourses, structured by the simulacrum and the virtual, and incorporating their own interpretive moment? In truth, the question remains of how to determine the structure of the substitute, and here of the image in information and in narration today. The substitute-image still refers to the very thing it replaces, even to the "truth" of its revelation. As we pointed out above (note 20), the substitute of the "modern" simulacrum ("live television," for example) takes the place of what it replaces and destroys, even the reference to the alterity of what it replaces, by means of its selective and interpretive performativity, and by means of the absolute and indubitable "truth effect" that it produces. Here, then, is doubtless the space of an absolute lie that *can always* survive indefinitely without anyone ever knowing anything about it or without anyone being there any longer to know it or remember it. It *can always do so, perhaps*, but we must maintain this regime of the *perhaps* and this clause of possibility if we want to avoid effacing once again the history of the lie into a history of the truth, into a theoretical knowledge that comes under the authority of determinant judgments.

24. On this question of the *bebaios* as the value of stability and fiability founded on stability, of fiastability, see my *Politiques de l'amitié* (Paris: Galilée, 1994), passim.

25. In a note to "Truth and Politics" (p. 298 n. 5), Arendt does in fact allude to a "crucial passage" of the *Republic* (414c). She recalls correctly that *pseudos* can signify in Greek "fiction," "error," or "lie according to context." But other than the fact that she never mentions, to my knowledge, Plato's explicit treatise on the lie, the *Hippias Minor*, it is not certain that a context is ever decidable enough to become decisive, ever determinable enough to carry out the determination of meaning.

26. As cited in a very fine article by Michèle Sinapi, "Le mensonge officieux dans la correspondance Jérôme-Augustin" (*Rue Descartes*, no. 8/9 [1993]), to which I hope to return elsewhere and to which I am here referring too implicitly and schematically. Through this correspondence, the author of the article, who also finds inspiration in Pierre Legendre, analyzes the crossing of two heterogeneous traditions, that of a "conception of speech supported by an image ontology" and that of "Roman law," of "trial science," and a "new elaboration of notions of proof and cause" (p. 65).

FENVES, "OUT OF THE BLUE"

1. See Hermann Diels, *Die Fragmente der Vorsokratiker*, 3d ed. (Berlin: Weidmann, 1912), 1: 101, fragment A 123.

2. Jacques Derrida, *Aporias*, trans. Thomas Dutoit (Stanford, Calif.: Stanford University Press, 1993), p. 81.

3. See Martin Heidegger, *Heraklit*, in *Gesammelte Schriften* (Frankfurt am Main: Klostermann, 1979), 55: 130: "Die Vorstufe für die Ausbildung der Leidenschaft [at issue is *philei* and, in the next section, *eros*] für die Psychologie ist das Christentum." For an analysis of this passage, see Jacques Derrida, *Politics of Friendship*, trans. G. Collins (New York: Verso, 1997), pp. 242–45; the French edition is *Politiques de l'amitié* (Paris: Galilée, 1994), pp. 271–73.

4. See Immanuel Kant, *Religion innerhalb der Grenzen der bloßen Vernunft* (1793), reprinted in *Kants Gesammelte Schriften*, ed. Königliche preußischen [later, Deutsche] Akademie der Wissenschaften (Berlin: de Gruyter, 1900–), 6: 12. Hereafter, references to *Kants Gesammelte Schriften* will use the abbreviation Ak. and the volume and page numbers. All translations are my own. For a translation of the *Religion* that gives the pagination of the Akademie edition, see *Religion Within the Boundaries of Mere Reason*, trans. George di Giovanni, in Immanuel Kant, *Religion and Rational Theology*, ed. Allen Wood and George de Giovanni (Cambridge, Eng.: Cambridge University Press, 1996). For an earlier and sometimes more accurate translation, which, however, does not include the Akademie pagination, see *Religion Within the Limits of Reason Alone*, trans. Theodore Greene and Hoyt Hudson (1934; reprint, New York: Harper and Row, 1960).

5. Derrida analyzes the function of the "parerga" in the General Remark to the first section of *Religion Within the Limits of Reason Alone* in association with Kant's explication of the concept of *parergon* in terms of clothing in the *Critique of Judgment*. See Jacques Derrida, "Parergon," in *The Truth in Painting*, trans. Geoff Bennington and Ian McLeod (Chicago: University of Chicago Press, 1987), pp. 55–56; the French edition is *La verité en peinture* (Paris: Flammarion, 1978), pp. 64–66.

6. Kant sometimes speaks of a purely rational revelation; see, for example, his justification for the distinction between "external" and "inward" revelation in Immanuel Kant, *Vorlesungen über die philosophische Religionslehre*, ed. Karl Heinrich Ludwig Pölitz (Leipzig: Franz, 1817), p. 220. A copy of this rare volume is available in the Deering collection of Northwestern University Library.

7. Immanuel Kant, *Kritik der praktischen Vernunft* (*Critique of Practical Reason*), Ak., 5: 47. Kant speaks sometimes of the "sole fact of pure reason" (e.g., Ak., 5: 31), sometimes of the "fact, as it were, of pure reason" (e.g., Ak., 5: 47), and sometimes of "practical data of reason" (e.g., *Critique of Pure Reason*, B xxii and xviii).

8. See Jacques Derrida, *Force de loi: Le "fondement mystique de l'autorité"* (Paris: Galilée, 1994), esp. pp. 29–33.

9. See Immanuel Kant, *Vorlesung über Logik*, Ak., 9: 25. See also Kant's letter to Carl Friedrick Staüdlin of May 4, 1793; Ak., 11: 414.

10. Two of the most influential English-language discussions of Kant's thesis fault him for not sufficiently addressing the reality of diabolical evil: see John Silber, "The Ethical Significance of Kant's *Religion*," reprinted in Kant, *Religion Within the Limits of Reason Alone*, trans. Greene and Hudson, esp. cxxix–cxxxii; and Emil Fackenheim, "Kant and Radical Evil," *University of Toronto Quarterly*, 23 (1954): 339–53. The question of diabolical versus radical evil has recently been much discussed, often from widely diverging perspectives. See, for example, Jean-Luc Nancy, "Le katègorein de l'excès," in *L'impératif catégorique* (Paris: Flammarion, 1983), pp. 5–32; and Gordon Michalson, *Fallen Freedom* (Cambridge, Eng.: Cambridge University Press, 1990), esp. pp. 73–88. Slavoj Žižek concurs with Silber and Fackenheim on this point, without acknowledging their works, and without recognizing that the point has become a commonplace over the course of 40 years; see his essay "On Radical Evil and Related Matters," in *Tarrying with the Negative* (Durham, N.C.: Duke University Press, 1993), pp. 83–124. Žižek may "tarry with the negative," but he certainly does not stay long with the text of Kant. The chapter on radical evil begins with a breezy discussion of the antinomies of pure reason, in which Žižek attributes the following opinion to Kant: "The crucial point, however, is that this illusion of the universe is not something we can 'realistically' renounce but is necessary, unavoidable, if our experience is to retain its consistency: if I do not represent to myself objects in the world as entities that exist in themselves, if I do not conceive of what I perceive as a partial aspect of some reality-in-itself—if, say, I do not assume that the house I see now has its back side which corresponds to its front [this is an entirely different question from that of 'reality-in-itself' since the back of a house is an object of possible experience, not something that exists regardless of human modes of intuition]—then my perceptual field disintegrates into an inconsistent, meaningless mess" (p. 85). This review of the antinomies of pure reason, which confuses Kant's aim with the aim of those who seek a phenomenology of perception, introduces a discussion of radical evil that begins with this unpromising thesis: "According to Kant, the ultimate proof[!] of the presence, in the human being, of a positive counterforce to this tendency toward Good [Kant never speaks of a tendency toward Good] is the fact that the subject experiences morality in himself as an unbearable traumatic pressure which humiliates his self-esteem and self-love" (p. 95). When one writes the phrase "according to Kant," one should indicate where Kant expresses the subsequent opinion. That Kant does not understand self-esteem or even self-love (happiness) as evil is perhaps the easiest "doctrine" to be found in the *Religion*: one need only read the chapter concerning dispositions toward the good, which include precisely self-love and self-esteem. But what does Žižek take to be evil? "That is to say," he writes, "what, precisely, *is* Evil?" Kant has a precise answer to this question, but Žižek neither quotes it nor refers to it. Instead, he answers his own question with glib

psychologisms: "Evil is another name for the 'death-drive,' for the fixation on some Thing which derails our customary life-circuit" (p. 96). Whether this definition has anything to do with Kant's exposition of evil is doubtful.

11. This footnote has been overlooked by Henry Allison in his interpretation of Kant's thesis of radical evil; see Henry E. Allison, *Kant's Theory of Freedom* (Cambridge, Eng.: Cambridge University Press, 1990), pp. 146–61. Allison tries to resolve the aporias of Kant's text by supplementing it: "The claim [of radical evil], then, is to be taken as a priori; indeed, as a postulate [this is Allison's term, not Kant's], it must be synthetic a priori. Consequently, it requires some sort of deduction or justification; and since Kant fails to provide one, we must attempt to do so" (p. 155). If Kant omits something so seemingly important, one might ask *why* before assuming the philosopher has failed and needs help. Allison's hermeneutic nonchalance would be less troubling if he had not misdiagnosed the omissions in Kant's text and rushed in with a cure: "Instead of offering a 'formal proof' of the universality of the propensity to evil, he [Kant] simply asserts the necessity for such a proof is obviated by 'the multitude of crying examples which experience *of the actions* of men put before our eyes'. . . . In short, he seems to treat it as an unproblematic empirical generalization" (p. 154). But immediately before the sentence Allison quotes, Kant makes clear that he leaves the matter of empirical generalization to the only authoritative—that is, scientific—mode of addressing this question, namely "anthropological research" (Ak., 6: 25). His "generalization," in other words, is far from "unproblematic." And soon after the sentence Allison quotes, Kant writes: "even if the existence of this propensity to evil in human nature can be demonstrated by experiential proofs of the real opposition, in time, of man's elective will, such proofs do not teach us the essential character of that propensity or the ground of this opposition" (Ak., 6: 35)—which indicates just how problematic Kant understood the thesis of radical evil to be. So little does Kant "obviate" the necessity of a "formal proof" that he adds a footnote to the section from which Allison draws his quotation: "The proper proof of this sentence of condemnation by morally judging reason is to be found in the preceding section rather than in this one" (Ak., 6: 39). Finally, at the very end of the section in which Kant, according to Allison, thoughtlessly offers only an empirical generalization, he asks his readers to decide by themselves whether "everyone has his price" (Ak., 6: 38)—which makes any talk of "unproblematic empirical generalization" ludicrous.

12. See Gotthold Ephraim Lessing, "Über den Beweis des Geistes und der Kraft," in *Lessings Werke*, ed. Kurt Wölfel (Frankfurt am Main: Insel, 1967), 3: 307–12.

13. On the difficult problematic surrounding the term "addiction," see Jacques Derrida, "Rhétorique de la drogue," in *Points de suspension: Entretiens*, ed. Elisabeth Weber (Paris: Galilée, 1992), pp. 241–67; see also Avital Ronell,

Crack Wars: Literature, Addiction, Mania (Lincoln: University of Nebraska Press, 1992).

14. See Immanuel Kant, *Grundlegung zur Metaphysik der Sitten* (*Laying the Ground for the Metaphysics of Morals*), Ak., 4: 425–26.

15. See, for example, Goethe's spirited letter to Herder of June 7, 1793: "Kant required a long lifetime to purify his philosophical mantle of many impurities and prejudices. And now he has wantonly tainted [*beschlabbert*] it with the shameful stain [*Schandfleck*] of radical evil, in order that Christians, too, might be attracted to kiss its hem" (J. W. v. Goethe, *Goethes Briefe*, ed. K. R. Mandelkow [Hamburg: Wegner, 1964], 2: 166; cf. Fackenheim's discussion in "Kant and Radical Evil," p. 340). The question how this *Schandfleck* sullies the "purity" of Kant's "philosophical mantle" will occupy us below, but at least this much can be said here: Goethe is, as far as I know, the only one who saw Kant's thesis in terms of a "taint" (*Fleck*), and instead of reading this "spot" as an extreme moment in the very act of "purifying" a "philosophical mantle," he interpreted it in a psychological manner as a failure on Kant's part. And Goethe fails to relate the "philosophical mantle" that Kant cleaned to the "naked reason" (*bloßen Vernunft*) of Kant's title. A mere consideration of Kant's strangely modest *bloß* might have altered Goethe's image of the *Fleck* transmitted by the thesis of radical evil.

16. Aristotle, quoted in Immanuel Kant, *Metaphysik der Sitten* (*Metaphysics of Morals*), Ak., 6: 470. For an extensive discussion of Kant's attraction to this sentence—and the sentence itself—see Derrida, *Politics of Friendship*, pp. 252–63; in French, *Politiques de l'amitié*, pp. 282–94. For an analysis of Derrida's encounter with the vanishing figure of the friend in Kant, see my essay "Politics of Friendship—Once Again," *Eighteenth Century Studies*, 32 (Winter 1998–99): 133–55.

17. See Derrida's analysis of Kant's predicament in "Mochlos," in Jacques Derrida, *Logomachia*, ed. Richard Rand (Lincoln: University of Nebraska Press, 1992), p. 19 and passim. The standard account of Kant's interaction with the Prussian authorities is an essay by Wilhelm Dilthey, "Der Streit Kants mit der Zensur über das Recht freier Religionsforschung," *Archiv für Geschichte der Philosophie*, 3 (1890): 418–50; reprinted in Wilhelm Dilthey, *Gesammelte Schriften*, 2d ed. (Stuttgart: Vandenhoech und Ruprecht, 1959), 4: 285–309. A summary of the conflict can be found in George di Giovanni's introduction to his translation, Kant, *Religion and Rational Theology*, pp. 41–48.

18. See Schopenhauer's famous—or notorious—polemic against academic philosophy, "Über die Universitätsphilosophie," in the first volume of *Parerga und Paralipomena*, reprinted in Arthur Schopenhauer, *Sämtliche Werke*, ed. A. Hübscher (Wiesbaden: Brockhaus, 1972), 5: 149–210. This is what Schopenhauer taught Nietzsche: "A scholar can never become a philosopher; for even Kant was

unable to do so" ("Schopenhauer als Erzieher," in *Unzeitgemässige Betrachtungen*, reprinted in Arthur Schopenhauer, *Werke*, ed. Karl Schlechta [Frankfurt am Main: Ullstein, 1983], 1: 370, §7). Although neither Schopenhauer nor Nietzsche acknowledged it, the most rigorous attack on Kant's honesty takes place in Hegel's famous discussion of the hypocrisy at the heart of moral consciousness; see Hegel's *Grundlinien der Philosophie des Rechts*, reprinted in G. W. F. Hegel, *Werke*, ed. Eva Moldenhauer and Karl Markus Michel (Frankfurt am Main: Suhrkamp, 1970), 7: 265–86, §140. Hegel, in his analysis of the self-defeating and self-deceptive irony into which *Moralität* lapses, himself lapses into irony by bringing Kant's practical philosophy into close association with an action of Count Leopold von Stolberg, about whom Kant—without actually naming him—makes several ironic asides in "Von einem neuerdings erhobenen vornehmen Ton in der Philosophie" (Ak., 8: 394–95). A thorough analysis of Hegel's discussion of *Gewissen* as subjective self-certainty (*Gewißheit*) cannot be undertaken here, but it should be noted that the radical secrecy in which actions take place, according to Kant, not only makes such certainty impossible but likewise undoes "conscience" as anything but a *figure* of right, the *image* of a tribunal, never the tribunal *itself*. An analysis of Heidegger's dismissal, in *Being and Time*, of Kant's figuration of conscience would be of some importance here (see Martin Heidegger, *Sein und Zeit* [Tübingen: Niemeyer, 1979], p. 293), as would Derrida's understanding, or overhearing, throughout *The Post Card*, of Heidegger's "call of conscience" (see Jacques Derrida, *La carte postale* [Paris: Aubier-Flammarion, 1980]).

19. See Kant, *Metaphysik der Sitten*, "Tugendlehre" ("The Doctrine of Virtue"), §9, Ak., 6: 430. On the question whether an "inner lie" is even possible—or only a figural expression—see Jacques Derrida, "History of the Lie," in this volume.

20. For an analysis of another moment when Kant resorts to the word *Verstimmung*, a moment, like this one, that concerns secrecy and self-deception, see Jacques Derrida, "On a Newly Arisen Apocalyptic Tone in Philosophy," in *Raising the Tone in Philosophy: Late Essays by Immanuel Kant, Transformative Critique by Jacques Derrida*, ed. Peter Fenves, trans. J. Leavey, Jr. (Baltimore: The Johns Hopkins University Press, 1993), pp. 131–33; the French edition is *D'un ton apocalyptique adopté naguère en philosophie* (Paris: Galilée, 1983), pp. 67–69.

21. The origin of the old and still frequently used expression *blauen Dunst vormachen* (to generate blue vapor, fool, humbug, hoodwink, blow smoke in one's face) remains unclear, as befits its meaning; but there is nevertheless a general agreement that the sense of this expression owes much to performances of magicians, alchemical experimentation, and the intoxicating smoke of tobacco. According to Keith Spalding, "the blue mist produced by mediaeval entertainers during their conjuring tricks contributed to this phrase"; see his *Historical Dic-*

tionary of German Figurative Usage (Oxford: Blackwell, 1952), 1: 334. See also the entry on *Dunst* in *Deutsches Wörterbuch von Jacob und Wilhelm Grimm*, rev. ed., Akademie der Wissenschaften der DDR im Zusammenarbeit mit der Akademie der Wissenschaften zu Göttingen (Leipzig: Hirzel, 1982), 6: 1525: "einbildung, vortäuschung phantasiegebilde; oft verstärkt durch das adjektiv *blau*" (with citations from the fifteenth century onward); cf. *Duden: Redewendungen und sprichwörtliche Redensarten* (Mannheim: Dudenverlag, 1992), 12: 163. The blueness of the "blue vapor" opens up other dimensions of this expression, as Spalding indicates: "presumably the blueness of distance" contributes to the sense of the expression. Moreover, in certain other phrases (*blaue Ente*, *blauer Nebel*, and *blaues Märchen*, for example) "blue" indicates lying, deception, and invention. Finally, "blue" not only indicates indeterminateness and openness but also conjures up the closely related sense of something unusual, out of the ordinary, or exceptional, as in the expressions "once in a blue moon" and "out of the blue" (*aus blauer Luft*). For one of Kant's infrequent uses of "blue" as indicative of something indeterminate and thus "hazy," see the essay entitled "Verkündigung des nahen Abschlusses eines Traktats zum ewigen Frieden in der Philosophie" ("Announcement of a Near Conclusion of a Treaty for Eternal Peace in Philosophy"): "[critical philosophy] begins its conquest with the investigation of the faculty of human reason . . . and does not ratiocinate into the blue heavens [*ins Blaue hinein vernünftelt*] when discussion comes around to philosophemes that no possible experience could vouchsafe" (Ak., 8: 416).

22. Instead of faulting Kant for failing to recognize absolute evil (see note 10 above) or for failing to give a proper proof of his thesis (see note 11 above), it would be more fruitful to understand the lingering sense that Kant's somehow failed in the opening section of the *Religion* as a consequence of his willingness to treat too quickly the problem posed by placid conscience. A longer meditation on "conscience at rest" might perhaps have produced a thesis of radical evil approximating what Hannah Arendt would later call "the banality of evil"; see her *Eichmann in Jerusalem: A Report on the Banality of Evil*, rev. and enlarged ed. (New York: Penguin, 1965). The complexities of Arendt's engagement with Kant's *Religion Within the Limits of Reason Alone* are immense, as the modest term *report* in her title already indicates. See also note 40 below.

23. See especially Kant's first—and from the perspective of his previous *Critiques* rather unexpected—discussion of *Stimmung* in the *Critique of Judgment* (§21): "But if cognitions are to be communicated, then the mental state, that is, the mood [*Stimmung*] of the cognitive powers, that is required for cognition in general—namely, that proportion suitable for turning a presentation (by which an object is given to us) into cognition—must also be universally communicable. For this *Stimmung* is the subjective condition of cognition, and without it cognition could not arise" (Ak., 5: 238). On the fleeting moments in which the

Stimmung of moral receptivity makes itself felt and gives rise to an otherwise unaccountable sense of thanks and praise, see a footnote to §86 of the *Critique of Judgment* (*Kritik der Urteilskraft*, Ak., 5: 445–46).

24. See Kant, *Metaphysik der Sitten*, Ak., 7: 437. For an analysis of Kant's exposition of conscience in the *Metaphysics of Morals*, see Werner Hamacher, "The Promise of Interpretation," in *Premises: Essays on Literature and Philosophy from Kant to Celan*, trans. Peter Fenves (Cambridge, Mass.: Harvard University Press, 1996), pp. 103–6.

25. See, in particular, Kant's discussion of "negative quantities"—a concept he first introduced in an early essay by this name (Ak., 2: 165–204)—in relation to the question he pursues in the opening of the *Religion*: are human beings, considered as a species, good or evil? (Ak., 6: 23).

26. See Kant, *Metaphysik der Sitten*, Ak., 6: 232–33.

27. Kant uses the same image in another, closely related connection—the end of philosophy: "Lying ('from the father of lies, through which all evil has come into the world') is the actual foul spot on human nature" (Ak., 8: 422).

28. See especially Kant, *Metaphysik der Sitten*, Ak., 6: 436.

29. Quotations are my translations of Luther's translation of the Bible: *Die Bibel nach der Übersetzung Martin Luthers*, rev. ed. (Stuttgart: Deutsche Bibelgesellschaft, 1985). Kant, of course, would have known this translation: "Was sagen wir denn nun? Haben wir Juden einen Vorzug? Gar keinen. Denn wir haben soeben bewiesen, daß alle, Juden wie Griechen, unter der Sünde sind, wie geschrieben steht: 'Da ist keiner, der gerecht ist, auch nicht einer'" (Rom. 3:9–10).

30. See Kant's cautious use of the term "providence" (*Vorsehung*) in his "Idea for a Universal History with a Cosmopolitan Intention" ("Idee zu einer allgemeinen Geschichte im weltbürglicher Absicht," Ak., 8: 30). In "Toward Eternal Peace," Kant becomes even more cautious and decides that the term "providence" is not quite humble enough ("Zum ewigen Frieden," Ak., 8: 362).

31. See Kant's extraordinarily complex discussion of the problem of debt-resolution (absolution from guilt) in the subsection of the second part of the *Religion*, entitled "Difficulties That Stand in the Way of the Reality of This Idea [of humanity pleasing to God], and Their Solution" ("Schwierigkeiten gegen die Realität dieser Idee und Auflösung derselben," Ak., 6: 66–79). The greatest of these difficulties, as Kant himself asserts, arises from the undeniable fact that, even if someone manages to overcome insubordination by subordinating all actions to the law of freedom, "*he nevertheless started out from evil*, and this is a debt that is impossible for him to wipe out" (Ak., 6: 72). From the apparent impossibility of debt-resolution Kant proceeds to a tortuous exposition of the "Son of God" as a "vicarious substitute" for punishment. Precisely the same difficulty leads Hermann Cohen to rewrite the *Religion* in a way expressed in his

title, *Religion Within the Limits of Naked Reason as Religion of Reason from the Source of Judaism*—with the significant proviso that Cohen understands the difficulty as one of repentance, not absolution; see Hermann Cohen, *Die Religion der Vernunft aus den Quellen des Judentums* (Leipzig: Fock, 1919). From the perspective of these two equivalent but asymmetrical books on religion within the arena circumscribed by reason, it is worth renewing the thought Derrida initiated under the title "Interpretations at War: Kant the Jew, Kant the German," trans. Moshe Ron, *New Literary History*, 22 (Winter 1991): 39–95.

32. On this hesitancy, see Jacques Derrida, *Specters of Marx: The State of Debt, the Work of Mourning, and the New International*, trans. Peggy Kamuf (New York: Routledge, 1994), pp. 265–68; the French edition is *Spectres de Marx: L'état de la dette, le travail du deuil et la nouvelle Internationale* (Paris: Galilée, 1993), pp. 268–70.

33. In Kant's first treatise, he presents the moment of self-conscious enlightenment in terms of a dissipating cloud; see Immanuel Kant, *Allgemeine Naturgeschichte und Theorie des Himmels* (*Universal Natural History and Theory of the Heavens*), Ak., 1: 356–57. In his famous essay "Answer to the Question: What Is Enlightenment?" ("Beantwortung der Frage: Was ist Aufklärung," Ak., 8: 33–42), Kant keeps his distance from imagery of light breaking into a cloudy, indistinct, or otherwise unclear atmosphere.

34. The three texts I am about to discuss do not, of course, constitute a comprehensive list of Derrida's confrontations with Kant—far from it. They leave out not only Derrida's extensive analysis of the *Critique of Judgment* in *Truth and Painting* but also, among other texts, Derrida's interrogation of the "secret article" (*geheimer Artikel*) Kant appends to "Toward Eternal Peace" (Derrida, *Aporias*, pp. 84–86) and Derrida's incisive interpretation of certain passages in the second preface to the *Critique of Pure Reason* where Kant discusses the conditions under which geometry was first discovered; see Edmund Husserl, *L'origine de la géométrie*, trans. and intro. J. Derrida (Paris: Presses Universitaires de France, 1962), pp. 21–25. In all of these texts, Derrida is concerned with the motif of hiding.

35. Kant, "Von einem neuerdings erhobenen vornehmen Ton in der Philosophie" (Ak., 8: 405), quoted by Derrida, "On a Newly Arisen Apocalyptic Tone," pp. 143–44; in French, *D'un ton apocalyptique adopté naguère*, p. 56–57.

36. Derrida, "On a Newly Arisen Apocalyptic Tone," p. 143; in French, p. 54.

37. Jacques Derrida, *Passions* (Paris: Galilée, 1993), p. 56 and passim; abbreviated hereafter as *P*. For a translation, see "Passions: 'An Oblique Offering,'" in Jacques Derrida, *On the Name*, ed. Thomas Dutoit, trans. David Wood (Stanford, Calif.: Stanford University Press, 1995), pp. 3–31. All references in my text are to the French edition; all quotations are my translations.

38. By drawing attention to the question of "politeness" in relation to the

Kantian critique of practical reason, Derrida repeats one of the original gestures through which philosophy becomes "post-Kantian": Schiller's elucidation of a "grace" (*Anmut*) that exceeds every moral demand. See Friedrich Schiller, "Über Anmut und Würde," in *Über das Schöne und die Kunst* (Munich: Hanser, 1984), pp. 44–93. Schiller's essay is of particular importance in the context of *Religion Within the Limits of Reason Alone* because Kant devotes a long footnote in his chapter on radical evil to refuting it. As in Kant's response to Schlosser in "On a Newly Arisen Superior Tone in Philosophy"—and Kant seems, strangely enough, to have confused Schiller and Schlosser (see Ak., 23: 195)—in the *Religion*, too, Kant insists upon the absolute priority of practical reason over "aesthetic presentation": the voice of reason precedes and gives shape to the image of the goddess, and it is for this reason, according to Kant, that Heracles had to labor before he was allowed to become "Musagagete" (Ak., 6: 18–19).

39. Jacques Derrida, "Faith and Knowledge: The Two Sources of 'Religion' at the Limit of Reason Alone" (abbreviated hereafter as FK), trans. Sam Weber, in *Religion*, ed. J. Derrida and G. Vattimo (Stanford, Calif.: Stanford University Press, 1998), pp. 1–78. The French text is "Foi et savoir: Les deux sources de la 'religion' aux limites de la simple raison" (abbreviated hereafter as FS), in *La religion*, ed. Jacques Derrida and Gianni Vattimo (Paris: Seuil, 1996), pp. 9–86. Quotations from this text are from Weber's translation. References in my text give the English page numbers first, followed by a slash and the French pages.

40. "Acting well," as Derrida seeks to understand it, corresponds to a phenomenon to which Arendt devotes some attention in *The Human Condition*—the "extreme" phenomenon of "good works" or "good deeds"; see Hannah Arendt, *The Human Condition* (Chicago: University of Chicago Press, 1958), pp. 73–78. Good works or good deeds remain radically concealed: "Good deeds can never keep anybody company; they must be forgotten the moment they are done, because even memory will destroy their quality of being 'good.' . . . Good works, because they must be forgotten instantly, can never become part of the world; they come and go, leaving no trace. They are truly not of this world" (p. 76). Least of all can those who perform "good works" know that they do so or who they are. If the doing of good deeds is not therefore to "annihilate human existence altogether," this action—not the actor, however, who remains ignorant of acting well—must be graced with an otherworldly "witness" (p. 76). If, moreover, action as such is revelatory, as Arendt seeks to demonstrate, then "good deeds" are "performative contradictions" brought to perfection: acts that deny a fundamental trait of action. And if, finally, there is something constitutively good about action—and Arendt certainly suggests as much when she presents it under the rubric of the "miraculous" (p. 246)—then those actions that fully and finally correspond to the trait that helps define them not only nullify the world but entirely conceal themselves, "leaving no trace." All Derrida's inquiries into

the possibility, necessity, and impossibility not only of the "trace" but also, accordingly, of hospitality, friendship, giving, acting well, and "over-duty" (*Aporias*, p. 16) can perhaps be understood as further interrogations of "good works" and "good deeds"—and the self-concealment of goodness that might nevertheless leave a trace of itself in the uneasy vacillation of the "well" of "acting well" between "work" and "deed." Needless to say, both Arendt's and Derrida's interrogations of these matters—which in the inadequate vocabulary of traditional European moral philosophy fall under the category of supererogation—take place in the shadow of Kant's thesis of radical evil. The two never sound more alike than when addressing this thesis: just as Derrida says of radical evil, "We now know [that it] is not *one*, nor given once and for all, as though it were capable only of inaugurating figures or tropes of itself" (FK, 9 / FS, 18), so Arendt says that it is one of those "offenses . . . about whose nature so little is known, even to us who have been exposed to one of their rare outbursts on the public scene" (*Human Condition*, p. 241).

HAMACHER, "LINGUA AMISSA"

1. See Jacques Derrida, *Spectres de Marx: L'état de la dette, le travail du deuil et la nouvelle Internationale* (Paris: Galilée 1993), p. 165. The corresponding English passages from *Specters of Marx: The State of Debt, the Work of Mourning, and the New International*, trans. Peggy Kamuf (New York: Routledge, 1994), pp. 100–101, which I have modified, are as follows: "The specter is also, among other things, what one imagines, what one thinks one sees and which one projects—on an imaginary screen [*écran*] where there is nothing to see. Not even the screen sometimes, and a screen always has, at bottom [*au fond qu'il est*] a structure of disappearing apparition [*de l'apparition disparaissant*]." Two pages earlier Derrida had written: "All phantasms are projected onto the screen [*écran*] of this ghost (that is, on something absent, for the screen itself is phantomatic, as in the television of the future . . .)" (p. 99; in French, p. 163). The screen, the cloth, is the ground-figure that appears only in disappearing and in which disappearing appears; thus the abyss as ground and the figure as none.

2. Karl Marx, *Capital: A Critique of Political Economy*, vol. 1, trans. Ben Fowkes (New York: Vintage, 1977), p. 143; abbreviated hereafter as *C*. The translation has been slightly modified where necessary.

3. In a footnote to the observation that the body of a commodity is the value-mirror of the other commodity, its body being the reflection of something disembodied and thus the incarnation of something general in an impossible simulacrum, Marx explains: "In a certain sense, a man is in the same situation as a commodity. As he neither enters the world in possession of a mirror, nor as a Fichtean philosopher who can say 'I am I,' a man first sees and recognizes himself in another man. Peter relates to himself as a man through his relation to

another man, Paul, in whom he recognizes his likeness. With this, however, Paul also becomes from head to toe, in his physical form as Paul, the form of appearance of the genus homo for Peter" (ibid., p. 144).

4. Marx makes the historicity of this ergontology clear in a note on the failure of the "great investigator" Aristotle in the face of value-form: Aristotle was not yet able to recognize "human labor" as the "common substance" of different commodities because the "concept of human equality" did not yet have the "permanence of a fixed popular opinion" (ibid., pp. 151–52). This also means that human labor in its function as a standard and value-substance has since then become not the truth of political economy but a "popular opinion" supporting the historical truth of capitalist economy.

5. [The pun, in Marx and Hamacher, on *Tisch* (table) and *Fetisch* (fetish) is lost in translation.—Trans.]

6. Karl Marx, *Capital, Volume* 3, quoted from *The Marx-Engels Reader*, ed. Robert Tucker (New York: Norton, 1972), pp. 319–20.

7. Karl Marx, *The German Ideology*, in *Marx-Engels Reader*, p. 157.

8. Ibid., pp. 149–50.

9. Aphorism CCXIV, in Friedrich Schelling, *Sämmtliche Werke*, pt. 1, vol. 7 (Stuttgart: Cotta, 1860), p. 238.

10. Derrida, *Specters of Marx*, p. 37; in French, *Spectres de Marx*, p. 69. Page references to these works are given hereafter in my text, with the English edition abbreviated as SE and the French edition as SF. My citations refer essentially to the Kamuf translation but deviate from it where required by the French text.

11. Jacques Derrida, *Glas* (Paris: Editions Galilée, 1974), p. 134b.

12. And again a little later: "a kind of double or brother" (*une sorte de double ou de frère*) (SE, 141 / SF, 224). Here Derrida takes up once more a theme of great importance in his reading of Lacan. See Jacques Derrida, "Le facteur de la vérité" in *La carte postale* (Paris: Aubier-Flammarion, 1980).

13. "I am," Derrida continues, "would then mean 'I am haunted': I am haunted by myself who am (haunted by myself who am haunted by myself who am . . . and so forth). Wherever there is Ego, *es spukt*, 'it spooks.' . . . The essential mode of self-presence of the *cogito* would be the haunting obsession of this '*es spukt*'" (SE, 133 / SF, 212).

14. What is sketched here and below I have developed in more detail in various works since 1983: first in "Das Versprechen der Auslegung" (in the Festschrift for Jacob Taubes, *Spiegel und Gleichnis*, ed. N. Bolz and W. Hübener [Würzburg: Könighausen and Neumann, 1983]; reprinted in my *Premises—Essays on Philosophy and Literature from Kant to Celan* [Cambridge, Mass.: Harvard University Press, 1996]), and then in "Lectio" and in "Afformative, Strike" (both in *Walter Benjamin's Philosophy*, ed. A. Benjamin and P. Osborne [London: Routledge, 1994]), etc. It always remains astonishing to me that the theme of the

promise that—prompted by Heidegger's analyses of the prestructure of being there—I first observed in Kant and Nietzsche has become one of the points of convergence between Derrida's work and my own.

15. On the concept of "ergontology" used here several times already, I refer to my "Working Through Working," *Modernism/Modernity*, 3, no. 1 (Jan. 1996): 23–55.

16. Derrida uses the word "perverformative" in *La carte postale*.

17. In inventing the word—or pre-word—"afformative" (which I used for the first time in "Afformative, Strike") or "biformative" (see W. Hamacher, "Afformative, Strike," trans. Dana Hollander, *Cardozo Law Review* 13, no. 4 [Dec. 1991], I allow myself the same license that Austin used for the introduction of the concept "performative." I recall—not to soften the peculiarity of these concepts but to emphasize the peculiarity of concepts codified and conventionalized since then—that Austin did not leave it at "performatives" but also speaks of "illocutives" and "perlocutives," of "verdictives," "exercitives," "commissives," "behabitives," and "expositives" (see John Austin, *How to Do Things with Words* [Cambridge, Mass.: Harvard University Press, 1962], pp. 153–64).

18. As far as I can see, the only author besides Ernst Bloch in the tradition of "messianic" Marxism who prepared this important difference was Walter Benjamin, in his "Theological-Political Fragment." The first sentences read: "Only the Messiah himself completes each historical event, and indeed in the sense that he himself first redeems, completes, creates its relation to the messianic. That is why the Kingdom of God is not the telos of historical *dynamis*; it cannot be made an objective. Seen historically, it is not an objective but an end" (Walter Benjamin, *Gesammelte Schriften*, ed. R. Tiedemann and H. Schweppenhäuser, vol. 2, pt. 1 [Frankfurt: Suhrkamp, 1977], p. 203). [My translation.—Trans.]. "The messianic" for Benjamin is end and not aim, eschaton and not telos—and is in fact even "a messianic" without a messiah, for he alone could complete and create the very reference to the messianic. Derrida's proximity to Benjamin is unmistakable at this point. The—minimal—distance is marked by the fact that for Benjamin there can be only the absolute paradox of a "messianic without the messianic," for the messianic cannot be a category of history. But, conversely, he also writes: "The profane (the historical) is thus not a category of the Kingdom, but a category, and indeed one of the most decisive, of his gentlest approach" (p. 204). It is only in this sense that Benjamin can write: "The relation of this order (of the profane) to the messianic is one of the most essential lessons of historical philosophy" (p. 203).

19. Jacques Derrida, "Foi et savoir: Les deux sources de la 'religion' aux limites de la simple raison," in *La religion*, ed. Jacques Derrida and Gianni Vattimo (Paris: Seuil, 1996), p. 59. [This and the following are my translations.—Trans.]

20. Ibid. p. 63.
21. Ibid. p. 40.
22. Ibid. p. 73.
23. Jacques Derrida, "Avances," in Serge Margel, *Le tombeau du dieu artisan* (Paris: Minuit, 1995), p. 26. [My translation.—Trans.]
24. Ibid., pp. 42–43.
25. Both "admissive" and "amissive" are modifications of *mittere*—throw, fling, send, dispatch, release—and both mean "let go, permit, give up, admit," *admittere* with an additional accent on "permit and let happen" and *amittere* with the accent on "give up, discard, lose, forfeit." Hence *fidem amittere* means "to break one's word," and *amissio* "loss (by death)." In the phrase *res publica amissa,* the meaning of admission has also been completely eclipsed by that of the loss of the republic.
26. "It [big industry]," Marx writes, "produced world history for the first time, insofar as it made all civilized nations and every individual member of them dependent for the satisfaction of their wants on the whole world, thus destroying the former natural exclusiveness of separate nations" (*German Ideology,* p. 149). This industrially produced "whole world" is still torn into classes under capitalist conditions of production; only the communist revolution could make of it a "world." Therefore we do not *know* what a world is.
27. Maurice Blanchot, "La parole prophétique," in *Le Livre à venir* (Paris: Gallimard, 1959), pp. 118–20. [My translation.—Trans.]
28. [The Hebrew *Laken* would be the paraphone of the German *Laken,* which also means "cloth."—Trans.]

RABATÉ, "MUJIC OF THE FOOTURE"

1. Jacques Derrida, *De la grammatologie* (Paris: Editions de Minuit, 1967), p. 14.
2. Jacques Derrida, "Archive Fever: A Freudian Impression," trans. Eric Prenowitz (Chicago: University of Chicago Press, 1996), p. 68. The French text is to be found in Jacques Derrida, *Mal d'archive* (Paris: Galilée, 1995), p. 109.
3. The passage, which Derrida also quotes in "Archive Fever," is as follows: "We know that the Jews were prohibited from investigating the future. The Torah and the prayers instruct them in remembrance, however, This stripped the future of its magic, to which all those succumb who turn to the soothsayers for enlightenment. This does not imply, however, that for the Jews the future turned into homogeneous, empty time. For every second of time was the strait gate through which the Messiah might enter." Walter Benjamin, "Theses on the Philosophy of History," in his *Illuminations,* trans. Harry Zohn (New York: Shocken Books, 1969), p. 264.
4. Blaise Pascal, *Pensées,* trans. A. J. Krailsheimer (London: Penguin, 1966),

p. 43. Hereafter, page references to this English edition will be given with the abbreviation *P*; I have slightly modified the translations as needed. There is no general agreement as to which French edition of the *Pensées* is the most reliable. For the sake of practicality, I have used Michel Le Guern's two-volume edition: Pascal, *Pensées* (Paris: Gallimard, Folio, 1977). The passage just quoted is from 1: 82: "Le passé et le présent sont nos moyens, le seul avenir est notre fin."

5. James Joyce "Grace," in *Dubliners*, ed. R. Scholes and A. Walton Litz (New York: Penguin and Viking, 1976), p. 173.

6. Le Guern refers to Pascal's *Treatise on the arithmetic triangle* for a definition of the word *parti* as "stakes" or "the money a player must be ready to lose as soon as he puts it on the table." The *parti* presupposes the notion of a *partie*, a game one is free to enter into or to leave at one's leisure. See Le Guern's edition, Pascal, *Pensées*, ed. Le Guern, 1: 290–91.

7. Ibid., 2: 11. Krailsheimer translates a little weakly: "Yes, but you must wager. There is no choice, you are already committed" (Pascal, *P*, 150).

8. Heidegger quotes Pascal in §1 of *Being and Time*; see Heidegger, *Basic Writings*, trans. David Farrell Krell (New York: Harper, 1993), p. 43.

9. Nicholas Rescher, *Pascal's Wager: A Study of Practical Reasoning in Philosophical Theology* (Notre Dame: University of Notre Dame Press, 1985), p. 7.

10. *Quand on lit trop vite ou trop doucement on n'entend rien.* Pascal, *Pensées*, quoted in Paul de Man, *Allegories of Reading* (New Haven, Conn.: Yale University Press, 1979), p. v; see *P*, 38.

11. I owe this point to Pierre Force's excellent *Pascal et l'herméneutique* (Paris: Vrin, 1989), p. 100 n. 2.

12. Here I have modified *P*, 106, since the translation seems to express exactly the opposite of Pascal's original idea. See also Pascal, *Pensées*, ed. Le Guern, 1: 180.

13. See Pascal, *Pensées*, ed. Le Guern, 1: 216 and 325, for the endnote.

14. Martin Heidegger, "What Are Poets For?" in *Poetry, Language, Thought*, trans. A. Hofstadter (New York: Harper, 1971), p. 12, §7. I also refer to the German edition, Martin Heidegger, *Wozu Dicter?* (1946), in *Holzwege* (Frankfort: Klostermann, 1950), p. 302. Hereafter, page references to the English edition will be given with the abbreviation WAPF.

15. Rainer Maria Rilke, *Duino Elegies*, trans. J. B. Leishman and S. Spender (New York: Norton, 1963), p. 77. As Leishman and Spender note on p. 113, one could also translate *überzähliges Dasein* as "existence beyond number, uncountable, infinite, endlessly open."

16. Rilke, quoted in Heidegger, WAPF, 99.

17. Heidegger, *Wozu Dichter?*, p. 275.

18. Heidegger, WAPF, 131, and Heidegger, *Wozu Dichter?*, p. 293.

19. Stéphane Mallarmé, *Correspondance*, ed. B. Marchal (Paris: Gallimard-Folio, 1994), p. 291; abbreviated hereafter as *C*. The translations are all mine.

20. Stéphane Mallarmé, *Collected Poems*, trans. Henry Weinfeld (Berkeley: University of California Press, 1994), p. 49.

21. Ibid., pp. 44–45.

22. Ibid., p. 55.

23. I have tried to develop some of these insights in two chapters of my *Ghosts of Modernity* (Gainesville: University Press of Florida, 1996), pp. 84–121.

24. See Maurice Blanchot, "Le Livre à venir," in *Le Livre à venir* (Paris: Gallimard, 1959), pp. 270–97. Blanchot refers to *Le "Livre" de Mallarmé*, ed. Jacques Schérer (Paris: Gallimard, 1957).

25. Roger Dragonetti, *Un fantôme dans le kiosque: Mallarmé et l'esthétique du quotidien* (Paris: Seuil, 1992).

26. Benjamin, "Theses on the Philosophy of History," pp. 257–58.

27. I have attempted to develop this idea in "Back to Beria! Genetic Joyce and Eco's 'Ideal Readers,'" in *Probes: Genetic Studies in Joyce, European Joyce Studies*, vol. 5 (Amsterdam: Rodolpi, 1995), pp. 65–84.

28. James Joyce, *Finnegans Wake* (London: Faber, 1939), p. 518, line 28.

29. James Joyce, *Selected Letters* (London: Faber, 1975). See also Joyce's letter in French to Jacques Mercanton (Jan. 9, 1940), p. 403.

30. Arthur Rimbaud, "Vagabonds," in his *Illuminations*, in *Arthur Rimbaud Oeuvre-Vie*, ed. Alain Borer (Paris: Arléa, 1991), p. 349.

31. Olivier Cadiot, *Futur, ancien, fugitif* (Paris: P.O.L., 1993), presentation of the text on the back cover.

WEBER, "ELIJAH'S FUTURES"

1. Walter Benjamin, *Illuminations*, trans. Harry Zohn (New York: Schocken, 1969), p. 264.

2. Walter Benjamin, *Gesammelte Schriften*, ed. R. Tiedemann and H. Schweppenhäuser, vol. 1.3 (Frankfurt: Suhrkamp, 1972), p. 1252. Further references to this volume, abbreviated *GS*, will be given in my text.

3. " . . . wie diese Arbeit—vergleichbar der Methode der Atomzertrümmerung—die ungeheuren Kräfte der Geschichte freimacht, die im 'Es war einmal' der klassischen Historie gebunden liegen." Walter Benjamin, *Gesammelte Schriften*, vol. 5.1, *Das Passagen-Werk*, ed. R. Tiedemann (Frankfurt: Suhrkamp, 1982), p. 578.

4. Ibid., p. 494.

5. Ibid., p. 490: "ein Versuch zur Technik des Erwachens. Ein Versuch, der dialektischen, der kopernikanischen Wendung des Eingedenkens inne zu werden."

6. Ibid., p. 495: "Das kommende Erwachen steht wie das Holzpferd der Griechen im Troja des Traumes."

7. One of the most prominent figures in this debate is Saul Friedländer. See, for example, his *Memory, History, and the Extermination of the Jews of Europe* (Bloomington: Indiana University Press, 1993).

8. Benjamin, *Passagen-Werk*, p. 589: "Daß die Geschichte nicht allein eine Wissenschaft sondern nicht minder eine Form des Eingedenkens ist. Was die Wissenschaft 'festgestellt' hat, kann das Eingedenken modifizieren. Das Eingedenken kann das Unabgeschlossene (das Glück) zu einem Abgeschlossenen und das Abgeschlossene (das Leid) zu einem Unabgeschlossenen machen. Das ist Theologie; aber im Eingedenken machen wir eine Erfahrung, die uns verbietet, die Geschichte grundsätzlich atheologisch zu begreifen, so wenig wir sie in unmittelbar theologischen Begriffen zu schreiben versuchen dürfen."

9. See Dominick LaCapra, *Representing the Holocaust: History, Theory, Trauma* (Ithaca, N.Y.: Cornell University Press, 1994), pp. 9 and 13. Friedländer, in his *Memory, History, and the Extermination of the Jews*, suggests that a "redemptive closure" with regard to the Shoah could be "desirable" ("comforting and healing in effect") only "at the individual level," but that this "seems largely impossible. At the collective level, however, regardless of the present salience of these events, there can hardly be any doubt that the passage of time will erase the 'excess'" (p. 133). In other words, such an "erasure" might well result from a narrative of redemption, which, as such, is a betrayal of the Shoah's "excess." In another essay in the same collection, Friedländer formulates the problem from a slightly different perspective. After quoting Benjamin's second thesis in the "Theses on the Philosophy of History," which postulates that every generation has been "endowed with a *weak* messianic power, a power to which the past has a claim," Friedländer comments: "If Benjamin's view of historical redemption implies the construction of meaning, we may be confronted with an insoluble paradox when facing the extermination of the Jews of Europe: on the one hand, the most diverse modes of evocation of the events abound; on the other hand, both in the representations of this past as well as in its interpretation, we are facing dilemmas which paralyze our 'weak redeeming powers.' One may wonder, though, whether such a situation is not appropriate" (p. 61). In other words: "Individual common memory, as well as collective memory, tends to restore or establish coherence, closure, and possibly a redemptive stance, notwithstanding the resistance of deep memory at the individual level. The question remains whether, at the collective level as well, an event such as the Shoah may, after all the survivors have disappeared, leave traces of a deep memory beyond individual recall, which will defy any attempts to give it meaning" (p. 119). The persistent absence of meaning would in any case be more faithful to this particular past than any "redemptive stance." James Young reads the "pointedly anti-redemptory" productions of "post-Holocaust literature and art" as a result of the "artists' contempt for the religious, political, or aesthetic linking of redemption and destruc-

tion" that "seemed to justify" a catastrophe such as the Holocaust "in the first place" ("Germany's Memorial Question: Memory, Counter-Memory, and the End of the Monument," *South Atlantic Quarterly*, 96, no. 4 [Fall 1997]: 856). However, just as Benjamin doubts that it is possible "to conceive of history in fundamentally atheological terms," Young, in commenting on Friedländer, asks "whether the very act of writing Holocaust history might also redeem these events with meaning." James Young, "The Holocaust as Vicarious Past: Art Spiegelman's *Maus* and the Afterimages of History," *Critical Inquiry* 24, no. 3 (Spring 1998): 666. See also J. Young, *The Texture of Memory: Holocaust Memorials and Meaning* (New Haven, Conn.: Yale University Press, 1993).

10. Friedländer, *Memory, History, and the Extermination of the Jews*, p. 119. See also Lawrence L. Langer, "Remembering Survival," in Geoffrey Hartman, ed., *Holocaust Remembrance: The Shapes of Memory* (Oxford: Blackwell, 1994).

11. Jacques Derrida, "Comment ne pas parler: Dénégations," in his *Psyché: Inventions de l'autre* (Paris: Galilée, 1987), pp. 535–95; Jacques Derrida, "Nombre de oui," in *Psyché*, pp. 639–50; and Jacques Derrida, *Sauf le nom* (Paris: Galilée, 1993). For a detailed study of Derrida's use of the "apophatic" and the status of religion in his work, see John D. Caputo, *The Prayers and Tears of Jacques Derrida: Religion Without Religion* (Bloomington: Indiana University Press, 1997). See also the chapter "God, For Example," in Rodolphe Gasché's important *Inventions of Difference* (Cambridge, Mass.: Harvard University Press, 1994), as well as the essays collected in H. Coward and T. Foshay, eds., *Derrida and Negative Theology* (Albany: SUNY Press, 1992).

12. One of Derrida's texts is entitled "Interpretations at War: Kant the Jew, Kant the German," trans. Moshe Ron, *New Literary History*, 22 (Winter 1991): 39–95; the French original is "Interpretations at War: Kant, le Juif, l'Allemand," in Miguel Abensour et al., *Phénoménologie et politique: Mélanges offerts à J. Taminiaux* (Bruxelles: Ousia, 1990).

13. This text was published first in English, as Jacques Derrida, "Post-Scriptum: Aporias, Ways and Voices" (abbreviated hereafter as PS), trans. John P. Leavey, Jr., in Coward and Foshay, *Derrida and Negative Theology*, pp. 283–323. It was published the following year (1993) in French under the title *Sauf le nom* (abbreviated hereafter as *SN*). Further references to these works will be given in my text. English quotations are from "Post-Scriptum" unless otherwise indicated.

14. Jacques Derrida, "Épreuves d'écriture," *Revue philosophique de la France et de l'Étranger*, no. 2 (Apr.–June 1990): 273.

15. Meister Eckhart, *The Essential Sermons, Commentaries, Treatises, and Defense*, ed. and trans. E. Colledge and B. McGinn (New York: Paulist Press, 1981), p. 187. "Now detachment approaches so closely to nothingness that there can be nothing between perfect detachment and nothingness" (ibid., p. 286).

"And as the soul attains this [i.e., detachment], it loses its name and it draws God into itself, so that in itself it becomes nothing, as the sun draws up the red dawn into itself so that it becomes nothing" (p. 292). See also Meister Eckhart, *Teacher and Preacher*, ed. and trans. B. McGinn (New York: Paulist Press, 1986): "When the soul enters the unmixed light, it plunges into its utter nothingness so distant from its created somethingness in its utter nothingness that it can in no way through its own power come back again to its created somethingness. But God sustains its utter nothingness with his uncreatedness and holds the soul in his utter somethingness" (p. 242).

16. The remark comes in his famous sketch of the ascent of Mount Carmel. See John of the Cross, *Selected Writings*, ed. Kieran Kavanaugh (New York: Paulist, 1987), p. 44.

17. Mechthild von Magdeburg, "Die woestin hat zwoelf ding" (The desert has twelve things), in her *Das fließende Licht der Gottheit* (The flowing light of the Godhead), ed. H. Neumann (Munich: Artemis Verlag, 1990), 1: 24–25.

18. Ibid., bk. 6, par. 25. God replies: "My divinity has burned you" (p. 234).

19. Marguerite Porete, *The Mirror of Simple Souls Who Are Annihilated and Who Only Remain in the Will and Desire for Love,* trans. E. Babinsky (New York: Paulist Press, 1993).

20. Hadewijch of Brabant, *The Complete Works*, trans. Mother C. Hart (New York: Paulist Press, 1980), pp. 239 and 290.

21. See Jacques Derrida, "Circumfession," in G. Bennington and J. Derrida, *Jacques Derrida*, trans. G. Bennington (Chicago: University of Chicago Press, 1993), pp. 46, 98, 130, and passim.

22. Derrida, PS, 299 / *SN*, 53. See also pp. 308 and 77, respectively.

23. "Le désert est aussi une figure du lieu pur. Mais la figuration en général tient à cette spatialité, à cette localité de la parole." Derrida, PS, 301 / *SN*, 58. Translation slightly modified.

24. Derrida, *SN*, 63. The last part of the sentence is not included in "Post-Scriptum" (p. 302): "Là-bas, vers le nom, vers l'au-delà du nom dans le nom." See also *SN*, 94.

25. *The Seminar of Jacques Lacan, Book VII: The Ethics of Psychoanalysis 1959–1960*, ed. J.-A. Miller, trans. D. Porter (New York: Norton, 1992). The French edition is Jacques Lacan, *Le séminaire, livre VII: L'éthique de la psychanalyse* (Paris: Seuil, 1986). Further references to these works will be given in my text, with the French edition abbreviated as EF and the English edition as EE. English quotations are from the Porter translation.

26. Alexandre Koyré, quoted in H. Floris Cohen, *The Scientific Revolution: A Historiographical Inquiry* (Chicago: University of Chicago Press, 1994), p. 80. For modern science, indeed, "the celestial bodies . . . could just as well not be there," since, as Lacan points out, for example in his seminar "The Psychoses,"

"our culture" is an "exception" insofar as the "mental presence of what goes on in the sky," which is attested in all other cultures, no longer plays its role (Jacques Lacan, *Le séminaire, livre III: Les psychoses* [Paris: Seuil, 1981], pp. 77–78). The formulation of celestial bodies that "could just as well not be there" also refers to the definition of "empirical sciences as subject to contingency and change": "In order to be considered empirical, a statement should meet two conditions: (1) the state of things it refers to should be directly or indirectly representable in space and time; (2) it should be possible to think of the state of things it refers to as different from what it is. . . . Karl Popper's criterion of falsifiability is but an application of condition (2)" (Jean-Claude Milner, "Lacan and the Ideal of Science," in Alexandre Leupin, ed., *Lacan and the Human Sciences* [Lincoln: University of Nebraska Press, 1991], p. 34). With regard to psychoanalysis, the following thesis needs to be deduced: "Psychoanalysis is possible only in a universe where a mathematized science deals with what could fail to be where it is or what could fail to be as it is" (ibid., p. 35).

27. Koyré, quoted in Cohen, *Scientific Revolution*, p. 87.

28. Jacques Lacan, "Science and Truth" (abbreviated hereafter as ST), trans. Bruce Fink, *Newsletter of the Freudian Field*, 3 (1989): 17–18. The French text, originally published in 1965, is "La science et la vérité" (abbreviated hereafter as SV), in Jacques Lacan, *Écrits* (Paris: Seuil, 1966): "La science, si l'on y regarde de près, n'a pas de mémoire. Elle oublie les péripéties dont elle est née, quand elle est constituée, autrement dit une dimension de la vérité que la psychanalyse met là hautement en exercice" (p. 869). Further references to these works will be given in my text. English quotations are from the Fink translation.

29. Lacan, ST, 8 / SV, 859: "Il n'y a pas de science de l'homme, parce que l'homme de la science n'existe pas, mais seulement son sujet." Lacan continues: "My lifelong repugnance for the appellation 'human sciences' is well known; it strikes me as the very call of servitude."

30. Lacan, ST, 6 / SV, 857: "It is unthinkable that psychoanalysis as a practice and the *Freudian* unconscious as a discovery, could have taken on their roles before the birth—in the century which has been called the century of genius, i.e. the seventeenth century—of science; 'science' should be taken in the absolute sense just indicated, a sense which hardly seems to efface what formerly went by the same name, but which, rather than detecting its archaism therein, draws to itself the latter's principle in such a way as to better demonstrate its difference from any other science."

31. Lacan, ST, 6 / SV, 857: "Une chose est sûre: si le sujet est bien là, au noeud de la différence, toute reférénce humaniste y devient superflue, car c'est à elle qu'il coupe court."

32. Wolf Kittler, "Lacan: Encore," forthcoming in the proceedings of the con-

ference organized by the American Lacanian Link, "The Subject—*Encore*," held in March 1999 at the University of California, Los Angeles. Manuscript, p. 4.

33. Ibid.

34. *The Seminar of Jacques Lacan, Book II: The Ego in Freud's Theory and in the Technique of Psychoanalysis*, trans. S. Tomaselli (New York: Norton, 1988), p. 299.

35. Ibid., p. 300. The French is from Jacques Lacan, *Le séminaire, livre II: Le moi dans la théorie de Freud et dans la technique de la psychanalyse* (Paris: Seuil, 1978), p. 346.

36. This sentence is omitted in Walshe's translation (see next note).

37. Meister Eckhart, *German Sermons and Treatises*, vol. 1, trans. and ed. M. O'C. Walshe (London: Watkins, 1979), pp. 43–44; see Meister Eckhart, *Deutsche Predigten und Traktate*, ed. J. Quint (Munich: Hanser, 1955), pp. 435–36.

38. Lacan, EE, p. 120. See also Jacques Lacan, *Le séminaire, livre XVII: L'envers de la psychanalyse*, ed. J.-A. Miller (Paris: Seuil, 1991), p. 187: "Cest en tant que la science ne se réfère qu'à une articulation qui ne se prend que de l'ordre signifiant, qu'elle se construit de quelque chose dont il n'y avait rien avant. Voilà ce qui est important à saisir, si nous voulons comprendre quelque chose à ce qu'il en est de quoi? De l'oubli de cet effet même."

39. Lacan stresses repeatedly that modern science could develop only in the Judeo-Christian tradition that had broken with Aristotle. See Lacan, *Le séminaire, livre III: Les psychoses*, pp. 77–78.

40. Cf. Samuel Weber, "Introduction to the 1988 Edition," in Daniel Paul Schreber, *Memoirs of my Nervous Illness*, trans. and ed. Ida Macalpine and Richard A. Hunter (Cambridge, Mass.: Harvard University Press, 1988), p. xlv.

41. Jacques Lacan, "Réponse au commentaire de Jean Hyppolite sur la '*Verneinung*' de Freud," in Lacan, *Écrits*, p. 388. (This text is not included in the English edition of the *Écrits*.)

42. Jacques Lacan, "On the Possible Treatment of Psychosis," in his *Écrits: A Selection*, trans. A. Sheridan (New York: Norton, 1977), pp. 200–201. The "real" differs fundamentally from "reality." According to Lacan, perception takes its "reality character" only through "symbolic articulations which interweave it with an entire world." If a subject is confronted, through psychotic hallucinations, with a symbol that has been "cut off" from the original *Bejahung*, this symbol constitutes for him or her something that in fact "does not exist." In Schreber's case, for example, "the content of the massively symbolic hallucination owes its apparition in the real to the fact that it does not exist for the subject" (Lacan, "Réponse au commentaire de Hyppolite," p. 392). In other words, Schreber is overwhelmed by something he has "never known," by the apparition of a "total strangeness [*étrangeté totale*] which will progressively bring along a radical sub-

mersion of all his categories" and ultimately force the subject to undertake a complete "reorganisation of his world [*jusqu'à le forcer à un véritable remaniement de son monde*]." A signification appears to Schreber "which comes from nowhere and which does not refer to anything, but is an essential signification concerning the subject. Certainly, at this moment, repression, which intervenes each time there is a conflict of orders, sets in." However, repression "does not function" in this case. Lacan, *Le séminaire, livre III: Les psychoses*, pp. 99–100.

43. *The Standard Edition of the Complete Psychological Works of Sigmund Freud*, ed. J. Strachey (London: Hogarth, 1953–74), 19: 235.

44. Derrida, "Nombre de oui," pp. 643–44.

45. Weber, "Introduction to the 1988 Edition," p. xlv.

46. Lacan, *Écrits: A Selection*, p. 201. The signifier, according to Lacan, is "the signifier of the law which organizes the world for a subject, according to the continuity and the anticipation that characterize the signified." Where its foreclosure tears a rent in the symbolic, the world collapses, the signified is dissolved (Alain Jurainville, *Lacan et la philosophie* [Paris: P.U.F., 1988], pp. 271–72; see also p. 274).

47. Derrida, "Nombre de oui," p. 640.

48. Lacan, *Écrits*, French ed., p. 388.

49. In this essay, I consider only Lacan's reflections on science as presented in his Seminar, Book VII: *Ethics of Psychoanalysis* and in "Science and Truth." An analysis of these questions as treated in Lacan's seminars from 1972 forward, as well as his use of the topology of the Borromean knot, must be reserved for a future study.

50. Lacan, ST, 10 and 24 / SV, 861 and 877, emphasis mine. The French text reads as follows: "Le sujet en question reste le corrélat de la science, mais un corrélat antinomique puisque la science s'avère définie par la non-issue de l'effort pour le suturer." In Alexandre Leupin's words, for Lacan, "there is a hole in the field of science that prevents its rational unification. . . . This linking of the impossibility of scientific suture and the incompleteness of truth is Lacan's main contribution to epistemology." Leupin, *Lacan and the Human Sciences*, Introduction, p. 7.

51. Lacan, ST, 22 / SV, 874: "La fécondité prodigieuse de notre science est à interroger dans sa relation à cet aspect dont la science se soutiendrait: que la vérité comme cause, elle n'en voudrait-rien-savoir. On reconnaît là la formule que je donne de la *Verwerfung* ou forclusion."

52. Bruce Fink, *The Lacanian Subject: Between Language and Jouissance* (Princeton, N.J.: Princeton University Press, 1995), pp. 139–40.

53. Kittler, "Lacan: Encore," ms. p. 6.

54. Fink, *Lacanian Subject*, p. 91.

55. Benjamin, *Illuminations*, p. 257; translation slightly modified.

56. Derrida, "Nombre de oui," p. 640.

57. Meister Eckhart lived c.1260–1327/28; Mechthild c.1207–c.1282; Marguerite Porete was executed in 1310; Hadewijch's works are dated c.1221–1240. This repression has to be analyzed in the context of a deep restructuring of Europe's societies: under a still-prevailing feudalism, increased urbanization brought with it not only a growing freedom of trade but also wars, famines, the plague, and terrible poverty of the lower classes, as well as a deep crisis of Christianity. The most significant sign of the mystics' questioning of ecclesiastic authority and hierarchy, and of their popularity, was their very language: in their sermons and writings, the official ecclesiastic language, Latin, was abandoned for the first time.

58. Fiona Bowie, ed., *Beguine Spirituality* (New York: Crossroad, 1989), p. 13.

59. Lacan, *Le séminaire, livre III: Les psychoses*, pp. 100–101.

60. Ibid., pp. 101–2: "Cette structure [du stade du miroir] fait d'avance du monde imaginaire de l'homme, quelque chose de décomposé. Nous le trouvons ici à son état développé, et c'est un des intérêts de l'analyse du délire comme tel. Les analystes l'ont toujours souligné, le délire nous montre le jeu des fantasmes dans son caractère absolument développé de duplicité. Les deux personnages auxquels le monde se réduit pour le président Schreber, sont faits l'un par rapport à l'autre, l'un offre à l'autre son image inversée. L'important est de voir en quoi cela répond à la demande, faite de biais d'intégrer ce qui a surgi dans le réel, et qui représente pour le sujet ce quelque chose de lui-même qu'il n'a jamais symbolisé. Une exigence de l'ordre symbolique, pour ne pouvoir être intégrée dans ce qui a déjà été mis en jeu dans le mouvement dialectique sur lequel a vécu le sujet, entraîne une désagrégation en chaîne, une soustraction de la trame dans la tapisserie, qui s'appelle un délire. Un délire n'est pas forcément sans rapport avec un discours normal, et le sujet est fort capable de nous en faire part, et de s'en satisfaire, à l'intérieur d'un monde 097 toute communication n'est pas rompue."

61. The English translation is Jacques Derrida, "No apocalypse, not now," *Diacritics*, the issue entitled "Nuclear Criticism" (abbreviated hereafter as NC), 14, no. 2 (Summer 1984); the quotation here is from p. 30. The French version is "*No apocalypse, not now* (à toute vitesse, sept missiles, sept missives)" (abbreviated hereafter as NA), in Derrida, *Psyché*, pp. 363–86. Since the French version of this text, which was published later than the English translation, includes slight modifications and additions, both paginations will be given in references when necessary.

62. Lacan, EE, 282. On the question of purity see the excellent book by Bernard Baas, *Le désir pur* (Louvain: Peeters, 1992).

63. Jacaques Lacan, *Le désir et son interprétation*, unpublished seminar, session of Nov. 12, 1958.

64. Jacques Lacan, *The Seminar of Jacques Lacan: On Feminine Sexuality. The Limits of Love and Knowledge, Book XX, Encore* 1972–1973, ed. Jacques-Alain Miller, trans. Bruce Fink (New York: Norton, 1998), p. 77; the French edition is *Le séminaire, livre XX: Encore* (Paris: Seuil, 1972), pp. 70–71.

65. "Da-sein heißt: Hineingehaltenheit in das Nichts." Martin Heidegger, "Was ist Metaphysik?" in *Wegmarken* (Frankfurt: Klostermann, 1978), p. 114.

66. Lacan, *Le désir et son interpretation*, session of June 3, 1959.

67. Derrida, "Épreuves d'écriture," p. 273.

68. Benjamin, *Passagen-Werk*, p. 586: "Mein Denken verhält sich zur Theologie wie das Löschblatt zur Tinte. Es ist ganz von ihr vollgesogen. Ginge es aber nach dem Löschblatt, so würde nichts was geschrieben ist, übrig bleiben."

69. The scope of the questions touched upon in this essay might seem far too ambitious for the essay's limited space in this collection. A more patient analysis will be attempted in a future book-length study.

70. See Lacan, *Ecrits: A Selection*, p. 89. See also Gilles Deleuze, *Difference and Repetition*, trans. Paul Patton (New York: Columbia University Press, 1994), pp. 106–7.

71. Derrida, "Circumfession," pp. 81, 95. As Derrida relates in this text, "Élie," "Elijah," is his second given name, one, however, that remained "hidden," "secret," since it was not inscribed on Derrida's birth certificate and Derrida himself learned only "very late that it was my name." "Circumfession," pp. 84, 87–90, 96.

72. Derrida, "Nombre de oui," p. 648.

73. Michel de Certeau, *La fable mystique* (Paris: Gallimard, 1982), p. 185.

74. Jacques Derrida, "How to Avoid Speaking: Denials," in Coward and Foshay, *Derrida and Negative Theology*, pp. 98–99.

Cultural Memory in the Present

Richard Rand, *Futures: Of Jacques Derrida*

William Rasch, *Niklas Luhmann's Modernity: The Paradoxes of Differentiation*

Jacques Derrida and Anne Dufourmantelle, *Of Hospitality*

Jean-François Lyotard, *The Confession of Augustine*

Kaja Silverman, *World Spectators*

Samuel Weber, *Institution and Interpretation*, second edition

Jeffrey S. Librett, *The Rhetoric of Cultural Dialogue: Jews and Germans in the Epoch of Emancipation*

Ulrich Baer, *Remnants of Song: Trauma and the Experience of Modernity in Charles Baudelaire and Paul Celan*

Samuel C. Wheeler III, *Deconstruction as Analytic Philosophy*

David S. Ferris, *Silent Urns: Romanticism, Hellenism, Modernity*

Rodolphe Gasché, *Of Minimal Things: Studies on the Notion of Relation*

Sarah Winter, *Freud and the Institution of Psychoanalytic Knowledge*

Samuel Weber, *The Legend of Freud*, second edition

Aris Fioretos, ed., *The Solid Letter: Readings of Friedrich Hölderlin*

J. Hillis Miller / Manuel Asensi, *Black Holes / J. Hillis Miller; or, Boustrophedonic Reading*

Miryam Sas, *Fault Lines: Cultural Memory and Japanese Surrealism*

Peter Schwenger, *Fantasm and Fiction: On Textual Envisioning*

Didier Maleuvre, *Museum Memories: History, Technology, Art*

Jacques Derrida, *Monolingualism of the Other; or, The Prosthesis of Origin*

Andrew Baruch Wachtel, *Making a Nation, Breaking a Nation: Literature and Cultural Politics in Yugoslavia*

Niklas Luhmann, *Love as Passion: The Codification of Intimacy*

Mieke Bal, ed., *The Practice of Cultural Analysis: Exposing Interdisciplinary Interpretation*

Jacques Derrida and Gianni Vattimo, eds., *Religion*